THE TEMPO OF DISCIPLESHIP

The Musical Rudiments and Rhythms of
Developing Followers of Christ

DAVID E. YAUK

The Tempo of Discipleship
THE MUSICAL RUDIMENTS AND RHYTHMS OF DEVELOPING FOLLOWERS OF CHRIST

by Dave Yauk

Copyright © 2020 by Garden City Productions and Publications

All rights reserved. No part of this book may be reproduced in any form or by any electronic or mechanical means, including information storage and retrieval systems, without written permission from the author, except for the use of brief quotations in a book review.

Produced in the United States of America

First Release, 2020

www.gardencityproject.com

PRINT ISBN: 978-0-9994673-7-4

Dedication
TO ALL THOSE ON A JOURNEY

Book Structure

Opening Act

God Gathers Us
The Melody Image
Participation

God's Word Speaks to Us
Musical Rudiments
Pitch
Something Old, Familiar & New

We Respond
Musical Conversation
Repetition & Remembrance
Transposition

God Sends Us
Rhythms
Form & Improvisation
Transience
Sustain & Resolve
Sound & Silence

Book Structure

Encore

Endnotes

Opening Act

Messy Discipleship: Confessions from my Journey.

Have you ever had that feeling that people are laughing more at you than with you? I get this feeling all the time. Whenever people tell me that I'm funny, I believe it has less to do with any actual comedic intellect and more to do with the humorous stupidity that often follows my day-to-day decisions. I don't have a quick wit about me as does Chris Rock, nor do I possess the brilliance to see down to the root of stupidity like Jeff Foxworthy. My approach to humor…well, I'm usually the guy at the bottom of the barrel making the hair-brain decisions that supply the comedic greats with their hilarious content.

I have contributed wildly to the content of redneck jokes. For example, there was the time a number of years ago when I refused to rent a moving truck when transporting the full contents of my house to another location. I thought I could do it cheaper and quicker making about two dozen trips with an extended bed pick-up truck. Thrifty, right? Where I thought I was brilliant, in the eyes of others I became a running joke and the hillbilly village idiot. Family and friends still recite what a sight it was to watch me driving 10 miles an hour down a highway with baby changing tables and sofas stacked a good 12 feet high.

Looking back on the journey I call my life, I could liken it to a comedy, perhaps a tragedy, or perhaps a bunch of intertwined events that just make up a really uncomfortable tale of a prince who did not strike gold in his choices at the end of every rainbow. Personally, this has caused me to laugh and cry at myself over the years.

Another story comes to mind. When I was 17 my friend and I thought it would be fun to go joyriding in a snowstorm in my parents' '89 Volkswagen Golf. We called it The Womb because in it we felt we were once again being hatched in the incubator of mommy's tummy. We got in this car and headed to the local and iced-over high school parking lot. The lot itself was like a lake of ice and we satisfied ourselves skidding and leaping around for about thirty minutes or so in the parking lot until the race track that led into the soccer field caught our attention.

If you can picture it, the road bordering the track was about quarter mile long and it dead-ended in a huge soccer field. We got to the end of the road, cranked up the music—the Stone Temple Pilots—and laid on the gas until we reached about 120 mph—screaming down the road as we approached the glorious snow covered turf. Unfortunately, we did not see, nor did we know about, the drainage ditch at the end of the road right before the field itself. Fortunately, it was a grass ditch, and when we reached it, our car was propelled up in the air like a rocket. We caught air and felt like we were suspended forever! We crashed down and skidded out with snow billowing over the hub of the car before we screeched to a halt in the once pristinely manicured field. All we could say was, "That was awesome."

The story above is from my teenage years. I'm an adult now, but I still tend to find myself acting before I think. Last story, I promise. I can remember a couple years ago when I became really intrigued with eating healthy, which led my wife and me to research gardening; this all culminated in planting a garden in our backyard. Now, if the story were that easy, you might think I had matured, right? Wrong.

We picked a place in our backyard that was covered with grass to make our plot. Our first step was to clear away the grass to prepare a healthy planting area. The tool I chose to accomplish this task was a high-powered rototiller. I drove to the shop to rent one and came back ready to fire it up. "I'm ready," I thought. "I'm feeling like a man! I can do this," I told myself. Little did I know, I was about to tickle the neighbors with my humorous display and inexperience.

Opening Act

Where we live, the ground is pure clay and hard as rock. When the tiller kicked in, it jumped all over the place like a bucking bull. I was being thrown everywhere! I pretended that I was controlling it, but I was really just trying to keep it from destroying my feet. It took only about ten minutes of trying to cattle rope this thing before I came up with another brilliant idea. I thought, "I'll tie a rope to each handle and put it around my waist. That will take the pressure off my arms as it jumps around." Great idea, right? It did make things easier, but it wrenched my back because this thin little rope was wedged into and grinding against my spine.

The next brilliant idea hit me as I brainstormed better ways to make myself look foolish. I thought, "I'll get a towel and make this belt-thing that goes around my back thicker and cushier." I ran in the house and grabbed a Hawaiian-print beach towel and set out to continue the job. There I was, this behemoth tiller bouncing around, and the only thing that was controlling it was a mere Hawaiian party towel and a flimsy rope wrapped around my waist, all of which I had found buried at the bottom of a drawer. In all the excitement, I forgot to put on work gloves, and the Mississippi heat was beading sweat off me, causing my hands to blister up like an albino who went to the beach without sunscreen.

Needless to say, I stumbled in at the end of the day broken, blistered, and bloodied. When I looked out at my garden, it was only about half an inch deep and the grass was still there. I laid down on the couch with nothing to show for my well-meaning work ethic, and that's when God revealed to me what a precious wife I have. She came over, gave me a kiss and a glass of water, and said, "I'm proud of you for working so hard." Now, I'm no fool, but men, in women language that means, "I've been watching your sorry idiocy all day long from the kitchen window laughing 'til my sides hurt, but to save face, and preserve your dignity, I'm going to say 'I'm proud of you.'" Even I wasn't proud of myself. I had once again fallen prey to my lack of planning, over-eagerness, and fantastical thinking.

Messy Sin Makes Everything a Mess

The reason I share my madness with you is to make one point. People are messy! We are foolish, and as the Bible tells us, we are chock-full of sin. I am messy! You are messy! We are a work in process. We make foolish decisions for foolish reasons, and we catch ourselves asking the question after we indulge in our stupidity, "What was I thinking?" If we are going to

Opening Act

undergo the process of following Jesus and leading others to do the same, we need to have our expectations set rightly. When people undergo a process to repent, change, and choose by faith to walk out of stupidity and into wisdom, it's going to make for some lively giggling for those watching. My own comedic journey and my observation of countless others I have discipled over the years taught me this: we humans are just a motley crew! We are a hopeless lot, and we make hasty and unwise decisions. Even though our sometimes flippant lives must cause God to chuckle, most of the time the pain brought on by our foolishness is anything but comedic; it's threatening to our lives and well-being. It's sin. This is why God describes our condition without him as "No good." [1]

It's true, however, that we have value. We are prized beyond measure. We hold dignity and worth that reach far deeper than any gold mine. Nevertheless, without the loving intervention of our heavenly Father, we are incapable of seeking out ANY true virtue. We go after trivial things, and we chase car rides and cheap thrills that only reveal our tasteless pursuit of recklessness and bondage. We resist change, and when we embrace it, we change slowly and clumsily. God describes the process of becoming a follower of Jesus as doing away with the old man. I think there is no secret as to why God describes the process this way. Jesus realizes that we are like an old burned-out rusty engine that is left of center. In order to recalibrate our lives there's much work to do. We need a full overhaul, a tune-up, an oil change, new plugs, new body, and a whole new engine for that matter. Jesus makes it very clear that to become a Christian, the me, myself, and I will have to die. [2]

Even after the overhaul—when God gives us our new life—after our becoming a Christian, our decision-making skills are still a bit thrown off. This happens simultaneously when people who are caught up in all kinds of bad habits, filthy practices, and worldly thinking, become filled with the Holy Spirit and begin to hear a Holy voice within. They become disconcerted when the foolishness and sin of their old lives now seems trivial. The newly formed union within them of Spirit/human is fresh and is anything but familiar. Without God, we are used to thinking on our own. We are good at messing things up and chasing after everything that is bad for us. When God starts to fill us, humble us, and perfect us, we sometimes get an uncertain voice in our minds that screams, "What do I do now?" The questions that rage and the internal battle between saint and sinner cause a dichotomy to form within us, and this makes the process of discipleship all the more complicated.

The Parable and Purpose of This Book

Our method of evaluating discipleship therefore must remain true to real human experience. If we approach discipleship solely through system theory, scientific analysis, statistics, or through cold hard data, we will never truly address the nature of this journey, for a journey comes to us with real flow, emotion, and dynamic progress. To embark upon this journey of being transformed, recalibrated, overhauled, and remade by the LORD into His image and likeness, we must carefully and soberly consider the seriousness of such a process. That is what this book will seek to consider as we endeavor to be very careful in our method of approaching this journey. Because discipleship is a messy process and unfolds in the context of movements we must consider it in light of both realities.

We need a better mindset, a better image, and a better picture to teach us how we are to think about the discipleship process. We need a better parable and metaphor. A parable, as used by Jesus, is a story or object lesson that put "real clothes" on hard-to-understand truths. To teach faith, Jesus used a mustard seed. To teach the kingdom of God, God used a box of treasure and a field. To teach salvation, God used seeds and soil. *I believe there is a better parable that will help us think about the real process of discipleship—I believe that parable, or "metaphor" to be music! Music is the parable that most correctly teaches us all we need to know about discipleship's deepest truths.*

Music is true to the discipleship experience and is a journey in itself. It produces many colors, directions, tensions, and highs and lows, both emotionally and tonally. It most reflects how real life truly moves. In this book I will seek to use music as one big parable—an object lesson that points to real truth. I will not seek to describe music or discipleship solely in theory, nor will I consider them in isolation from one another, but I will seek to ponder God *through* music in the hope that we might find better ways of seeing things within our own context. Together, we will consider music's culture, form, interaction, and effects, and in doing so we will find a better way to describe the rudiments and rhythms that God uses to form and create people who follow Him.

Before we delve into the thrust of this work in which we deal with music as a journey and how it illustrates God and his creative methods to teach and train his children, let us first take a look at some of the common parables and images already used in Scripture to describe the nature of a disciple.

The Soldier, The Builder, The Athlete, The Farmer, & The Body

Since sin entered the world, our main desires do not seek to please the Lord. Until the Lord recaptures our affections with His grace, we are bound. In 2 Timothy, Paul writes to his protégée Timothy, who was still young and fairly inexperienced in the ministry, giving him this advice: "Share in suffering as a good soldier of Christ Jesus. No soldier gets entangled in civilian pursuits, since his aim is to please the one who enlisted him." [3] Paul's purpose in speaking to Timothy this way is to develop in Timothy's mind a way to rightly view his task of being a disciple and in discipling others: it involves suffering, fighting, battling to stay focused and free of entanglement. It involves obeying orders from our Lord and "General" in order to become holy and set free from the sin that is so pervasive. It involves sacrifice and mission. It's not as if Timothy is going off half-cocked in order to gamble and drink his life away. Paul simply realizes the tendency of human nature to leave the command of our General in Command and to become distracted. With grace, God reclaims for us the goal of His discipleship process. Grace is the enabling power to battle in this fashion. The intention in Paul's words is that Timothy connect God's grace to the victory that has already been won at Cavalry.

The work of Timothy therefore is to work *from* this grace, not simply to try to set in place life patterns of trying to become a "better person." Only by grace can the battle be waged, and our goal is to please our Master in heaven, the one who has enlisted us. This grace works powerfully in and through us, but it also undergoes real opposition. That is why Paul here uses the language of a militant speaking of a battle. From the very moment Adam and Eve stepped foot on garden ground, Satan was lurking in the shadows. He was, from the beginning, perched to distract us from the fight!

A soldier has to have focus and must be willing to become one who possesses a readiness to suffer the greater cause of Christ—and this means war. [4] This is what disciples are. This is what disciples do. Our expectations must be set rightly in dealing with ourselves and others. We must realize that we are, as followers of Christ, in the business of stealing real people from evil clutches and training them up to be soldiers in the Lord's army. The enemy does not like losing the ones he has deceived, and he

Opening Act

really does not like looking into the whites of their eyes as they stare him down once they have switched to God's team—advancing God's kingdom right over his head. Becoming part of the people of God means that God's people have switched sides, and such a shift requires a new form of training. Christ enlists disciples as soldiers. Consider the life of David for example.

We see in David's life that life and disciples are messy! David was given the title by God as a "man after God's own heart," and yet his laundry list of sins during his reign included adultery, deception, and murder. This makes David arguably one of the most glorious and most deplorable disciples that ever lived as a human. Why would God call David by such an honorable title when many of his sins were so blatantly evil? It's true he was a warrior for the people and for the ways of God, but we also know his comedic, tragic, and murderous history. Why did God give this man such a profound title? I think it had something to do with the very authentic tension that was in David's life.

David was an eclectic guy. He was such a valiant warrior that he inspired the women to fawn over him singing, "Saul has struck down his thousands, and David his ten thousands." [5] However, this same brute who advanced war in God's name, and who destroyed the masses with the might of his sword—whose courage won the day against a deceitfully intentioned and falsely jovial Giant—was also the man who played his lyre at night, writing songs of worship. Alone in his room, we can almost see him, sipping chai tea while sitting upon his down comforter, all the while peering out the window at ladies bathing naked (reference the Story of David and his adultery with Bathsheba) [6]. This same warrior, who fought God's battles on the battlefield, lost his way when at home among the world's desires. Instead of fighting and being in the battle as he should have been, he relaxed, wasted his time, became lost in what's attractive rather than what's chivalrous, and these distractions made a mess of things. Irony surrounds David's life. His lust drove him to sleep with and impregnate his friend's wife. When his attempts to cover the situation failed, he devised a plan to kill one of his most loyal soldier. Yet this same David could also duplicitously worship God unashamedly by dancing skimpily through the streets in his underwear as God's ark returned to Jerusalem. [7]

People are messy. God's work to rip us from our idolatry is war-like business and it's going take a fight on our part and on behalf of the body of Christ to enrich us. We are soldiers who are untrained and undisciplined, but God is up to the challenge of walking through the ups and downs and the ins and outs with us. This is particularly why he likens discipleship to the rigors of boot camp and battle.

The Builder

Paul, in the New Testament, goes on to liken discipleship to a master builder crafting and constructing a structure. He calls himself a master builder laying a foundation in excellence and building upon it. [8] Paul viewed himself as one skilled in craftsmanship. As a contractor measures every angle, counts every detail, plans for every nail, masters all the blue prints, and manages the people and the process of each project, so does the hand of God as the Almighty builds His kingdom through His people. Ephesians 2:19-22 profoundly exclaims, "So then you are no longer strangers and aliens, but you are fellow citizens with the saints and members of the *household* of God, *built* on the *foundation* of the apostles and prophets, Christ Jesus himself being the *cornerstone*, in whom the whole *structure*, being joined together, grows into a holy *temple* in the Lord. In him you also are being *built* together into a *dwelling* place for God by the Spirit." Notice the construction language when Jesus speaks of the very nature by which He builds His people. The Word likens us to the temple—the Old Testament residence for the presence of God Himself. Jesus approaches the task of building His house with the same tenacity that a builder tends to every detail of someone's dream home.

In your down time, start reading 2 Chronicles 3 in the Bible and notice the pain-staking detail God used in building the temple that typifies the cosmos and the believer's heart. You'll see the detail and seriousness that God puts into building His family and home. Jesus cautions us in how we build our house, His house, His people, lest it be worthless in the day of reckoning. He wants our work to truly reap a harvest of riches in that it was done for God and God alone. [9] As He builds us He wants us to keep in mind that He's working with raw materials to manufacture something beautiful and Holy; and if something proper emerges from this task, we have no one else to thank but God alone.

The Athlete

Further, the Bible likens discipleship to yet another analogy, an athlete.

Opening Act

Greco Roman athletes were the fiercest and most focused of competitors. Their regimen of diet, exercise, strategic rest, and even a healthy dose of music was part of their training to becoming not only sound in body and physicality, but equipped with the ability to focus with intensity in the most heated of situations. When Paul speaks of athletics in 1 Corinthians, he says this as he compares it to his own approach to living the Christian life: "So I do not run aimlessly; I do not box as one beating the air. But I discipline my body and keep it under control, lest after preaching to others I myself should be disqualified." [10] A Christ-like disciple is an athlete who stands in courage and integrity—following the rules and winning the crown. Discipleship is seen as a gridiron athletic undertaking where the competitor competes in the most strenuous triathlon and gladiator event.

What Paul stresses in the life of a follower of Christ is the fact that not only are we in a war, and not only are we being built into a walled city that is surrounded by the protection of the Lord and filled with the riches of His rule, we are also competing in a very real competition. The Bible very clearly outlines the struggle that the athlete will face in an uphill sprint against temptation, enemy forces, limitations, suffering, and weakness. Scripture also communicates candidly what the rewards will be like when we reach the summit. God promises rewards to those who do something with the faith that is given to them by Christ's gift of unearned grace:

The Victor's Crown: This crown was an ornament awarded to the Greco athletes after they had competed, overcome all the challenges, and emerged victorious (1 Cor. 9:25; 2 Tim. 2:5). It was also given at the *parousia* or return of a king.

The Incorruptible Crown: This crown indicates the Christian's mastery over sin by the power of the Holy Spirit. This is the crown Paul speaks of as he beats his body into submission and as he wars against the temptations of giving into the comforts of his flesh.

The Crown of Righteousness: In 2 Timothy 4:7-8, Paul recalls the life he has lived and the fight that he has fought for Christ. He praises God for making him faithful as a follower and he passes the torch to other men such as Timothy to keep advancing God's mission. This is living righteously.

The Crown of Life: This crown is given to those who continue through the trials of life and remain faithful (Jms. 1:12; Rev. 2:10). "Blessed is the man who perseveres under trial, because when he has stood the test, he will receive the crown of life that God has promised to those who love him." Continuing, "do not be afraid of what you are about to suffer. I tell you the devil will put some of you in prison to test you, and you will suffer persecution for ten days. Be faithful, even to the point of death, and I will give you the crown of life."

The Crown of Joy: This crown is given to those who influence others toward righteousness (Ph. 4:1; 1 Th. 2:19). An example of how this crown is earned is given in the Thessolonica church when Paul was accused of not caring for and being committed to them deeply enough. In reading the letter we can see that was why Paul reiterated his love for them as that of a parent to his children. [11] He suggested his care should be obvious to them, for he also knew his love for them would result in a crown for him if he succeeded.

The Crown of Glory: The greatest achievement is to finish the calling to which God called you, and to finish the work He gave you to do (1 Pt. 5:4). This crown extends to all those who sought after what God created them to be as they served Him.

The rewards listed are not promised on the basis that we "earn" or gain salvation. The Bible is very clear that our place in heaven is secured through Christ's first-place finish. [12] However, though Christ has run the race perfectly for us, He also doubles back and runs alongside us, carrying us through the race, teaching us how He ran the race, and aiding us in avoiding the pitfalls. He attacked the struggle of life with the intensity of an athlete and this is how we also should live as we follow Him.

The Farmer

Then there's the analogy that resounds even a bit closer to my heart, as I am a wannabe gardener. Discipleship is likened to farming. Think about it. We call the ministry of multiplying churches "church planting." Even Paul likens the growth of God's church to that of a garden. [13] I remember working in farming for a few summers—up at 4 a.m. and home by 8 p.m. It was strenuous work. The intensity of farming and gardening is extremely instructive to us in living. The Bible tells us that discipleship is like a hardworking farmer who has first claims on his crops. [14] The first fruits rightly go to the one who has worked the ground with such patience and tenacity. In the same way, the tilling of a person's heart is hard work, but the first fruits glorify the Gardener and exalt the joy of the person being farmed.

It's very important that discipleship be seen as something that is laborious in work but rewarding in result. The Scripture makes it very clear that discipleship will be a life spent in the dirt. Seeds will be planted and watered. Some seeds will fall on dry rock and die before germination. Other seeds will fall on rocky soil and grow up weakly only to die quickly. Yet other seeds will root deeply in rich soil and grow up to reap a rich harvest. The farmer will need to plow, fertilize, dig, trench, and cultivate appropriately in every situation. Throughout the growth process, the growing disciple will also need the careful nurturing by the Trinity—the Master Gardener—and by all those in Christ's body. There are times when a disciple will need watering. There will be times when water is the last thing a disciple needs. As most gardeners know, a plant will always desire water, but the loving gardener withdraws nourishment for a time so that the plant is forced to forge its roots deeper into the soil in order to seek out deeper wells—ultimately making the plant more resilient and strong.

Each person, like plants, will need a specified regimen of nutrients to survive and thrive. Some plants prefer alkaline or acidic soil, others like proteins and calcium more than others, and others prefer lime and so on and so forth. The disciple/gardener recognizes the uniqueness of each environment, culture, person, family, and situation and is able to pastor it like a gardener wisps a fragile and dying vine off the ground in order to stake it up for greater growth. On the other hand, there are times when a disciple is likened to a tomato plant that grows so healthy that the only way to keep it growing is to cut it back, seemingly injuring it in an effort to produce greater fruitfulness. This is the life of a gardener, as it also is with a disciple.

The Body

Still another analogy of discipleship comes to us in the form of a body building itself up in love. [15] The image of God's family as being a singular "body" causes us to see discipleship in a different light.

I believe that there's a tendency in discipleship today to "disciple-down." What I mean by this is that we (the discipler) get with people who are, in our eyes, "lesser" than we are in some way (disciple-eee). It could be that they lack spiritual maturity, their social status is in a lower class, or we perceive them as needing something from us. The trouble is that, oftentimes, the discipleship relationship is built in order to make the one discipling feel better about their own identity. This is not so in the human body. If one part of the body suffers, everyone suffers. If one part of the body flourishes it all flourishes. There is no downward trajectory of value in the human body. There are systems in the body that may seem to fulfill greater functions like the brain, the heart, or the liver, but in all reality, if any part, no matter how seemingly insignificant, were to be cut off—like a pinkie-toe for example which controls the balance of a person—that person would tend to fall over.

The body teaches us that we are interconnected. We may have parts that are seemingly less than, equal to, or greater when held in comparison in the whole, but relationships with all three are needed to ensure proper function.

This analogy is also healthy to hear for those of us who are in an independent culture. Discipleship goes beyond our personal quiet time or one-on-one mentorship or life-coaching. Our understanding of God and life is forged in the same way the Trinity does things—in community. The Trinity is a community, and so is the nature of the body. The nutrients are brought in, assimilated, and outsourced by various organs and systems into regions with needs, and, in specific ways, they receive and process those supplies. When there's a wound, the body compensates and gives up some of its resources to send more blood and life to the injured part. This interconnected communal function of the body teaches us something about discipleship.

Jesus is the Master Disciple Maker

It is most certainly seen that the Bible contains many variables and analogies that assist us in grasping what God's nature is really like. In all our thinking, we must ultimately begin with and culminate in the image of God alone! Our God is the master discipleship maker. He's the greatest analogy of perfection. Jesus builds His church like a master craftsman.[16] He strenuously lays out the blueprints, attends to every detail, and, like an artist, crafts His raw material world into a structure that will stand. He is agriculturally minded in that He lovingly tends to his flock like a shepherd to a lamb and a farmer to a sinewy new plant just striving to survive.[15]

His kindness is what leads His people to life and growth, and His attention to us is fatherly, priestly, and can be likened to that of a counselor and encourager.

On the flip-side, He can show His not so cuddly, warrior-like side when needed. He comes all tatted up in the end with the brawn of "King of Kings, Lord of Lords" etched on His thigh. [19] His love and His wrath work in tandem as He fights for his family against intruders that have come into His house seeking to destroy. Only after the battle is over does He sit down, and put on an apron—restraining and covering the blood from the battle—in order to serve us, just as He served us in His time on Earth. He caters and dines with us in the Wedding Supper of the Lamb. [20]

Is this not a picture of a God who is INDESCRIBABLE? Is this not the pitch to which every human should seek to harmonize? If our goal is to guide people into this image—to bear His likeness—we are most certainly going to have to deal with the means as well as the ends.

The results and aims of discipleship have been presented in hard-core images and truth, but the process of arriving at these conclusions is most certainly going to require an artful approach.

Jesus is an Artist

Though God defends us like a brute, disciplines us as a gardener tenderly prunes a vine, develops us as a master architect builds a structure, and feeds us like the mouth feeds the body, He does this along the moving line of an unfolding journey. Like a potter makes a pot, like an artist paints a canvas, and like a musician writes a song, God composes us into a singing chorus. His plan for us travels along life's page like the well-written score of a classical piece. He creates and writes in moments of rest, dips of dissonance, profound harmonies, dynamic decrescendos and crescendos, climaxes, endings, structure and even the improvisation of new melodies.

And through it all …

He composes a symphony. All the individual parts come together to make a grand opus that tells the same story from beginning to end. Each instrument chimes in to paint the mood, the emotion, and the rise and fall of reality. He crafts the world like an artist, and His posture toward us is that of a God singing over us. [21]

Though it is true that to best understand the call of Christ, we are to view it as war, responsibility, training, cultivation, and connection, I also believe that to actually do discipleship or be a disciple, it would be best for us to perceive the process as a creative work art. Remember, people are messy, and therefore, each individual person requires a delicate mastery of a fine-tuned method of training that will best embrace one's reality—forming an individual into Christlikeness, and kingdom truths. For God to reorganize us and capture all our moments into a storyline that leads toward a happy ending, He can not merely mold our lives like one might do within a cold science of facts. He can not tend to our lives like an agricultural experiment or supply us with nourishment as a body in need of nutrition. He must certainly do all this, but not only this. He must take us physically, emotionally, spiritually, mentally, and socially and begin to craft and form the parts together—this is His musical masterpiece.

Music's Goal: Equipping People for REAL LIFE...

I have been leading music for fifteen years now. I have led music in worship contexts within almost every denominational framework. I have traveled and led music in almost every state and in over seventeen countries, rubbing elbows with amateurs, professionals, perfectionists, and realists. When people ask me what I believe my role and goal is as a leader of music and a cultivator of worship in God's people, I tell them that my goal is "to equip people for real life."

Now, you might be wondering why I hop-skipped over from the topic of discipleship to leading music in a corporate worship context, but hang with me because the connection is there. What I mean by the above statement is that my goal is to teach people how Christ-likeness looks and is crafted within the ebbs and flows of real life. What this means for me is that when I begin to plan a worship service, I begin to think of rhythms and patterns that best reflect the path of the normal person's real journey. People in their real day-to-day lives experience times of loud and soft, full and empty, wordy and brief, tension and resolve, familiar and unfamiliar, form and improvisation, stimulus and response ... An individual might find themselves in a particularly academic environment with moments of high solitude in study and reflection before a season of intense application and assessment. A person might find themselves in the home exposed to schedules that seem to move from loud to soft, from busy to busier. Yet even within a person's spiritual journey, one may move along in intense learning, seeming only to keep up on the heels of all that God is saying only to find that God suddenly silences one with a period of waiting in hopes that He might act on their new training. This is real life! It moves. It comes in shades of many colors, and it is constantly building on the moment preceding its next movement.

As the worship service and plan evolves, I might choose a wordy hymn that teaches the theologically rich nature of God and inspires our minds to move faster and brighter. When profound learning happens however, the natural real life response is *not* to keep singing word after word in order to fill every moment. On the contrary, when God profoundly communicates His truths to us, we naturally come to a place of silence to pause for reflection, insight, and contemplation. I may resort in a corporate worship context to using a silent reflection, a prayer, or a still motion to create this reality. Our times are varied with a flood of loud and soft, times of praise and times of sadness and lament. The process of allowing for tension is *purposeful.* We do not always need to resolve every detail like a lament, question, or grievance before the Lord because life does not always resolve every tension with concrete answers. The song of our life might sound in a minor key, that at one point evokes sadness in order to paint the tone of our sin. It then may move into a major key that evokes cheer to express the audio of grace as it sounds into our darkness its joyful hope.

This is the art of taking human experience and painting it as is to help the individual find God in each and every moment. To paint God only in praise and joy would be to create a disconnect for a person who needs to know how to relate to God in their depression. To sing about a God who is only an idea and a theology that is certain—a thought that is grasped fully in the mind—is to make the mind anemic to God when real life brings about times of uncertainty and grey. This is why "church leaders are to design their orders of worship to communicate the truths of Scripture, touch the hearts of worshipers with the implications of those truths, and then equip believers to live faithfully in the world as witnesses to those truths." [22] To do this, the truth of Scripture must not only be preached, it must also be painted. The tone of the message is as important as the content. Tone and text intertwine and hold hands with each other.

This has everything to do with discipleship

The reason for the excursus in dealing with the planning of worship services is because many times worship is connected to the idea of music (albeit, music is only one small aspect of our worship to God), and it's because discipleship is very much like a song that is sung! As music moves in countless ways and forms, people also move in real life, and experience times with very real moments of plenty and want. There are times where we are up and then we are down. There are times that we are stirred up to question everything we believe and others when we are profoundly firm in our conclusions. The point is our lives are ever unique in how the tune sings its way out through each of us.

Unfortunately, discipleship, as I see it presented in many books and churches, seems to be thought of solely as a small group meeting, a one-on-one lunch date, a Sunday school class and a sermon preached. The process of discipleship seems to take on a once-and-for-all type of teaching that will provide a "mountain-top" experience that will ever hold its intensity. Though moments and aspects like these are all important, this rhythm and motion is not true to how reality truly moves. This is why we must embrace discipleship as an art, not merely a cold science. Life is a mess to be ordered and an open canvas of imagination. To make faith, worship, discipleship, and theology more relatable to real life, it is proposed that we need to explore how much music can benefit Theology. [23] What can music's movement teach us about how the plan of God really moves? What would it be to learn truth rightly (*logos*), to position our whole selves in a posture that can rightly feel those truths (*empatheia*), and to relate to them in real living (*ethos*)? What would it mean not only to theologize *about* music but also *through* music [24] using the dynamics, tones, rest and requiem, highs and celebrations, to understand how truths move and feel in our affections and passions? In this way, music becomes a brilliant analogy and parable that we must explore in order to teach ourselves how real truths are going to integrate and harmonize with our life's real melody.

This is not a new thought regarding contemplation in and through music. In ancient pagan rituals, music typically had at least one of three magical functions: *Euphemia*, to produce good omens; *apostrophe*, to ward off evil demons or the anger of the gods; and *epiclesis*, to summon the gods. [25] Considering that music has always seemed to be associated with a spiritual power or connection, it would seem that maybe within God's creation of song we can gain a picture and glimpse of how He works. Andrew Fletcher recognizes the power of music's pull and imagery to create environments of influence. He says, "Let me make the songs of a nation and I won't care

Opening Act

who makes its laws." [26] He simply recognizes that cold hard truths are just that—cold and hard—until they are told in a story, a song, or a sonnet. When truths are told in full-orbed ways, they come alive with meaning and are more deeply embraced. Isn't that how the Bible is written? It sings the story of God in song, story, poem, proclamation, metaphor, imagery, and in the real substance that makes up the real human passage.

The outline of this book

Life has a tempo—which is its timing. That's why this book is called *The Tempo of Discipleship*. As people come to reflect Christ more and more they come to it in roundabout ways. We have to be patient with God's craftsmanship and be conscientious of the composer as He writes the song in tempo and time. All this is so we can be ready to jump in and play our part in contribution to the piece.

This book not only addresses timing in how God forms and crafts his sons and daughters, but also deals with the musical form He uses in which to do it. This book is purposefully outlined in what I believe to be God's musical form in leading us. This form is what is known as the 4-fold order of how God disciples, forms, and captivates His people, (to be explained more in Chapter 10). In brief, a rhythm of interaction between God and his people can be observed. God Gathers us out of and from our stupidity (even though we are caught in our '89 Volkswagen mistake), He teaches us His Word and His ways, we Respond to Him in becoming more like Him in repentance, and He sends us out to impact others. This is the simple form and pattern to God's song as seen throughout Scripture. This is his verse, pre-chorus, chorus, and bridge. God's rhythm of working in our lives most certainly continues on in day-to-day living, and it comes to us through the same form. He's always gathering us, teaching, asking us to respond and sending us to gather others. This is God's process for discipleship.

This bears resemblance to the dynamic of modern music's effect on people. The artist promotes and gathers people to their event. They teach in song, art, and message. The crowd responds with hands in the air—sacrificing money on the altar of merchandise and product—and they leave to share the experience and recruit more groupies and fans to the band and cause. The power of music engages people on a mental, social, physical, emotional, and spiritual level, and it is one of the only things in creation that engages all five of humanity's spheres of being. It has content. It connects people. It stirs the body to move. It outlets the passions, and it nurtures, grows, and expresses what we worship, honor, respect, and believe. Considering that this pattern is the natural movement in how God trains us, I not only structure the book's Table of Contents around this pattern, but I will also seek to end every chapter with some practical insights for living out the truths that are discovered. In analyzing different aspects of music, and relating them to the life of discipleship, I will conclude every chapter with a section entitled *The Tempo of Discipleship*. Each ending section will include three subheadings. The three headings are entitled Theology (Head), Biography (Heart), and Doxology (Hands). The reason these subheadings were chosen is to show that discipleship is a holistic process. Discipleship captures the head, the heart, and the hands, and this is one of the reasons why music presents such a formidable parable for how all of this actually takes place.

The Theology section will assimilate the truths of each chapter into how we learn to know "God" and learn about Him. Our approach in learning His character is vital not only in *content* but in *construct*. What I mean by this is that theology not only contains very real truths, but also that those truths are best understood within certain environments and structures. Without the combination of *learning* and *walking* out the Bible's truths in our real spaces of living, theology is just dead weight.

The next section will deal with our Biography and life story. In this ending thought, we will seek to apply the truths we have learned to the real and tangible world of our lives and ponder ways in which our stories are impacted by the information that we will cover. This Biography section is important because it will teach us how truth interacts with authentic living and maturity formation.

Finally, we will look at what we *do*. We will look at what truth causes us to do in response to what we have learned. The word we use for this is Doxology. The word comes from a combination of two words, *doxas*, meaning "glory and/or praise," and *logy*, meaning "logic." In other words, it is the logic of our praise. How I explain this to people is by saying, "the logical end to learning about God, and learning about His place in our lives, is to praise and glorify Him." Therefore, every concept in our learning, and every endeavor of our life, should lead to a more robust worship of God's glory. Learning should lead us to expressive and creative response. If, after embracing a set of truths, we do not find ourselves standing in awe of

Opening Act

Christ and longing to live more in the light of His love, then our learning has been aimed in the wrong direction.

It is hoped that, by the end of this book, the reader will have an approach and patience for the timing and journey of their own personal growth and messy discipleship, as well as an approach to how they can aid in the development of others. History and people are not static, nor are they predictable and uniform; as such, each person is like a note, an instrument, a song that is best sung when played as it should be—sounded individually with all the flavor, pitch, range, and dynamic that it possesses and also played beautifully within community. God made us to be played in the right place, in the right time, and in the correct way. Though our song may bring moments of discord, we can know that God is committed to resolve all tension as the grand song of history winds to an end.

1

The Melody of Image

> *God sings a melody to us. It rings sweetly, penetrates in our ears and beckons us to 'Come'— come and participate. 'Come,' God says, 'and harmonize with me as I sing over you, and let us together build a symphony of sound that plays my glory.'*

The Top 100 Charts

When we are out on the open road, we all love to turn the radio up and tune into our favorite station or search in our iPod for a song that most rightly fits our mood, the journey, and the destination. Undoubtedly, as we spin the wheel-of-song-fortune long enough, eventually we land on "the song." When we hear "the song," it grips us and captures us up into its swells. The song's tune is much more than a group of notes punching out sound through our audio speakers. This song's theme is iconic. It gathers us and it calls us into the world it has created within its form. Soon we find ourselves not only singing along in the present, but remembering the moments from the past that were also sound-tracked by this melody. We remember the special instances, the victories, the holidays, the history. We attach personal, generational, and historical meaning to these simple recordings.

There are songs that have the power not only to equip us for a good car ride, but they also become so powerful that, like *My Generation* by The Who, they come to define actual points in history. Jimi Hendrix defined a period with *All Along the Watchtower;* U2's *With or Without You* formed relationships, and again we find that a song's influence not only carries the ability to encapsulate a generation, but also to become the universal love song for romantic relationships all around the world.

Songs influence people on different levels. For example, classical compositions such as Gioachino Rossini's *Morning Song* became powerfully attached to events like a sunrise in a cartoon and are forever associated with this in our minds. J.S. Bach's *Joy of Man's Desiring* is iconic in religious settings, as well as Handel's *Messiah*, for they have the ability to move the soul toward thoughts of God's grandeur and beauty. Even today on a simpler and more popular level, we have songs like Beyoncé's *Single Ladies (Put a Ring on it)* that defines not only a mantra for a new generation, or a relationship, but promotes a dance craze, much like Chubby Checker's *The Twist*. People resort to mimicking it, promoting it, and stylizing themselves after the phenomenon. In the briefest of moments, the fad passes, or ceases to be "cool," and the next hit artist draws the nations to attention with a new hook and beat.

Melody

What all this boils down to is the power of a song's *melody*. Melody is the part of a song that grabs us. It's what songwriters call the "memorable hook." It grips our attention in any moment with its catchiness and causes the song to be easily remembered. As the audience, we carry these melodies in our heads, and we sing them throughout the day at apropos times. Sometimes these melodies become so lodged in our brains that we can't help but think of anything BUT their seductive tune.

It's not only the audience that corrals around such a hook. The band does as well. The artist chooses lyrics that fit the melody's tone, imagery, and sound—for to put a happy melody with a sad hook would be unthinkable. This melody is like a magnet to which all the other parts cling. When the hook is written, the drums emphasize it with the beat and the piano, electric guitar, bass guitar, and synthesizers surround it, undergird it, and play around it in a way that propels it out into the audience's ear with intensity. The sound engineer pushes it up in volume so everyone can hear it, the dancers punctuate it and make it visual, and the light show, screens, hype, and atmosphere enliven the crowd to draw into and be captivated by the experience. This is the power of melody. It's the original song that is written and formed in hopes that all involved might come and form themselves around it.

Trinity Song

In Genesis 1:26, God in Himself is and was the first melody that has ever been heard. God is heard in these first few verses in Scripture resounding like an audio concert saying, "let us make man in *our image.*" His melody and hook exploded into all of creation and became the song to which the whole world would conform. Everything in land, sea, and sky reflected, sounded, tuned to, and painted the nature of the Creator. It is in this beginning time that the song of creation is profoundly the most clear.

God's unity in heaven propelled this melody forth. He did not just sing this melody alone, but He sounded it in a Triune chord that shook the darkness. His use of the language *"us"* in Genesis 1 defined God's ensemble as plural, and in this dramatic act of collaboration He sparked and implemented His new idea.

Yet even in this "plural-ness" of God's harmony, the most resounding claim God makes about Himself in the Bible is that in His plurality He is also One. [27] He exists in melody. So how can this Trinity the Scripture speaks of as being comprised of the Father, Son, and Holy Spirit also be *one*? It seems throughout the centuries that this is the much debated question. This mystery of the Trinity, the 3-in-1, has been likened to so many things, and every analogy leaves the human mind puzzled as to how to resolve the tension.

The concept of music can inform our thinking about this conundrum. Though there is one melody line within music, one can surround each individual note with two other notes and create what is called a *triadic chord*—or harmony. Each note surrounding the melody makes up a 3-note *triad* and allows musicians to sound one note together, and in unison and uniqueness, and still have the pitches intertwine with one another—and this chord makes sense. This is the foundation upon which all of music is built. The Trinity in like fashion, made up of "three tones, sound ... none of them is in a place; or better, they are all in the same place, namely everywhere ... no difference of places keeps them apart; yet they remain audible as different tones ... the tones connected in the triad sound *through one another."* [28]

In a very similar way to how music intertwines and holds conversation within itself, we can see the same kind of plural unity in the Trinity and in the human image that reflects His nature. We are made up of a mind (logic, reasoning), a heart/soul (life, emotions), and a strength (will and action) that all work together in one body to produce forward motion. If it is true that we have been given "the royal office or calling as God's representatives and agents in the world, with granted authorized power to share in God's rule or administration of the earth's resources and creatures," [29] then it would definitely be helpful to us to consider God's nature before we determine how we are going to go about acting out ours. James K.A. Smith puts it this way, "we are commissioned as God's image bearers, his vice-regents, charged with the task of ruling and caring for creation, which includes the task of cultivating it, unfolding it in all its possibilities, in human making—in short through culture. Imaging God thus involves representing and perhaps extending in some way God's rule on earth through ordinary communal practices of human sociocultural life." [30] We had better get started.

C.R.O.S.S.

The unity of the Trinity is fascinating, albeit mystical. It seems that if we are to ponder and try to understand such a complex being as God, we will only end up chasing a mere shadow of what is actual reality. Our quest to understand God, however, is similar to the quest that drives people to understand earth's elements and the scientific periodic table. Though everything in all of creation demonstrates a plurality in containing multiple scientific elements that make up its fabric, we see within this multiplicity that there is singularity. A tree, a river stream, an egg, and a rock all contain a combination of elements, but they still make up one "thing." In our search to explain how "three" is "one" we do not have to stretch very far into our imagination in which to do it. Into the very fabric of the universe, this plural-oneness is woven.

Though we cannot fully understand the way the Trinity works, I do believe we can derive some unifying principles in regards to how the Trinity holds together in their unique melodic plurality. The insights to be gained from our contemplation can provide us with some considerable insight into the human experience, informing us in how we are to *image* our Creator. In an effort to connect the complex themes of God's character as expressed across the whole Bible, I'll attempt an easy approach by using the acronym C.R.O.S.S. This acronym will serve as a brief encompassing framework for us to follow here in describing the image of God. It is suggested in this acrostic that the Trinity is predominantly united and intertwined in five ways as revealed in Scripture (all of which can be seen in Genesis 1-3 and in the totality of Bible):

Community: The Trinity's melodious harmony is made up of "one another," and they relate to each in friendship and unconditional love. In *how they relate*, the Godhead is united, and this is why "one another" is spoken of over 200 times in Scripture in how humans are to also conduct relationships. Though God's community toward humanity is built through *covenant* promise and steadfast commitment, his community within himself is sheer *communion*. It is enjoyment. This is foundational to understanding the context of love as well as all the other good things present in the universe. It shows us the importance of the melody of God's community. We, as humans, are to harmonize to His tune in how He relates and loves.

Reasoning: The Trinity is also united in *how they do things*. In Ephesians 1-2, it speaks of God's establishment of the world. His works are depicted as being in "accordance to his purpose." In Scripture, He uses the word "will," the word "plan," and the word "promises" to describe the nature of His method. He links all these things to the culminating work and personhood of Jesus Christ. In this way, every method of His design points toward the gospel that is finished in Christ. This reasoning filters into how He does family, marriage, parenting, church, government, work, recreation, rest, etc. His truth is not just *audio*, it's *video*! This means that God's truth is not just something that is audible as it is proclaimed, but it is something visual. He shows forth His truth in how He constructs family, marriage, church, etc. God is very ordered and very creative in His method as we see in creation. If we are to play off His melody, we are to consider how He does things.

Organization: The Trinity is also united in *how they organize*. Though they are ONE, it is clear throughout Scripture that they serve each other within a real *authority* and real *submission* structure. The Father is always showing His nature in Jesus, and has submitted and entrusted His likeness to Jesus to perfectly display; yet Jesus is always seen to be doing the Father's will. [31] Jesus is always praying to, praising, and serving the Father's will in submission, yet all authority in heaven and earth has been given to Him. [32] Similarly, the Holy Spirit is always drawing attention to Jesus and perfecting the Father's commands in submission, yet holds authority to carry out God's plans on earth. This very real culture of heaven—one of submission and authority—is a melody to which we must also remain in sync for our own betterment and protection.

Scripture: The Trinity is united also in *what they believe*. In reading the Bible, we gain insight into how the Trinity communicates with one another. The Bible gives us their language. In reading their words, we learn not only how they speak to one another, but we also learn what they believe, value, and esteem above all else as a unified team. Their melody of belief is one we are to sing and embody in the content of our own living song.

Signature Mission: The Trinity is lastly harmonized in *how they lead*. Ephesians 3:9-11 says "God who created all things, so that through the church the manifold wisdom of God might now be made known to the rulers and authorities in the heavenly places. This was according to the *eternal purpose* that he has realized in *Christ Jesus* our Lord." The signature mission to save humanity has been in play since the creation of the world. Jesus clearly explains in Luke 24:27 that all the Scriptures proclaim Him as the center that pieces together all of history. Jesus ineffably knew we would fall away from His melody, pitch, and key into the dissonant chord of sin. That's why the melody and mission of the cosmos has been to bring this grand song back to resolve through belief in Christ.

When we look at the totality of Scripture and analyze God's work from start to finish, these sub-headings provide a nice framework in helping us to understand what it means to be "made in his image." To become like him, all of these facets must be considered in our own living. When it comes to music, it is helpful for us to think of God's likeness as the melody to which we all harmonize, and that's where we turn our attention now.

Community

When God made man in His image, He called us "good." By saying the word "good," He measured man by His standards, which is *perfection*. We were perfect. We came from and out of God himself. When God sat back and reveled in the fellowship, friendship, and love that He enjoyed within Himself, He erupted in joy and made us perfectly as the offspring of that love. We were then caught up in the perfect union of God. The *communion* love that holds the Godhead together held us together. This love went far deeper than human ability and stretched far higher than human understanding; this love toward humanity was also one of *covenant*.

Covenant connotes the idea of absolute, unadulterated, uninhibited, and unconditional loyalty and affection. This is the DNA which makes up how God made us and the reason for which we were created ... to love and be loved. Within God's nature, it is impossible for Him to be anything less than pure and Holy, and, thus, it is impossible for Him to turn His back on His commitment to us. His love and affection for us is anchored in His nature and being. This is what ensured that the culture of the Garden was equipped with protective safety, productive care, and the pervading presence of God Himself.

In Genesis 3:1-9, when tension and discord entered the Garden through a temptation, a fall, and the sin of Adam and Eve, something more was at stake than a mere taste test between apple trees. The perfection of humans had been forever scarred—made imperfect. No longer could humanity reflect God anymore—perfection. The attack made on humans was an attack on God's nature itself. Notice how in the Genesis passage, the serpent does not challenge humanity as much as He calls into question the goodness, loyalty, and true worthiness of God;

Now the serpent was more crafty than any other beast of the field that the Lord God had made.

He said to the woman, *Did God <u>actually</u> say*, 'You shall not eat of any tree in the garden?' And the woman said to the serpent, 'We may eat of the fruit of the trees in the garden,' but God said, 'You shall not eat of the fruit of the tree that is in the midst of the garden, neither shall you touch it, lest you die.' But the serpent said to the woman, '*You will not* surely die. For *God knows* that when you eat of it your eyes will be opened, and you will be like God, knowing good and evil.' So when the woman saw that the tree was good for food, and that it was a delight to the eyes, and that the tree was to be desired to make one wise, she took of its fruit and ate, and she also gave some to her husband who was with her, and he ate. *Then the eyes of both were opened*, and they knew that they were naked. And they sewed fig leaves together and made themselves loincloths.

And they heard the sound of the Lord God walking in the garden in the cool of the day, and the man and his wife hid themselves from the presence of the Lord God among the trees of the garden.

Satan first caused Adam and Eve to doubt God's word, and from there he began to cause them to question God's character. When they began to feel as if God had kept something from them, they entered into a new type of love, a *conditional contract* not a *communal covenant*. They treated the unconditional love of God like a lease, and as soon as they felt that they did not get what they wanted or deserved, they divorced God. The Bible says that "their eyes were opened," and they were open to the fact that they had shamed their perfection. They had broken the law and code of law that was in the Garden—the law of love. They had not only forsaken God, but they had also destroyed and murdered their happiness by choosing what is altogether flawed.

When God came walking through the Garden looking for them, He found them, and He sentenced them. Their treason against God's law of love was punishable by annihilation and death. Though this seems harsh, it is also just. The perfect law of love and of complete trust and unhindered relationship had been broken by spiritual adultery. Humanity had strayed and had transgressed God's perfect holiness. However, in mercy, it appears that in God's dealings with Adam and Eve, He held something back and possibly even relented a bit in His justice. Or did He? He did not kill them, but it is true that God chose to curse the ground for the man and to add pain and penalty to the legacy of the woman rather than start over. They did not get away scot-free. God, in order to be truly God, had to reveal not only his love and mercy, but had to also satisfy His justice. In Genesis 3:21, God outlets the penalty of death upon an animal instead, and clothed humanity in "garments of skins" to cover their shame.

The implication here is that the first death in creation had taken place, and an animal had taken Adam and Eve's place for their due punishment. This is what theologians call the *proto evangelion;* the "first gospel." The good news. It is God's commitment to the melody of His covenant as it still rings out through Creation. Though we had left, He had not. Though we had failed, He would not. Though our leaving Him resulted in fear, death, and worry, God promised still to remain with us as He continued through all of Scripture to sound one of the most resonant promises, "Fear not, I am with you."

This theme, or melody, of the death of something or someone standing in place of humanity, begins in this passage, and is developed throughout the Scriptures until the grand climax in Revelation. This great crimson thread of atonement is woven throughout the following passages: Genesis 22:8; Exodus 12; Leviticus 16; Isaiah 53; John 1:29, 36; Acts 8:26ff; 1 Peter 1:18-20; Revelation 5:9, 12; 6:15-17; 7:9-17; 17:14; 19:11-21; 21:7-9, 22, to name just a few. The ultimate fulfillment of sacrifice on behalf of our sin, is found in Jesus, the Lamb of God who takes away the sin of the world, dying in the place of humanity and paying for our sins. [33] Later, Paul calls believers in Jesus by the name of "living sacrifices" through Christ's sacrifice and God's *poiema*, a word translated to "workmanship" and related to our word *poem*. [34] God's sacrifice poetically holds the theme of His covenant communion love together, and as God's word is crafted to the prose of covenant, so are we to write a similar rhyme of sacrificial love.

The death brought about in the first covenant made with Adam produced a series of following promises that God makes in order to ensure humanity would remain firm in their hope that God would never leave. His first covenant to Adam provided a framework for the covenant that would soon follow—the one made to Noah. [35] After Adam and Eve's fall, the evil on the earth quickly increased to a disastrous place, causing God to start over with a global flood. Though many died, Peter reminds us of how God "did not spare the ancient world, but saved Noah, one of eight people, a preacher of righteousness, bringing in the flood on the world of the ungodly" (2 Peter 2:5). Once again, the defiance of humans resulted in punishable death, but God, through the grace of a wooden ark upon the flood, foreshadowed a wooden cross on which Christ would ride through the waters of judgment in order to start a new race. This ark, like the cross of Christ, portrays God holding firm to His commitment to us; for even when we leave and fail, He does not and will not.

Then came the covenant made to Abraham. In Genesis 15, God *cuts* a covenant with Abraham [36], by which He divides animals in half, lets their blood run down the center of two adjacent hills, and God Himself then walks through the blood. This act on God's behalf is symbolic, and "the sacrifice reminded both parties of the weight of their oath. Should the covenant be broken by one of the members, such violence should be expected in retribution." [37] God symbolizes His unwavering oath and promise to His people through a vow—a covenant marriage vow.

This act of communal covenant is where we get the symbolism for marriage. This imagery in God's covenant to Abraham demonstrates a marital devotion within God's commitment to us. Even today, at a traditional wedding, the two families are divided on two sides just as the animals were divided. A red or white (purity) runner divides the aisle symbolizing the walk through the blood which the bride and the father walk through to meet the groom at the front. Just like Abraham did not walk through the blood, neither does the groom. This is to symbolize that the father is committed to this covenant beyond what humans can do. After the groom puts the sign of eternity on the bride's finger (the ring), the couple walks back down the red aisle between the families as a commitment to God, family, and country that this covenant is 'til death do us part.

This mentality of God, a mentality of marriage, was and is how He relates to His people, and it continues into the Mosaic covenant, [38] the following Davidic covenant, [39] and on into the new covenant agreement reached in Jesus, a descendant of the line of David who was born in Bethlehem.

The gospel of Matthew starts off by showing Christ as the "Son of David," [40] and thus he has the right to rule over God's people. Peter preached that Jesus Christ was a fulfillment of God's promise to David, [41] and Paul later proclaimed Christ to be a fulfillment also of the law of Moses. [42] Jesus is the perfect sacrificial lamb offered once and for all in the place of humanity. He died so our sin could die. He rose to life so we could be born again into His family, and He ascended into heaven to secure our citizenship in His garden once again. This is God's communal and covenantal ethic, culture, and nature.

Reasoning

Flowing from this real and loyal love is a methodology in how God does things. If His mode of emotional expression is one of love, hospitality, peace, and generosity, then His method for expressing such love must follow suit. Not only did God, in the Garden, create a community of fellowship, but the *context* through which He desired for His DNA to spread is equally important. God wanted to propel His image out into His creation, and He did not see fit to begin in creating a sports team, a stock exchange, a Fortune 500, a Para Church 501c3, a democracy, or a metropolitan city to grow and portray His image. Rather, He decided to hide His most valuable possession, the reflection of Himself, within the fabric of a *family*. His method for advancement is hidden within the family. It is in the union between the husband and wife and in their relationship to their future children that God is going to produce the liveliest and truest covenant picture of His own storyline.

The man became the Head of the Garden as Christ is the Head of the Church, and the woman became the one called alongside to reflect the Holy Spirit's role within the Trinity as expressed in human form. The Father officiated the wedding and ruled the marriage, and under His leadership, Adam and Eve were caught up in a genuine display of the divine. God then told them to multiply, to be fruitful, and to tap into the same joy that He had when He spawned His children. He wanted Adam and Eve to create as He had created, from the overflow of joy in one another. This marriage was to show forth God's image.

After a marriage consummation, what naturally soon follows suit is the producing of offspring. Not knowing for sure that Adam and Eve ever had kids before the Fall, we may only be able to think hypothetically about what their parenting would have looked like, but we can extrapolate some methodology of what the "home" may have been like in the Garden by looking at some of the nuggets of God's wisdom in other parts of Scripture. For example, Proverbs tell us that the children are to honor their father and mother. This honor and authority structure within the family paints a picture of how God relates within Himself. Adam and Eve would have been very real authorities to their children, and their children would have joyfully resolved to love their parents in safe submission. This culture of the Trinity—one of honor and respect for each member's value and position—would have certainly been normal in the pre-Fall family. The Scriptures tell us that human parents are also called to train up children in the way they should go. This dynamic of *training* would have also been the norm in the Garden economy. The training coming from the parents down toward the children would have been received and applied by the children in a way that reflected the parent's values and image—the same way the Trinity designed humanity to interact with Himself. The Proverbs portrayal of the concept of training goes much deeper than the post-fall necessity for spanking and the like. This training is to reap a fruit much deeper than mere obedience—it is to multiply the image and love of God. The Proverbs idea of training is encapsulated in this respect in the Hebrew word *paideia*.

Paideia was understood in the Old Testament Jewish mind as the whole of a person. Over 800 times, the word "heart" is also used in Scripture to indicate this idea of whole. The idea is that a child and person is composed of an emotional, social, physical, spiritual, and mental make-up, and the parent is required to train, teach, instruct, provide balance, give ideas, nurture, and craft each area of a child's life. The purpose in all of this is not to produce *good* families as the end goal, but to raise children that grow up into the same desires as their parents and of their Trinitarian parents (the Godhead)—namely that they hold the desire to resemble the glory and image of God themselves.

One can only imagine what humanity would have become if the Fall would never have happened and God's method of expansion would have continued to grow unhindered, but this was not the plan. What's the bottom line in all of this? We must still continue to imagine a world where the family unit is the hot-bed for training character and Godliness within God's kids, and it is the very source from which all other productivity on earth should come. Discipleship, leadership, and any other kind of "ship" is forged and measured not outside the home, but inside of the home. This is how God does things. Everything springs from here.

ORGANIZATION

Unfortunately, with earth's parents firmly putting a trajectory of disobedience into play, the culture of the Garden was not able to permeate outward into the rest of the world. Not only did God's grace need to restore the broken community and the broken methodology, He also had to restore the broken order. Humanity usurped the chain of command that ensured their protection, and they had stepped outside the family's protective walls and right out into a counterfeit worldview. Because of this, family not only

The Tempo of Discipleship

became decentralized and de-prioritized—as we see in our world today—but it became tangled and confused.

We must note, first and foremost, that God is not surprised by this; rather, He planned it and expected it from before the beginning (Eph. 3:8-10). This anticipated disobedience ignited a long chain reaction that ultimately revealed the Trinity in an even greater glory—in the crucifixion of Christ and in the gospel. To understand the effect this had on the organization of the world and God's plan in allowing this, we must first understand that this apparent detour was "according to the eternal purpose that He has realized in Christ Jesus our Lord." [43] As discussed previously, God's thread of payment for humanity's sin is a melodic DNA that permeates its strain all through human history: when Jesus arrived on the scene in the New Testament and died on the cross only to rise again. He is found in Luke 24:25-27 having a conversation with a slow-to-understand mix of disciples. In the conversation, it is clearly seen that the disciples did not understand the Torah and the strain of grace and sacrifice that ran through it due to the Fall of Humanity. Jesus says to them, "'O foolish ones, and slow of heart to believe all that the prophets have spoken! Was it not necessary that the Christ should suffer these things and enter into his glory?' *Thus, beginning with Moses and all the Prophets,* **he interpreted** *to them in all the Scriptures the things concerning himself.*"

Jesus clearly understood Himself to be the covenant melody of the entire Bible to which all of humanity harmonizes. He understood Himself even to be the melody of the Garden. [44] In allowing the Fall of mankind, Jesus' authority over the earth was not undone, but humanity's relationship to His authority was. Humanity now turned their sights to a different leader—themselves. Christ's rescue mission now went forth into the rest of history to reveal His intended glory in making this planned moment of sinful perversity right again. The foundation of earth had been shaken, and it was up to Christ to restore the order in putting humanity back under His Headship once again.

To do this, God would have to proverbially rebuild the family house that had been broken down to the foundation. In Ephesians 2, Paul describes Christ as the *cornerstone*, likening the world and all we know to a building. Author Constance Cherry describes the cornerstone this way: "the cornerstone was a masonry block that established the corner of the building. Everything was measured out from this critical building block. The cornerstone had to be laid straight and true; if not, it compromised the stability and beauty of the entire building. The cornerstone was the first stone laid —usually at the outer corner closest to the street. It had to be true, level, and flawless in form or else the rest of the stones in the wall would set askew." [45] Jesus' perspective was that all of human history started in His perfection within the Trinity—the cornerstone. Thus, for humanity to return to the state it once had in the Garden, the cornerstone had to realign the world in perfection so humanity would no longer be searching and struggling to align and organize themselves according to Adam's crookedness. Our order had to once again be found in Jesus. Jesus thus reminds us that "...Worship starts with God. It begins in the loving relationship of the Trinity, where the Father exalts the Son, the Son exalts the Father, and the Spirit celebrates them both." [46] For our melody to begin we must start with God as the cornerstone.

ORGANIZATIONAL HARMONY

The dynamic image of the Trinity is what laid the cornerstone of creation. The relationship of the Trinity, although built on community, is ordered and organized. In discussing humanities' restoration, we must think through this Trinitarian hierarchy and chain of interaction if our broken world is to rediscover its own lost image. To discuss this organization, we must talk not only in oneness but also discuss the plural harmony of how God works together within Himself. The covenant commitment is the melody God sings, and from this He harmonizes all of His being, His house, His government, His ethics, His work and recreation, and all of His plans to this sustaining theme.

In music, the idea of melody carries the *hook* of the song and is the memorable strand that provides the theme around which the whole of the band and instrumentation organizes. *Harmony* in music is what organizes itself around the melody as it complements, reinforces, and supports the piece. In music there are different types of harmony:

> **Organum:** One of the earliest forms of harmony, organum is a means of greater emphasis, or of reinforcing the sound to carry through the larger churches. It consisted of adding a

voice that exactly paralleled the original melody at the interval of a fourth or fifth.

Descant: From Latin *discantus,* meaning 'song apart.' This is a countermelody either composed or improvised above a familiar melody. In late medieval music, *discantus* referred to a particular style of organum featuring one or more countermelodies added to a newly rhythmicized plainsong melody.

Faux-bourdon: French for false bass, this is a technique of musical harmonization used in the late Middle Ages and early Renaissance, which involves three voices, two of which are written and another added or improvised. In its simplest form, faux-bourdon consists of the cantus firmus and two other parts—a sixth and a perfect fourth below.

Polytonality: Developed primarily by French composer Darius Milhaud, this is the simultaneous use of two or more different tonalities or keys in a single piece of music. [47]

JUST AS THERE IS FOUND A HARMONY IN MUSIC, THERE IS ALSO ONE WITH God. Though God is One, He works together in an organized community within Himself in harmonious unity. This unity can be described in the words of *authority* and *submission.* Elizabeth Elliot calls it the "Glorious Hierarchy." [48] The Father, in authority, maintains the will, plans, purposes, and promises that the Godhead has made to humanity. He administrates the Trinity, and even Jesus Himself acknowledges this. Jesus, on the other hand, in authority, prays for, leads, is head of, builds, and stands in perfection in the place of His people—the church. He is the God-man and our representative in heaven, carrying out on our behalf the functions that Adam failed to accomplish. The Holy Spirit, the Trinity's hands and feet, leads the authoritative work of God to unite all things to Himself as He counsels, comforts, convicts, proclaims, and transforms God's children into those once again under His rule and reign.

Though they are all in authority, they all submit to one another. Servanthood and love within the Trinity is not the prerequisite for greatness, it is the *stan-*

dard of greatness. [49] The Father loves us through Christ and shows us what He looks like in Christ. The Father clearly delegates all of His nature and visibility to Jesus. Christ, in response, glorifies and works toward the fame of the Father and follows the Father's commands in a perfect effort to show forth the Father's image wholly. The Spirit draws everyone's attention to Jesus, so that all might see the Father, and fills humanity with the Father's love. It's as if they are all together providing the *organum* in exactly pairing with each other, the *descant* in that they improvise and play off each other, the *fauxbourdon* as the Father and the Son resound the finished work, and the Spirit improvises upon it to bring things to completion, and finally the *polytonality* in that God's character resonates in pairing attributes through it all; love/anger, justice/mercy, wrath/grace, etc.—seemingly dissonant themes all operating at the same time to provide a glorious tension and mixture of grace.

This same harmony filters into human relationships and organization in like fashion. God's *authority* and *submission* structure first entered creation when God <u>said</u>… God told creation what to do, and creation obeyed. God provided the authority, and the creation submitted. This is the intended government structure of God's kingdom. God worked through His hosts like the sun to accomplish His purposes. God worked through His living animals to proclaim His character and nature. And when Adam and Eve were created, He told them that they would resemble Him, and they listened.

In Genesis 1-2, God created Adam to be first in the Garden. Adam was to protect, expand, and steward the health of God's creation under God's rule. When Eve came along, God took her from Adam's side, his rib. God set up the order not only of His Creation, but also of His households on earth. Eve was not made from Adam's spine in that she should walk behind him as a slave, nor was she made from Adam's sternum that she should walk in front of him as his leader. She came from his side, a helper, a complementary person to help him. She was to be intimate with her husband in face to face *perochoresis* like that of the Triune God, and she was also to serve side by side with her husband in carrying out God's image upon the earth. In the New Testament, as mentioned previously, the man is related to Christ, the Head—the leader. In the New Testament, the Holy Spirit, the *paraclete*, is the one "called alongside" to *help*. Thus, the woman and man were to work in tandem as Jesus and the Holy Spirit do within the Godhead. God had given them a *co-mission* and a *sub-mission* as they walked with each other to function in different roles and strengths in order to completely show forth the glory of the Triune God.

Many in our culture recoil from this idea of making the male and female distinct in this manner. Even if we clearly affirm both the male and female's equality in dignity, value, and worth, the world still wants men and women to be equal in role and function. Clearly, if we "take away differences in role we no longer have distinct persons (this alludes to the Trinity's unity and plurality); there is nothing that makes the Son to be the Son rather than the Father, or the Spirit to be the Spirit rather than the Father, or the Son. If we abandon eternal differences in role, then we also abandon the Trinity." [50] The tragedy in this regard emerges; that the battle over gender role and function has nothing to do with gender at all. It is an assault on the Trinity! It is that humanity has walked away from Christ, the cornerstone, and no longer works outward from Him as the starting place. As time has passed, this out-of-balance genesis has propelled people, tribes, and whole nations into refusing to obey God's chain of loving command.

Even God's people, Israel, did not honor God's order, and they found themselves moving in and out of slavery and war due to their misunderstanding of authority and submission. Israel in particular was taken captive and oppressed under evil governments such as Egyptian rule. They refused God's instruction and leadership, and the result was bondage under a false system of authority. When God freed them from over 400 years of slavery in the book of Exodus and led them toward the Promised Land in Numbers, God had to recalibrate His people. They disdained authority, for they had been abused. God had to take them into an authority/submission rehab and teach them how to love and serve all over again.

In Numbers 1-3, God ordered the people into families first (very important), then chiefs, tribes, and standards. The structure of the family was still the bedrock of God's ordinance. Then His system grew up into a leader of families—a chief. Then it expanded itself into a cluster of families within 12 tribes under 12 main leaders. Then there were tribes grouped together around the temple in standards (networks) for the purpose of land ownership, governance, battle, and defense. Clearly God's Triune family harmonized His nature, and as it grew, His *plurality* (meaning more than one) of leadership in the Twelve tribes of Israel resembled His heartbeat. This structure was not merely to organize people, but also to position people's hearts to understand the framework and kingdom culture of heaven itself.

A kingdom ethic is made up of a culture of leading and following. Everyone is in authority to someone, and everyone is submitting to someone. It ensures a holistic good for everyone involved, and the protection and preservation of everyone involved—man, woman, and child.

This same phenomenon appears in Acts. After God's people had once again compromised His message and forsaken His authority, Jesus came and freed His people once again from the slavery of the law. In Acts 2, after Christ's death, resurrection, and ascension, 3,000 people were saved in one day through Peter sharing the gospel. God ordered them into homes to be led by apostles, overseen by multiple elders, and to be helped along by deacons/deaconesses. This harmony of structure aligns with God's nature. Once again, it establishes an ethic and values for the home, church, government, workplace, recreation, and on into any other location in which one might be found. We are supposed to follow His tune, otherwise the song our life plays sounds like an out-of-pitch tryout from an American Idol contestant.

God's melody streams constantly forth, and our worship and honor is to resonate. Harold Best calls this harmonizing process worship; as it is a continuous outpouring proceeding from this tune of God. He describes that God's Trinitarian melody cannot help but pour forth; "He cannot but give of himself, reveal himself, pour himself out. Even before he chooses to create, and before he chooses to reveal himself beyond himself, he eternally pours himself out to his triune Self in unending fellowship, ceaseless conversation and immeasurable love unto and infinity of the same." [51] God's endless conversation and Trinitarian nature is continually communicating itself to us. We either ignore it and try to fight, only to be caught up within God's authority whether we like it or not, or we serve and follow it willingly and experience His peace.

SCRIPTURE

The reality that God's song is heard in all of creation, and that each pitch we play is to harmonize to Him, is now important to preserve in principle for all generations. In order to preserve people's connection to Himself, God wrote things down. It was part of His plan as the composer to chart out the notes, the themes, the dynamics, and the instrumentation so that the Creation could follow his conductor's score and lead chart. God thus took the language of heaven, the dialect of the Trinity, and translated it into human understanding. When He wrote the Bible over a period of 1,500 years in 66 books through more than 40 different authors from all walks of life, yet writing the same storyline, He was describing to and through them the story that He was trying to tell.

Scripture provides the bridge between God's song and the directions in how He enables humanity to sing along. As *creatives* all around the world work to capture people's imaginations, it is nice to know that God gives us a wonderfully creative book in the Bible and invites us to engage that imagination. [52] The Bible is the "Christian version of the idea of world harmony, a 'prose hymn' that reveals an 'upward striving from the visible world harmony to the invisible will of the Creator.' In it 'nature and man unite in a concert of softly singing waves and pious songs.'" [53] God sings His song and ways to us and we respond, either to leave this composition behind and decide that we would very much like to play the notes in the way we think they should sound, or we read the composition and allow it to lead us in the direction of His choosing.

As God crafted the words, His goal was not so much the words themselves, but the people reading them. The notes are the template, but people are the instruments. We are supposed to sound His purposes. Tragically, our instruments became broken and useless at the Fall. Because of this, Scripture's words are not merely a composition in themselves, but they are written to re-compose people and transform them back into resonance with the Creator.

To do this, God had to undergo a process of composition in not only writing the notes, but stripping away the sins of His people that cloud the original song. This simplifying process applies to the process of composition, which Tavener describes as "an act of repentance, stripping away of unessentials, ever more naked, ever more simple ... one might even say, ever more 'foolish.'" [54] This is what a songwriter does, and this is what the Scripture then serves to do. It serves to provide a simple manual of love. It corrects and remedies the complicated existence that humanity has created for itself. Humanity has become confused by embracing false affections and chasing dark rabbit holes, and God has made a way back for us into the simplicity of what His life is like without tragedy, death, and the murderous intent of sin. In writing the Bible, then, as a master composer and craftsman, He exposes false notes, accidentals, and things outside the musical key. He not only removes them in calling us to repent, but He replaces our drunk affections with the "expulsive power of new affections." [55] He writes in new notes, new trills and motifs that restore the beauty to His and our song—that motif is His own glory.

2 Timothy 3:15-17 records that "All Scripture is breathed out by God and profitable for teaching, for reproof, for correction, and for training in righteousness, that the man of God may be complete, equipped for every good work." And Hebrews 4:12 follows by stating, "that the word of God is living and active, sharper than any two-edged sword, piercing to the division of soul and of spirit, of joints and of marrow, and discerning the thoughts and intentions of the heart." The implications of these two verses work in tandem. In one sense, we have a "greatest hits" album playing inside ourselves that resonates only with sin, folly, foolishness, and deception. When we come to the Bible singing our song, God rebukes us, corrects us, knocks us down, and possibly knocks us out in order that we might take the headphones off. He puts His ear buds in that we might listen to His greatest hits album. When the process happens of Him stripping us of our song, we feel the sting of His sword. We feel almost as if He's killing us. But as we start to listen to His Word, we find that the sword is more like a Doctor's scalpel. Though it cuts and hurts, it operates on our cancerous tumor and removes the growth so that we can go into remission and ultimately live life once again the way it is intended.

God's language is like a loving and violent scalpel. Its attack is devastating to us, but the motive of God is one of love and healing. It is God's very language that performs the operation. God, in a very great way, translates the language and dialect of heaven into the form of the people, into a language we ourselves can understand for the purpose of our healing. Mike Cosper says it this way, "language includes and excludes; illuminates or confuses," [56] and God, being a great communicator, did not let a word slip by without thinking about a way in which to say things so we would understand it.

Just as He created the world when He *said* ... He recreates us as a new person in the same way. Each word cuts through the darkness of our psyche and into the depth of our void and says "let there be light."

Signature Mission

The Tempo of Discipleship

When God sings, we harmonize, and when He recalibrates us to His pitch, we join together in a symphony with Him that echoes into all of Creation. This symphony resounds with many instruments from many nations, in many languages and cultural expressions, and it all forms a new culture—a new kingdom.

This is where we come back to some of our discipleship analogies. As a Christian community, we are called the body of Christ. This is how we connect and interrelate to each other across denominations within national and international borders. We do not seek to break from each other, we seek to equip one another. We realize that one of us is the hand and a hand needs the mind; one of us is the mouth and we need the feet. Early Christian movements grasped this deeply, such as the Moravians, who made sure that their potential converts understood from the outset that commitment to Jesus meant commitment to His group. [57] The body needs the other parts to build it up and support it. Jesus, in an effort to heighten the weight of the commitment to the kingdom family and body, publicly disowned allegiance to His own blood family (Mark 3:31-35). He called James and John to leave their natural families (Mark 1:18-20). He commanded a man who wished to provide for his father's burial, in accordance with traditional Jewish family piety, to instead follow Him and "let the dead bury their own dead" (Matt 8:22).

Though Jesus supported and supports the family unit, He nonetheless stresses that human blood cannot bind in the same manner as heavenly DNA. We are blood relatives of Jesus if we are in His family as Christians, and our family ties to the church are much stronger than our ties to the world. This is the first tempo of discipleship in that it connects the disciple to the mission of God in His body. This means a disciple's first mission is to that of his/her family within God's larger household. The disciple's first "light bulb" moment is to see themselves as family members in the community, and thus, their decisions hold the potential to either help or hurt that community. Disciples need to undergo a mind shift in how they make decisions. Decisions are best made in community and in the context of the church family. The closer a Christian group approximates the strong-group church family model that characterized early Christianity, the better the decisions will be amongst the group's individual members and nuclear family units. [58]

The next tempo of discipleship is to realize that this new covenant reasoning takes time to forge. People are used to thinking in terms of wants and contracts. When we do not get what we want, we run! This is the individual default mode of the human heart. In order for a disciple to grow in their mission to the body of Christ, they need to begin to see all of their life in relationship to the whole. This can be helped along by the culture and methodology of the environment itself. Since we are talking about music, let's first mention songs.

Many wonderful songs reflect on our personal relationship with Jesus but tend to ignore the connection between God and His people as a group. Songs can help in forming the believer to understand their relationship to God as well as to others. The theology in songs is very important and cannot be simply sung to God, but it has to have moments of singing to the believer about God in order to connect us as a family around His truth.

Another dimension to restoring order to earth's broken anarchy, is to place a disciple in a place where they are exposed to God's order and teachings. Matt 23:8-12 says, "But as for you, do not be called 'Rabbi,' because you have one Teacher, and you are all brothers. Do not call anyone on earth your father, because you have one Father, who is in heaven. And do not be called masters either, because you have one Master, the Messiah. The greatest among you will be your servant. Whoever exalts himself will be humbled, and whoever humbles himself will be exalted." Here, Jesus clearly teaches his ethic of *authority and submission*, and He highlights the plural nature of the Trinity's leadership in how important it is to walk within order as we do mission. Even in heaven we see 24 elders around God's throne. *Plurality* and servant leadership are designed to be central to God's model of the church as a strong-group family. As one learns to share the mission of God and gospel of good news with others, they need to have the protection of a Biblical force of Generals that are assembling the army for strategic mission out in the field. In a very real way, for our own protection in the field, we need to have people *over us, beside us, and under us* in order to fully fight the good fight. This process of coming around the melody of God's image is a holistic one and is a messy process; as humans, we carry with us an aversion to community, an addiction to independence, and a rebellious heart toward the ways and leadership of God. However, when a disciple is taught about their subjection to all these things, and that it is to their betterment, they can begin to operate freely within the new culture of joy and safety.

One element that is amplified in this becomes the spiritual gifts. The disciple can now feel a motivation not only to be served in God's home, but also to serve. This is the Trinitarian image. A new ethic begins to propel the disciple on into the Great Commission as they are not only saved and baptized to *sit*, but also sent to teach and train others in how to *walk*. God equips them for this mission in gracing them with supernatural ministries that He aids them to accomplish. Paul's writings can help us here in understanding the integration of these ministries.

In 1 Cor. 12:1, a passage heavily dealing with spiritual gifts, Paul introduces the subject of a disciple's gifts in the terms preferred by his Corinthian readers using the word πνευματιόν *(pneumatikon)*. Interestingly though, he quickly changes terms through Chapter 12 to use the term he himself prefers for the spiritual ministries (gifts), χισμα (charisma). But what does he achieve by this change, and how does it help our discussion here?

The Corinthian church had begun to make the mission of God individualized—once again threatening the Trinitarian mindset of togetherness as a body—and had begun to turn the *gifts* into supposed abilities or superpowers. They began to follow more the pattern of sorcery that was conducted in amongst pagans. The Pagan temples used ecstatic gifts as well. One of which, *glossalalia*, was known to create connections with the gods, and Christians were beginning to try to pervert spiritual gifts, namely tongues, in the same way. Because of this, Paul wanted to create a distinction between what it is to serve like the world and what is to serve like God.

Pneumatikon, for example, was not used anywhere else by Paul to refer to miraculous abilities on an individualized scale, nor should it be assumed to be used as such in 1 Corinthians. Paul's use of this word is specific and purposeful here. A big danger loomed in Paul's mind as it should ours; "The quest for an individualizing and self-centered form of 'spirituality' was in danger of denying the source of all true spiritual gifts, the unbounded grace of God." [59] The people of Corinth had become so obsessed with individual rights and abilities that they had lost their focus on what service to the body really meant. Because of this, Paul did not mean to depreciate the term πνευματιόν *(pneumatikon);* for elsewhere in his epistle, with only one possible exception, Paul always uses the word with positive overtones of spiritual maturity. But Paul's use here, in this context, and the switch to χισμα (charisma) in the following verses in Corinthians, seems to lay emphasis on a community of grace.

Paul's emphasis in talking about the spiritual gifts (preferred translation here: "spiritual ministries") was in the context of the body. The so-called spiritual ministries should *not* be viewed here as special abilities to do ministry (focused on the individual); rather, they should be viewed as the corporate ministries themselves. [60] And as we see in 1 Corinthians, well over 250 ministries are listed by Paul, so we can assume that the gifts lists given are not exhaustive. Rather, they are examples of family ministry (in the context of community), not referring to abilities that were owned, [61] but instead these gifts are given by God to believers for specific points in time as the body has need.

In seeing spiritual gifting this way, and in seeing that spiritual ministries are given, not owned (there is no evidence of a person's ownership of these gifts [62]), a person's thinking turns from entitlement (that's my gift), to a place of asking the question, "where can I serve." In this fashion, the spiritual ministries become like the percussion section in the grand symphony. Together they play their part, and they accent and contribute to the whole of God's melody. There are times when the trumpets chime in with loud voices, and other moments when they rest and stay quiet. In a sense, the writing of the composer and songwriter determines when the gift sounds and when the gift lays dormant. The composer might also determine when a ministry and melody may disappear from the song altogether. The decision of when to play their talent is not up to the instrumentalists. They may possess the potential to play, but only the grace of the composer allows them to play in the appropriate timing. Thinking in this manner helps those who follow Christ as disciples to embrace his serving outreach to the world within the community, and in the manner in which He intends.

THE TEMPO OF DISCIPLESHIP

What music has taught us about real discipleship is that melody, harmony, and symphony are connected. This bears implications on discipleship methods and practice:

THEOLOGIES' MELODY: THE MELODY OF GOD IS HIS *COMMUNION* WITHIN Himself, and His *covenant image and nature* toward all He has made. Our nature without God is one of *contract and conformation*. We, because of sin, are forever bent—a crooked and depraved generation—toward exalting, glorifying, making much of, and worshipping ourselves. Therefore, we seek deals that provide for our needs and selfish wants. If we deem something to be bent toward making much of us (it's called self-esteem), we naturally will comply and conform to the situation we worship until it violates our agreement. As soon as it steps outside our policy, we buck and break contract only to move onto something else that most satisfies our need for worship. To break out of our self-focus we need first to ask, *Who is God?* When we ask this question, we set our sights toward right thinking and position ourselves for Him to communicate covenant practice to us. This helps us rest secure in Him, as well as become like Him in how we extend His character toward others.

BIOGRAPHIES' HARMONY: I KNOW IT GOES WITHOUT SAYING, BUT GOD IS different altogether than us. This bears considerable weight in how we are to think of ALL OF LIFE. A disciple is to consider the covenant thinking of God, and must ponder His Community (*how he relates*), His Reasoning (*how He does things*), His Organization (*how He organizes*), His Scriptural ethics (*how He believes*), and His Signature Mission (*how He leads*). To learn to act out of this wisdom effectively in harmony, a disciple must be provided with a variety of situations, environments, and settings. God, the composer, along with a possible mentor, provides places of work, church, home, marriage, parenting, recreation, media, and so on as stimuli to unearth contract thinking in His people and to expose our fallen nature. This provides the opportunity for a person in particular to fall back in line with God's song. In situations where sin is seen, repentance can happen, and the Trinity can be pondered and thought of in how the Godhead's *image* might remedy the situation. Once the melody is heard of the Trinity's image, the disciple can then maneuver their life around it in how they do community, how they organize, and how they lead. The disciple's response to seeing God is to ask, *Who am I?* and to reform one's self accordingly.

DOXOLOGIES' SYMPHONY: A HUMAN RACE THAT IS CAUGHT UP IN THE disconnected melody of "me, myself and **I**," must also see through to "the **we**"—the symphony. It is curious in Genesis 3, that when Eve was first tempted by the snake in the Garden, she responds to the serpent's attempts in saying things like "***we*** may eat the fruit from the trees in the Garden, just not the one that is forbidden." (Genesis 3:2). Notice how she refers to herself and Adam as *we.* After they sin, and when they are caught by God in their shame, the language surprisingly turns to "***I.***" This once perfect humanity that viewed identity in a plural-unity, now falls into individuality. The "we-ness" of creation had been usurped. From then on, our response has been to isolate and pull away from true community, and because of this, mission and message has suffered.

An idea that comes from African tribes might prove helpful here in our conclusion and in helping us bring restoration to "**we**" thinking. They carry on a tradition called *unbuntu*. This word holds the concept that "**I**" and "**we**" are intertwined. In saying "**I**" we are considering the whole, because without the whole, "**I**" could not be. This way of thinking is hard for independents. We think we are self-sufficient. But ask a person to tell you for example, who built their house, who crafted the chair they sit in, who manufactured the car they drive? Quickly they will see how dependent their "**I**" is on the "**we**." A disciple needs to think in *unbuntu*. We need to turn our sights toward the whole—serving the family and serving those who need the family through the spiritual ministries God gives us. We must ask, "*Who are we?*" This gives traction and real effect to our gifting and image, and we become more like God in the process.

2

The Participation

Hands flail in the air, voices scream loudly, the smell of concessions is in the air as the show of a lifetime is about to start. The energy that a concert brings to a room, a stadium, or to any platform is thrilling. I've been to well over a hundred concerts as a spectator, and the culture of the event is fascinating to me. Eager fans pour in from everywhere and sacrifice tons of money just to hear a few hit songs that they have already been playing on their listening device at home. If we were to try and figure out why people attend such an event when they've already put plenty of mileage in listening to the music during their commute to work, we inevitably conclude that they attend an event for more than just the songs. The music is more than the songs, it's about the participation. It's about the gathering. It's about the songs with skin on. In attending the event, the groupie not only gets to sing their favorite song, they get to participate in the culture it creates. It creates a culture of worship.

The Grateful Dead were known for the culture they created. Their groupies were even affectionately known as "dead heads." Why? Well, that's easy. Pot! If you listen to a Grateful Dead album you will hear that the musicianship leaves little to be desired. The musical talent of the Grateful Dead is not what attracts people. It is the culture and escape that the music created. People from everywhere who sought escape, comfort, community, and experience came to spend face time with this band/icon/idol that served them up the banquet that their hearts most earnestly desired. For the Grateful Dead, their banquet supplied a culture of proposed freedom; a culture of expression and experimentation. In the last 30 years, artists like Kurt Cobain and Nirvana have followed suit in building cult followings that cultivate a grunge and indie culture of uniqueness, outcasts, and rebels. Into today, artists like Lady Gaga draw people in who still seek to live on the fringe—the edge.

Music has the ability to involve us in its changing sounds, ebbs and flows, highs and lows, and to invigorate our senses and emotions as it captures us into the story that it is telling. In one instance we hear it, but we also feel its beat. We emotionally connect to its tone. We socially connect to the people in the room, and, in many cases, one can spiritually and mentally relate to, believe in, honor, and even worship its message or performer. Music is like a miracle of creativity which "passes through the human personality, sensibility and historical-cultural background of the artist. When the music is played—the listener hears it in a context which may well mark the meaning of that song in that person's lived experience for every other time he or she hears it." [63] Depending on the flavor of the music, it tends to draw certain people with certain preferences, and when they arrive, they are sucked into its culture. Whether it be a drug culture, an angry culture, a sexual culture, an exercise/competition/sports event culture, or a Biblical worship culture, the music plays a part in *forming people*.

An interesting study was done by Dorothy Retallack in 1973 on how melody not only affects people, but living things in general. [64] Her experiment involved plant life, which was based on her experiments of music's effects on vegetation. She found out that out of the plants in three different chambers with different conditions, those exposed to soothing music grew better than the others. In one case, the plants had bent towards the soothing music playing. In another case, plants listening to the harsh music had withered and died. Further research has even shown that the song of birds singing throughout creation provides the musical soundtrack that causes plants to flourish, as the song sung over them helps them grow and germinate. It's amazing to think about the implications of this upon the spiritual formation of a person.

Music holds in itself a power store of manipulative effects that can lead people to false or true affections. This art forms us. Regardless of how this all works, we must consider how this relates to faith. God Himself is shown in Scripture as singing over His people. [65] His song of delight, pleasure, and love causes us to grow and flourish—it forms us. He seeks to wrap us up in His warm culture and form us into His image. This is how He gathers us! He performs His melody, teaches us the harmony, and then invites us to participate in the performance itself.

When you think about it, all of art maintains this power. Art, movies, poetry, drama, etc., all have the ability to invite us into a story that is much bigger than ourselves. This is very informative for how we look at the nature of Scripture itself.

BIBLE AS NARRATIVE

One must first be conscious of how Scripture is told. Scripture is a story. It is an art form—it invites us to enter into its world. Many may presume that viewing Scripture this way might trivialize it or even erase some of its deeper theological implications upon our belief. Rather than viewing the story of Scripture in such a reductionist manner, one must see that the story of Scripture does not dilute belief, but rather it forms belief. [66] Often, misconceptions can be adopted when a person does not make the necessary connections between what the Bible teaches and what the undertones of the Bible actually paint. What this means is that the Bible almost seemingly has two layers to it. It has the *information* layer and the *transformation* layer. If the Bible is only read through historical, redacted, literary, evidential lenses, then it will merely be embraced or rejected as another piece of literature or even as an artifact. This is the level where the Bible is "just like any other book" in that it holds words on a page. However, the second level of transformation is when the disciple seeks to understand the world of the inspired words accompanied by the power of the Holy Spirit. The reader not only seeks to take each word as a banquet served up to the soul, but also tries to understand the emotional cues affiliated with such words and experiences within the storyline. This helps the interpreter to enter into the story of God which is found within the lace and framework of God's Holy words. This proves to be the far more enlightening level. It is at this story level that God begins to shape our thinking, and in the story He connects thinking with doing.

The forming of belief has to take place in the context of real life. Real experience brings moments of loud and soft, slow and fast, full and empty, up and down, in and out. Therefore, the best container for human application is within the context of a journey. This is why the narrative of the Bible, though written on pages, is meant to craft for us a world of drama that is to be entered. It is not that one leaves the wisdom of the Bible behind in this approach. No! It is rather that the Bible is the informant for all we do. The story provides the nutrition, but it is through the exercise of its truth that one fully allows its nutrients to supply every root and every nerve ending of our being. Philemon 1:6 says, "I pray that in the *sharing of your faith* you may *become effective* for the *full knowledge* of every good thing that is in us for the sake of Christ." [67] This verse supports the idea that only in performing our faith do we truly experience its depth. Paul links the growth of a Christian not merely to that of studying the truth, but to a person's diligence in exercising and sharing it. Paul knows that once we begin to use the truth, we will see where we have holes and gaps in our thinking, and this will cause greater diligence on our part to fill in our places of immaturity.

If one perceives themselves to be merely a spectator of God's account rather than viewing themselves in relationship with it, then the reader and text feel disconnected. If a person views themselves as a character within the grand plot of God's movie and unfolding chronicle for the world, the relationship between text and life is changed. Characters within the story have a particular way of viewing the world and orienting themselves in it.

The Old Testament documents the particular journey of a quaint people known as the Israelites, who themselves were woven into God's story of redemption. The people of Israel knew no division between God's story and their place within it. They believed that the glory of God filled the world and that everything in the world told of this glory. The comings and goings of ordinary life held glory; the narrative lifted the veil of the ordinary and let it shine. Second, the narratives not only revealed (and reveal) God's glory in events, but they also draw the hearers more fully into God's work in the world. Stories are a type of what we later in the history of faith will call *catechesis*. They form people spiritually and instruct them in the truths of the faith. Third, the authority exercised by the narrator suggests a setting in worship. The narrator demonstrates a privileged knowledge of events, knowledge of people's thoughts and motives, of conversations overheard, and of the movements of God.

The view expressed above helps us to capture the mentality of a character within the narrative of God. Israel did not separate holy things from unholy things, but rather saw how they intertwined. Scripture is a narrative and as such, should be approached from a performance/drama angle. Doing so is paramount to hermeneutically (proper way of learning and teaching) interpreting and applying Scripture correctly.

PERFORMANCES

In order to convey the reality that we are caught up in the story of God, "performances were also a central and an integral part of the early Christian experience of the compositions that have now come down to us in written form in the Second Testament. The collections of Second Testament writings we now have are records of what early Christians experienced in speech by performers in the community." [68] The performances were not only artful expressions of God's text, but they were essential unto themselves. In the Roman world, as little as five to eight percent of the people (and perhaps less) were able to read, a much smaller percentage were able to write, and even fewer could do either with facility. [69] For the most part, writing served the efforts of empires and elites to establish and maintain hegemony—through records, laws, propaganda, official communications, inscriptions, commerce, and so on. [70] Due to this factor, many of the people were shaped in their knowledge of the truth by these performances. Truth was not merely read, it was acted out and expressed.

Many in the church today may have been trained, either formally or informally, to see the Bible as solely history rather than as drama. This is not the mindset of those in the early church, nor of Jesus Himself. People today have been trained to imagine the narrator as a scribe who gathers historical facts and arranges them chronologically rather than as a playwright who felt the movement of God's Spirit in human affairs. [71] However, this is the not the complete timbre of the melody of the Bible's song. It sings of artistry, movement, and is tantalizing for the real senses. It calls for participation.

How might our experience of God and His word change if we viewed faith this way?

I think that viewing life and faith this way may have profound implications upon how we live out our faith. It may also help us to better understand the culture of the Bible itself. The reality is that the Bible is written in genres such as music and poetry, history and mystery, drama and comedy. This is for the purpose of communicating how its contents are to best be experienced and lived out. The Bible is part of an oral tradition that people not only learned about, but in which they participated. Fathers passed on this tradition to their children and Bible exposition may have felt, in many cases, more like a story given around a campfire than that of the context of Western traditional classrooms. The context of story is lively, energetic, inspirational, and motivating. It captures us and causes us to respond in interactive ways, rather than just spectating in a mere cerebral posture. The art form invites us to participate within it, not apart from it.

Orality Forms Community

In oral cultures, performance and presentation form a community identity for those speaking and those listening. There were physical locations and socio-historical circumstances that shape the performances and the reception. [72] This makes theology instructive and also communally synergetic and transformational. In Paul's mind, he was forming people and churches not merely theologically, but he was sending a *person* to represent him, not primarily a letter. [73] We know that the letters of Paul were composed orally by Paul [74] and recorded by a scribe or amanuensis [75], perhaps in several sessions—a possibility that may explain the stops and starts of a letter such as Philippians. Even in his writing process, the idea of presentation was most likely taking place. His goal was to put the full effect of the text on display in the life and flesh of a person speaking God's words; the words themselves were spoken while animated by the very personality and *imago dei* (image of God) of the messenger. Martin McGuire writes, "The personal representative or messenger, the visitor or traveler, was almost the sole means of communication between nations and individuals." [76]

Therefore, the connection made in oral (spoken) presentation runs far deeper than mere interpretation; it is a means to connect the heart and soul of the global philosophy of the church. That philosophy is one of story, and it is transmitted in relationship. Dietrich Bonheoffer, "in a provocative essay unfinished at the time of his death, argued that truth and truth-telling are relational in their essence, part of a total reality seeking expression, and that for a word to be 'true,' it must first of all fit the relational requirements of a particular encounter." [77] Where it would seem odd for the text of the Bible to be read un-relationally in the context of a pub or coffee shop, in light of performance, the Bible, if memorized, pondered, and lived out in the flesh of human day to day living, could breathe in and out of everyday conversation simply because its DNA possesses the same ethic.

It is in this moment that the relationship between interpreter and text takes on the properties of vivid presence in the power of performance—when all things come together to affect a quality greater than the sum of them as separate. [78] This is a reality that collides and rests not only on the performer, but also within God's work itself. God's revealing of Himself in Jesus Christ is and was a performative event, [79] and, as such, it is also characterized by call, choice, commitment, calculation, and a common goal.

Our Continued Tradition

Considering all the thoughts presented causes us to re-think our various approaches to discipleship. Are we too formal in our training? Perhaps. Are we too Western in our methods? Absolutely. Are we more dependent on written text than lively performance? Without a doubt!

The church is called to develop practices that release and enable the Great Commission to move forward. This commission is one that includes all nations, and so the milieu of the people and their communication styles must be prioritized in good worship, discipleship, and educational modes of operation. For example, studies have been done within and on various cultures of the South Pacific. These cultures conventionally give standing to dance, ritual, and ceremony and are primarily communal. [80] John D. Arcy May says this means that "the community does theology by reaching a consensus in reflecting on its practice." [81] The plain fact is that South Pacific cultures are oral cultures, for which the producing of material in written form is culturally alien. [82] The demographic of the South Pacific is merely one example, but, in all seriousness, most of earth's contexts are communally and orally focused. Predominantly, most of the world reflects the time and place of Jesus' life. It was in this very culturally oral framework that he made known His mysteries. It would do us well to put ourselves into this mode of thinking when trying to communicate all that he said and did.

Therefore, "if a denomination which has a predominantly oral society depends primarily upon written material for most of its Bible study and teaching, then at the heart of its ministry such a denomination is not indigenous." [83] Without anchoring itself within the living, participatory, and continuing tradition of oral transmission, the modern church will have no long-term collective memory, and therefore no self-identity that will enable it to judge the novelties and fleeting fashions of the day in light of the enduring truth of the Scripture which it purports to uphold. [84] What this very brief snapshot and overview of the South Pacific mentality gives us is a mindset for discipleship, worship, and outreach that must reach beyond the most recent fad in materials. It influences the primary mode of our transmitting the truth, preaching and proclaiming. Since we have come to appreciate that orality is not just the lack of literacy—orality and literacy both presuppose a mindset, a way of experiencing the world that is not commensurate one with the other [85]—preaching should acknowledge this mindset and reach much further than just establishing doctrine, although it must wholeheartedly do this, as well. Preaching should delve further into nurturing and instructing the imagination. [86] People need to participate in the truth and *go there* in their minds and bodies.

In any case, the preacher's own interpretation of the Scriptures should be informed by how he/she interprets culture around them. Having eyes and ears tuned to all the facets of real life action will give the preacher more sensitivity to the inflection of the real life action that also took place in the narrative of the Bible—and vice versa. Teaching and materials created solely from a written viewpoint proves to be confusing to students of the faith from other cultures, and this is precisely why broader methodologies must be reconsidered. What is at stake in our practice is the very globalization of the gospel to which we have been called.

Liturgy

True discipleship places a predominant focus upon a believer's participation within the story of God. Like any art form, music included, story has the ability to wrap a person up within itself and leave the person feeling as if they've left their world and have been enraptured into another. Art is culture-forming. Art forms people. In the world of theology, the theologically coy and oftentimes overused idea that alludes to this idea of rich participation is the word *liturgy*. So often, this word is thrown around in different environments without a basic knowledge of what it actually means. I have personally been in churches where liturgy is treated like a swear word. To the congregation, it stinks of traditionalism. While, in other churches, liturgy is heartily embraced and taught as a rich and deep experience. It seems almost foolish that some embrace liturgy and others reject it, but it all comes down to how we understand it. Liturgy refers to work that is done on behalf of a community. It assumes that people are not merely hearing a truth, but they are entering its world and participating in its service. Any work done on behalf of a sole individual or for the benefit of another is what the Scripture understands as a liturgy. Liturgy as understood by Paul in his use of it in Romans 13 and 15 is that is both a *cultic* (religious) and *civic* duty. The truth of the matter is that we all have liturgies —whether for the purpose of religion or just daily life.

Another way to look at liturgies is to use the word "schedule" or "rhythm" (to be looked at more in the coming chapters). We observe both of these in order to better conduct our living and to participate more fully in life's story on behalf of our own well being and what we believe to be for the well-being of others. In our church services, and in our daily lives, we have schedules, habits, and rhythms that form us. James K. A. Smith in *Desiring the Kingdom* says that we have *thick and thin* rhythms. Thin rhythms can be things like brushing our teeth, combing our hair, eating our Wheaties, commuting, attending meetings, and performing our rituals before we go to sleep. Thick rhythms are things like family time, church, devotions, small group, etc. The difference in our habits and rhythms throughout the day, whether they are thick or thin, only appears in how we use them. Oftentimes we assume that thinner rhythms have lesser value, and so we assign to them titles of "less meaningful." When, in all reality, assigning greater and lesser value to things is not the correct approach at all, for everything we spend our time on in *working and doing* eventually begins to form us.

Liturgy in churches and discipleship is no different. Thin rhythms can be text messages, announcements, bulletins, newsletters, blogs, etc., whereas thick rhythms can be our call to worship, assurance of pardon, confession, the word, our response, communion, etc. The bottom line is that, "Liturgics, the art of crafting and *doing* liturgy, is concerned with the *sequence* of *communal* acts, verbal and nonverbal, that together form and shape the worship event." [87] What we worship comes out in the forms and shapes that we adopt for our living.

Ideally this shape and form for life should rise from the Scriptures [88] but then should seek to tell the story with all the life and depth that its richness warrants. We see this idea carried out in how the Scripture refers to liturgies and various types of service. In Lk. 1:23, Zechariah served in a profound way within the temple, and when his liturgy or service ended in the temple, he went home. In 2 Cor. 9:12 the *leiturgia* and ministry of giving is mentioned. In Ph. 2:17, the Scripture mentions the sacrificial offering of believers to God. In Ph. 2:30, Paul calls us to serve other brothers on behalf of the work of Christ. And further, Heb. 8:6 proclaims that "Christ obtained a ministry that is as much more excellent than the old as the covenant he mediates is better, since it is enacted on better promises." Jesus' work is mentioned in line with the priestly work of the Levitical priests in their ministry of blood sprinkling. [89]

Ultimately, the point to be seen here is that all of life is connected in one growing liturgical action in that all the habits and rhythms that we partake and participate in play a role in this grand story of Redemption, of which Christ has completed the final say in all our work. Everything Christ did forms our story, and everything we do plays a part in the story of his redemptive plan. Robert Webber says this about the *work* or *liturgy* of Jesus on our behalf: "This story is the good news *(evangelion)*. In worship we signify it *(leiturgia)*; in evangelism we proclaim it *(kerygma)*; in fellowship we experience it *(koinonia)*; in our ministry to each other and in our service to others we live it *(deaconia)*. It is the very heartbeat of who we are." [90] Because the work of salvation was done, it is now to be received and celebrated by faith. It is a vibrant story that we can participate in. This is why men like Martin Luther understood worship as God's gift to the people. He saw the freedom in Christ's gift, in that through Christ's incarnation heaven collides with earth's brokenness and wraps it up in healing arms again, only to bridge the divide that keeps us from participating with Christ in His life and work. Through the liturgy, God's people can now praise Him for grace already completed in Christ's finished work of salvation. [91]

The influences continue into how the liturgy of our discipleship and everyday living is to be crafted, designed, and approached. In his book *Worship in the Shape of Scripture*, F. Russell Mitman coins the term *organic liturgy*. [92] What he means by this is that all expressions should reinforce one another so that the whole is more than the sum of the parts. The liturgy, and all the parts, should resonate with the actual real-life work of the people. It should be grafted from the very soil and DNA of people and context and be fleshed out in parts that reflect the whole.

Our soil and DNA of "real" life is EVERYTHING we do. We form patterns or habits in how we relate to EVERYTHING. It's part of our story. When we come home from work, we have our habits. Some shoot through the door, get changed out of grubby work clothes, and hit the sofa to watch the game and play video games for 6 hours. That's a liturgy. It's forming. Some run in, receive an embrace from their spouse, finding that two ankle-biting toddlers are clinging to their legs, and they fall down to their knees to begin an evening of tickle wars, wrestling, face time with the family, and bed time routine. That's a liturgy. It's a habit, and it's forming. We participate in story, in the performance of living out out life, and the issue needing to be addressed is this formed in this question: What are we participating in, and how is it forming us?

FOUR-FOLD ORDER

In the same way that we form these liturgies and patterns of story in our lives, and in how we relate to everything—from home to work to play to church, and so on and so forth—we also need to observe our rhythms in how we participate with God in His story. The pattern of God is everywhere. He has thick and thin rhythms of participation spinning constantly in every direction and in every place. Bryan Chappell says, "gospel understanding is not only embedded in physical structures, but it is also communicated in the worship patterns in all of life—including the church." [93] God's melody teaches us that we are to be formed to His theme and crafted by His beat.

Throughout church history this rhythmic and interactive participation with God has a four-fold nature to it. Implied is that though God is creative with the specifics of how He leads disciples and calls them to worship, He's very consistent with the *form*. He calls and gathers us (1), teaches us (2), invites our response (3), and sends us (4). Our approach to everything, regardless of our tradition, musical style, religion, or culture, is shaping our hearts and minds in this four fold rhythm. Because God shaped this into the very fabric of the cosmos, it cannot be avoided by us, but only obeyed or perverted in our use of it. As we consider the four-fold order, to be presented in brief below, take note of how this reflects the ways in which the copy-cat world we live in has hijacked this method in everything from marketing to entertainment to politics, etc. The truth is, we can't escape God's framework, for we are always teaching, shaping, and painting a picture of what the good life looks like. [94] Some people shape and form their reality around unbiblical shapes, and this is where discipleship comes in. The framework and training of God is needed to help disciples recalibrate their mode for relating to the world and to God.

The brief four-fold pattern is Gathering, Word, Response, and Sending. This pattern of God and humanity acts like a human skeleton. It provides the underlying framework of our relationship with all things. We can then hang the meat and skin onto our schedules and liturgies with the specifics that are tuned specifically to us. Bryan Chapell, in his book *Christ Centered Worship*, does a phenomenal and complete job of showing God's pattern and skeleton framework as traced through Scripture (I would highly recommend it for in depth study), but for content purposes let's deal with one instance this forming takes place, namely the first one—in Genesis 1.

In Genesis 1:1-2, we read the account of God aligning the world in a way to ensure that it worships and reflects Himself. As an artist and musician takes center stage before an on-looking audience, God took his place as His Spirit hovered over the deep in Act 1 of the drama of creation. We see Him in these verses standing over the darkened void, which at this point was unprepared to support life. He needed to *gather* the chaos into order. In a very real sense, God prepared His creation for light. The creation was dark, empty, teeming with chaos, and lacked any desire or ability to call itself into order. In a very real way, the creation foreshadows the dark nature of sin in its confusion, its disorder, and its bewilderment. This creation needed a real God to prepare it, to gather it together and make some sense and purpose out of it. The darkness served only as the canvas on which God was prepared to paint His art. Like an artist, He was about to bring together unrelated, raw, and disconnected material in order to prepare and to make all that is meaningful out of all that was seemingly hopeless.

If one were to have been observing this concert, one would have learned and seen two things. They would have seen the Holiness of God, and they would have seen and understood the nature of chaos. The contrast must have been spectacular. God was revealing His perfection, and when the dark collided with His nature, it was revealed for what it is—dark! We can only imagine the kind of tension that must have been in the studio here as God created His masterpiece. In light of Him, we, in the same way as He

The Tempo of Discipleship

gathers us, are revealed for what we are. We are in tension with His ways and we need resolve.

God's gaze gripped and held creation in fierce embrace as He proceeded to the next step—the *Word*. Scripture tells us that then "God said…" He said, "let there be light." He said "let there be animals." Every moment of creation came out of His mouth! It was His Word that drilled through the concrete chaos and began to cause divisions of order. When He speaks, notice that in chapter one of Genesis, the chaos obeys. The starry hosts move when He says "move." The earth teems with life in the seas and on land. In a very real event, everything that God was pondering in the privacy of His mind was made public in His creation. His word and His creation became testimonies that undeniably pointed to His character and nature.

All creation, which had been spoken to, was forced to *respond*. It not only heard the word, but it was enabled and encouraged to join into the play and drama itself. In obeying the Word of God, it found itself stepping out of darkness into light. It found the jagged pieces of disarray being ordered and arranged into purpose, promise, and potential. Some pieces of the darkness withdrew to the ocean deep in response to God's light, almost as if they were repellent to God's light as the polar end of a magnet naturally runs away from the pursuit of another magnet. Others attracted toward His magnetic pull as material rose into the mountain peaks, almost as if the creation could not get enough of His truth. Each part moved. Each part responded.

Then God *sent* each responding piece to its corner in the universe to serve its intended function. The sun was sent to provide daylight, and the moon was assigned to the night. The fish were sent to fill the seas, as those breathing air were assigned to serve on land, beneath the sky. In this rhythm that can be observed in all of creation and throughout great events in this history of God, we see God dealing with His people. This is how He disciples and teaches His creation.

GATHERING:

As humans, we are not exempt from this participatory rhythm. It is everywhere. Whether we are gathered and taught by the stadium, the mall, or Toy's 'R Us, we are, all the same, solicited to respond to a message and sold a vision of the good life that seeks to tantalize our imagination. The vision of the good life we succumb to profoundly forms us. We ought to think carefully about the things we are allowing into our formation process.

The church upholds these rhythms as well. Let's look at the structure of a real life church service or liturgy. This example will not solely look at all of God's creation as it participates in His dance, but will consider the human responsibility to join into the responding chorus. Usually, every worship service has a "Gathering." The Gathering in a worship service is too often seen as that "opening stuff" in most people's minds, the requisite assortment of hymns and prayers that we need to chug through prior to the "real thing"—the Sermon. [95] However, it is much more important than this. In God gathering us, He calls us to worship and He invites us (*the invocation*) to worship Him. In receiving His calling, we turn to listen to Him call.

Have you ever noticed that most churches begin church by singing or speaking something? Have you ever noticed that the first thing anyone do when we sing or speak is *take a breath*? We prepare to sing or say words of praise (*the Gloria, The Thanksgiving*) or words of humility in response to His glory (*Confession*), and as we breath the importance of *breathing* in the act of singing becomes an "embodied effort … when done consciously and as an act of prayer, it is spiritually and corporally very uplifting, as the whole person is involved."[96] Breathing as a musician prepares one to play and sing, as it invites air into the body. Fascinatingly, the Holy Spirit is likened to wind and breath in the Scriptures. Our breath is symbolic of receiving God's call to us, and we are going to invite and breathe Him into us in order that He might order our chaos. This is God gathering us.

God inhabits the gathered church when we breathe in because we, as scattered worshippers, are all temples who together, make a greater temple (Eph. 2:19-22). When this temple (us) gathers, something otherworldly takes place. It's an outpost of hope in a dying world, a fellowship of resurrected sinners, whose presence in the world is a foretaste of a greater transformation to come. [97] When this takes place, one of two things happens. The weight of this moment produces a darkness over our life *(the Kyrie*—"*Lord have mercy," the Confession)* as we come in contact with a Holy God who reveals our imperfections. Secondly, though He first reveals our sin in light of His perfection, only then does He calm us with His grace (*The Assurance of Pardon, Thanksgiving, Petition*). He not only levels our pride, but assures us of His pleasure, and we are not pushed out of the heavenly courts, but rather drawn near in confidence into His presence.

Word / Instruction:

Like a hen gathering her chicks or an eagle overshadowing its young in its wings, God pulls us in like a loving Father. He secures His creation in an intimate embrace through and in Jesus. He then pulls us up on His knee to command us, to teach us, to train us, to speak to us, to affirm us, to counsel us, and to disciple us. His words breathe through us. This beautiful picture is even the rhythm in how God calls His very own Son. "For the church, then, worship is participation in Jesus' own worship of the Father by the power of the Spirit. It's initiated by the Spirit's prompting, made possible by the Son's work, and is all about the Trinity's glory." [98]

When God speaks, He speaks through His language, His dialect, and His ethics. He indoctrinates us with His values by using the Bible and His Creation as His curriculum. When the Word of God is preached and spoken into a disciple's life in faithful and true manner, Jesus still speaks to His church by His Spirit in the hearts of His people. When the command of Jesus is heralded, it collides with our reality. It's like a symphony, consuming us in its song as it whisks us out of stress and worldly cares and sucks us up in its majestic story. This is why men like John Calvin saw the whole Christ-centered Scripture as gospel-focused. He saw each moment of human history as an imperfect drama that needed redemption—just like the foundation of creation needed the same. In some way or another, either directly (reading, preaching, praying, and singing) or indirectly as responses to the Word (confessing, faith, saying the "Amen"), all things are caused by God's word spoken to us. [99]

Table / Response:

The moment then appears in a church service. Our participation in God's work is now summoned. When the light collides with the dark, the dark is either forced to relinquish all its powers to the light, and give up its hold in an act of rebellion against the light, or it can see the light as a positive thing as it provides an opportunity to participate in redemption. Again, the Word of God gathers and speaks to us, and the creation always responds.

Imagine you were at the creation event. I believe, whatever it must have been like, it must have sounded like a Big Bang. As darkness scattered, the deep divided, fissures erupted, the crust cracked open, islands shot up through the ocean swells, and continents formed as they rose in seconds to almost touch the sky, it must have been a terrifying spectacle. Out of all the thunderous noise came beautiful seascapes, mountains, rivers, and the like. All of what we call *beautiful* came out of what was then *chaos*.

The creation was all responding, singing, and participating in God's commands. Some parts retreated, as if in rebellion, and others were made more lovely, as if in obedience. The rhythm of God's creation was established. He gathers, He speaks, and all that is created responds.

In a worship setting, we may participate in response to God's call on our lives through things such as singing, giving, prayer, counsel, and, most importantly, communion. We do so because "we participate in an event of communion conceived in terms of the bilateral, reciprocal giving which is realized in Christ's relationship with the Father in the Spirit and in which we are liberated to participate ... by the Spirit." [100] This is why the event of the Lord's Supper has always been central to the worship of the early church. [101] As the bread breaks and the wine imparts its aroma, we observe the doorway into God's creation (Christ's body and blood). At the table of His feast, we are forced to make a decision—will we eat dinner with Him or will we retreat? His light comes through His table.

If we say yes to God's call, it is surely a sign that His light has awakened us, for our darkness cannot understand how to *choose* light. As His light warms us, we sing, we pray, we move toward Him and toward each other in generosity, encouragement, praise, and thanksgiving, etc. On the flip side, when His light goes out into the people, the darkness also runs. Those who do not want to partake and participate in His household story will reject His feast and choose to search for their power, provision, and protection from some other source. Ultimately, whatever source one chooses to draw from will begin to define every action of their life.

Sending/Charge/Blessing:

This powerful Gathering, Word, and Response now brings with it a Sending, a charge, and a challenge to go and do something. Jesus says, "go and die." When Isaiah, in Isaiah 6, was called into the holy place of God to view the angelic chorus around God's throne, he is gathered to hear the word of holiness. God pulled Him up from humanity and preached to Him about what perfection is like. When Isaiah hears it and sees it, he responds, "I am a man of unclean lips." Though his response is profound, it is not complete. His response is not the end. He did not fully understood what God's story was all about. God then spoke a powerful word of action—of sending—and benediction. He touched Isaiah's mouth and purified him with a hot coal, and, in the closing of God's worship service, brings Isaiah to utter in Is. 6:8 "Here I am, send me."

When I read this verse, it's as if Isaiah's heart was like a bowl. It was a bowl filled with uncleanliness. The thing about a bowl is that it can only hold so much liquid, so if that heart/bowl is filled with dirty filth, over time the only place for that hate to go is to overflow. However, the human heart can also only hold so much love, as well. As God began to pour His love into Isaiah, it turned Isaiah's insides to mud and the overflow became a stench in Isaiah's nose, but this was not God's end. God knows that the human heart can only hold so much hate or so much love. He kept filling Isaiah, until Isaiah's only response was to overflow in love. This is the sending.

Chapell calls this the Gospel Sequence. [102] Edmund Clowney calls this full-circle event "Doxological Evangelism." [103] The cycle of true worship participation and forming is complete when we are not only gathered before God's heavenly throne in a concert of praise, nor only when He sings His word to us to teach us His message, nor only when we respond with our giving, our pledges, and our vows in response, but true *forming and participation* occurs when we leave His concert hall and enter the home, the workplace, the community, and all the spheres of life with an intentional attitude of sending that says, "Here am I! I'll do it!" This forming is complete only when we overflow.

James K. A. Smith says, "It's as if the story we've been hearing and rehearsing now comes with live illustrations." [104] The truth of God begins to overflow in our *liturgies*—our schedules, our budget, our talents—the participation in God's kingdom is not only something we dream about, but it's something we experience and overflow with in our own five senses. God invites us into His artwork through imagination and story. He wants us to enter into His way of life in all our spheres. He wants to overwhelm our family with His leadership. He wants to govern our churches with His code of love. He wants to challenge our workplace integrity and policy with His unending character and purpose. This is what it means to be a disciple; not only to hear the melody, but to harmonize with it and overflow with it into story.

The Tempo of Discipleship

So, let's deal with the implications of what participation implies upon the very formation of a disciple's song:

Theology: Participation in God's story should cause us to deal with what we *input*. Everything is forming, from the words spoken to the beliefs embraced, to the very liturgies and forms of our church, everyday schedules, events, and formats. Therefore, the input we digest, and the content we swallow should not only be correct in meaning, but it should resonate in tone. This means that we are not to command people to obey what God has not commanded. We are also not free to permit what God has forbidden. We must pay close attention to the tone and pitch in how He speaks about things. Oral cultures understood this fully. The dynamics of the performance, of the art, and of the song bring to life not only the content of God's truth in how it should resonate in our minds, but it also captured the grandeur of how it should resonate in our hearts.

We must find creative ways to enrapture people up into environments of learning. We must utilize visual, kinesthetic, digital, and auditory forms liberally and with great Gospel precision. We must be as shrewd as a serpent in picking content that amplifies the words of theology into real tangible expression and as gentle as a dove in our presentation. All of this is an effort to make the transmission of theological learning feel more like a story than that of an academic lecture.

Biography: In participation, we are to be conscious of our *throughput*. As our story unfolds within the story of God, we are to pay close attention to how our soul is intertwining with God's reality. Galatians 5:22-23 gives us a list of the fruit of the Spirit to help us in becoming aware of our interaction with God: "love, joy, peace, patience, kindness, goodness, faithfulness, gentleness, and self-control." It is surprising how many of these are very emotional and deep words. It's almost as if God wants us to be conscious of our emotions as they are like evidence to the health of our soul. They tell us the truth about the storyline we are joining into and what is truly forming us. If we're plugged into the world's formation, it forms stress-ridden, anxiety-filled worriers and people who are hateful, self-centered, brash, and proud. This is the world's cookie sheet and this is their form. The true part however of what's forming us should be God's Spirit. The Bible encourages us never to *quench* His fruit by plugging up the water pipe that He flows through.

DOXOLOGY: BE CAREFUL OF THE *OUTPUT*. THIS IS NOT JUST A CAUTION TO the individual, but an exhortation for the disciple to begin to see everything as forming. Every gimmick, T-shirt, artist, politician, and church is utilizing God's system, whether in good or perverse ways, to form people. Everything is theological! Everyone is Gathering followers with Facebook "likes," they are speaking their Word and message, they ask for Response in our sacrifice of what is most valuable to us, and they Send us out as their ambassadors to model and represent them. In the process they redefine words like friendship, like, social, and countless other biblical words.

Everything on planet earth is performing in this exact same way. Everything on the planet is forming us and beckoning us into its storyline. It's the ploy of marketing, advertising, consumer markets, and salesmanship. This is not a bad approach, for it is Godly—God made this form. It's His invention! Nevertheless, in living, we need to be conscious of the output message by which we are being formed. Our fleshly heart draws us to indulge our five senses in immoral and disgusting ways (throughput) and in giving into such temptations we will eventually finalize our habits and character. Though this is true, and even scary, we must focus on the freedom of realizing the same thing, formation, happens with good intention for those who seek the Spirit's leading.

3

Musical Rudiments

> *God teaches us His Word. Its content is firm and foundational, and yet its pitch ever moves with the timbre of life. He teaches us His language in words old, familiar, and new, and the Word of God trains us to be more like Him.*

Over the last 17 years, I have had a lot of people come through my business seeking individual instruction in various areas of music and art. When a person sits down with me and begins asking me questions about how to enroll their son or daughter in my studio, I first begin by asking them about their goal for instruction. Some people come in seeking an extra-curricular activity to round out their children in the arts. Some are parents who have been playing music all their lives and want to pass on the skill to their kids. Still others come in not knowing what to expect, and others come in with a definite style, sound, instrument, and direction that they want to pursue. My reason for wanting to understand their goal before I proceed is to assess whether I can best create a form-fit lesson plan that will help the student and/or parents arrive at their desired outcome.

Once I learn the student's goal(s), I begin to tailor-make a plan that best fits them. As this creation process takes place, it really becomes quite an art. Each person holds their own unique personality and design, and each student approaches learning in an altogether different way. Some learners are visual. Some are kinesthetic. Some are auditory. Some personalities desire connection and personal relationship as the highest value to learning. Others desire ideas, tasks, and efficiency in their approach. Still others need time to think, process, and grow in their skills while others appreciate a lot of feedback and sharing.

This is the dynamic of real people. We have our different preferences, flavors, tastes, and things that work for us. If a teacher does not recognize these differences and teach in ways that the student understands the information, then the instruction will fall flat on its face before ever gaining steam.

Needless to say, teaching people is a unique endeavor, for everyone holds a different perspective and approach to their way of doing things. Regardless, there are also truly foundational items that lie at the core of every practice that we need to consider. Foundational items, or what I call "rudiments," are like the floor in any house. If the floor's base is not constructed properly, the building or house, no matter how beautiful it is, will eventually reach a point of collapse.

Everything brings with it these same principles and fundamentals. In sports, the fundamentals are dribbling, shooting, passing, defense, offense, sportsmanship, and so forth. In fly fishing, the fundamentals are river ecosystems, gear, technique, supplies, and destination. In writing there is pencil grip, words, sentence structure, grammar, and genre. If a basketball player fails to learn how to dribble, they will find every other aspect of their game will suffer. They may get by for a while just passing and shooting, but it will not last long. A writer can get by with pencil grip, words, and sentence structure, but if they lack good grammatical sense, their stories and work will never catch the eye of a seasoned reader. These are the fundamentals, and everything we do in life possesses these things.

When it comes to music, those who play wind instruments first learn the importance of *embrasure*. They learn that if their mouths cannot form to the mouth piece in the correct way, they may never be able to make an instrument sound. The percussionist learns very quickly how to hold the sticks, play straight up and down, play loose, and use a combination of elbow, wrist, and finger techniques. If the drummer does not learn these techniques, they will be slower, unable to play harder rhythm, and, over time, they may even develop tendonitis.

The Postmodern Pizza and Rudiments

Everyone may possess their own personalities, tastes, desires, and beliefs that form everything they do, but without first learning the fundamentals, any person in any craft, belief, or skill will quickly learn they are forever hindered by their lack of knowledge in the basics. What the fundamentals do is provide the anchor. When a basketball player learns to dribble, a fisherman learns to cast, and a writer learns to use grammar, it changes everything—it opens up creativity.

I explain this musically to my students by showing them that musical notes are like words, rhythms are like sentences, and that a piece of music is like a paragraph in a story. Without understanding the basics of words, the reader will never be able to enter into the sentences themselves, much less understand the story. In learning the words, the writer and reader are able to connect ideas and push them out in stories that then captivate the imagination and spur on boundless moments of creativity. It all starts with the basics. Because of this, rudiments should be considered useful not only in learning music, but also in how we sound and play aspects of faith.

In society today, we experience a culture of post-modernity, meaning that everyone's personal preference is considered paramount and equally correct. Through post modern thinking we have tried to erase the fundamentals and basics of human life. This is a useless and impossible quest needless to say, in that in the very framework of the universe the fundamentals are built in.

In the postmodern culture, everything is "truth." The belief is that as long as everything is personalized to you, then it's right ... whatever works for you! It's like a pizza pie world. We get to pick the toppings, the practices, and the beliefs and make our own pizza. The only problem with this is that the universe contains the presence of *absolutes*. Absolutes are governing laws like thermodynamics and elements of time, energy and space that govern our universe. We can choose not to "want" them, or even try to convince ourselves that they are not true to our "preferential pizza," but the reality is, these absolutes will not go away. I can pretend that gravity is not there, but it is. An atheist can say "there is no God," but there is. Saying there is no fundamental Creator to our world is like fighting gravity. Why? To answer this, I'll respond to the atheist in theory. I might ask the atheist, so, "your belief is that there is no god." The atheist would respond with an ecstatic "of course." I would then say, "that is an absolute statement," and without God an atheist cannot even make such a statement. Why? They believe we live in an evolved and irrational universe. In their very statement, the atheist is tapping into foundational laws that cannot be present without something absolutely true. A person cannot say something "absolutely" unless something "absolutely" does and does not exist. The reality of God is the only thing that makes this possible.

The atheist always looks dumbfounded when I say this to them because they cannot see this logical inconsistency in their blindness. The problem they run into is that the very presence of logical and absolute truths destroys their whole system. How can true logic proceed from the illogical? That's not logical.

Basic Principles

The reality is, a divine mind or an ordered "something" had to have preceded creation in order to make creation make sense. Now, this is not a book on apologetics, but as Christians we have a Triune God who claims to have been there before the beginning and will continue to exist after the end. This God is the Father, the Son, and the Holy Spirit. When He designed creation, He made Himself as the absolute to the universe. This means that everything in creation points to Him, and if we fail to make Jesus the *rudiment* or basic *cornerstone* to everything we see, then nothing will make sense. God spoke this world into being and "narrated into antiquity even to the beginning of the world ... and the Bible pours forth a thesaurus of words that creates a new religious vocabulary and a cornucopia of scenes and images that stir literary and artistic imagination as well as theological thought." [105] Within the pages of Scripture, we find the basic principles and absolutes that God weaves into the tapestry of creation's fabric. If a person, a disciple, is to follow God, these basic principles must first begin their journey. If not, a disciple's faith will be like a basketball player who doesn't know how to dribble or a drummer who doesn't know how to hold a stick. Eventually, the lack of foundational training will cause their skyscraper-life to build itself up, only to lean to the point of toppling over. Honing the rudiments of faith will ensure that as people grow in their knowledge of God, they will not have to be forever stuck on trivial things like words and grammar. The mastery of the fundamentals will enable people with the ability to move on into a life of freely composing and creating an existence of beauty and majesty that pays homage and respect to a Majestic Creator God.

Hebrews 5:12-14 confronts us with this reality: "For though by this time you ought to be teachers, you need someone to teach you again the *basic principles* of the oracles of God. You need milk, not solid food, for everyone who lives on milk is unskilled in the word of righteousness, since he is a child. Solid food is for the mature, for those who have their powers of discernment trained by constant practice to distinguish good from evil." The author of Hebrews is addressing unbelieving Jewish people here. They had, in one respect, been part of a rich family lineage of grandparents who had been there when God had parted the Red Sea, made the sun stand still, and caused a whale to spit a prophet out of its mouth; yet they still were unbelieving. With all the training they'd received, their faith should have been vibrant, energetic, and inspiring to the masses, and yet they were still bound in *words, grammar, and line-by-line reading*—like little first graders reading "little pig, little pig." These people had missed the basic principle of God Himself. They missed Jesus, they overlooked Jesus, and they got the whole Torah wrong. God clearly equates maturity not with *what* you know, but with *who* you know. This is why, in Luke 24:27, Jesus had to go back and re-teach them everything in the Old Testament in what it "taught concerning Himself." The disciples thought it was about something different. They missed the Savior because of their lack of skill in dribbling and their atrocious writing technique and misrepresentation of the heart of God's law.

This is what happens to people who do not understand the bedrock elements of any practice, especially faith. Not only can they not create, but they are drawn away into foolish things. Like a fisherman untrained in the power of the river, a person can get into the water thinking that it seems harmless. Their lack of training proves fatal, for they quickly find out that a simple stream contains power sufficient to rip a person off their feet and quickly drown them. Colossians 2:8 says, "See to it that no one takes you captive by philosophy and empty deceit, according to human tradition, according to the *elemental* spirits of the world, and not according to Christ."

· · ·

Learn your ABC's

The word used in Greek concerning the word "elemental" in the Colossians 2:8 verse above is the word *stoikhā'on*—it literally is the music term "rudiment." The writer is telling us that there are elemental rules that govern the way people think in this world, and they are as basic as the fundamentals are to music and the ABC's are to the alphabet. They are primary, simple, effortless, primal, and natural to how we live and think as sinful humans. The world carries with it doctrines and theologies just like any other system. Burger King says, "Have it your way;" Coke sounds its mantra, "Everything goes better with Coke;" and Nike resounds, "Just do it." If taken literally, these marketing slogans preach the primal and most basic principles of the world.

When strung together, slogans like these do nicely to dole up a path to a ruined life. In "just doing" everything that comes to you "your way," you'll find yourself a slave and captive to your own greed and feelings. [106] We always tend to look to what is most natural to us, and we often find comfort in things we think make us safe. When we are comfortable, we are easily mastered by things that reduce us to weakness and imprison us in worthless bondage. [107] We easily give in to products that promise us empty happiness [108] and promote our immature thinking and practice. [109] The world's precepts, philosophy, and psychology [110] are what God tells us will burn up and be eaten up in the last days much like that of a garment in a moth's McDonald's Happy Meal. [111]

When we reach to the root of all of these principles and try to find one "big idea" that labels how the world works, I believe the bedrock core of humanity's basic principles is *religion*.

You might find my use of this word odd, but in all matter of speaking, the entire world is very religious. Martin Luther once summed up the fact that religion is the default mode of the human heart. Religion actually means to "bind back." What this means is that we feel like we all hold within ourselves this nagging feeling that we have lost something. We feel we have lost some sense of value, esteem, worth, fame, or piece of ourselves, and because of this, we have to forever try various avenues to try and bind back or work back to where we feel most whole. We humans begin striving, stressing, worrying, and wandering, trying to scrape about in the darkness. Some of us find our identity in success, others in sex. Some find identity in family or even in ministry. The bottom line is that we are trying to desperately prove to ourselves that we are good people and worthy of something, although there's a nagging feeling in us that tells us somehow that we've lost it, and that we just cannot be good!

Jesus hates this mentality of binding back! Jesus hates religion! He hates the repugnant stench of anyone who tries to earn His approval on their own terms. To Him, our efforts are, as Paul says in Philippians, a pile of rubbish. The word in the Greek for rubbish here, literally implies a steaming pile of %$&#. The reason for such strong language, is that our own ABC's are made up of trying to prove ourselves apart from God.

The religious people in Jesus' day tried to "bind back." They asked Jesus, "Why do your disciples break the tradition of the elders?" These Pharisees were serious about their religion and the traditions they had set up. The only thing was that it was hopeless. They made such an effort to keep God's commands that they not only ignored them by adding to them, but they added so much to them that they lost them altogether. They judged God's law as not good enough, and they judged themselves to be better! This ultimate act of pride flew in the face of Jesus' words as He likens disobeying or adding to the commandments as being the same as *leaving God*. [112] Jesus had no use for people striving to gauge who is good and who is bad (remember in the Garden … that's the Tree He didn't want us to touch—the tree of *knowledge of good and evil*). God never desired us to know good and bad, nor desire religion, He only wanted us to measure things how He measures them, in perfect and imperfect.

These Pharisees, and we as religious humans, cannot earn our way back to God through tradition or our own primal and natural laws. Our set of religious fundamentals and elemental worldly principles seem only to bind us up and imprison us more completely. Our own set of traditions are good only when they enrich faith, not when they become the object of our faith. Jaroslav Pelikan said, "Tradition is the living faith of the dead; traditionalism is the dead faith of the living." [113] He captures that tradition is good and rich when it's God's history we are describing, but it's death if it becomes the mountain we try to climb to reach Him by our own good works. The truth is, Christ is the only one that began at the top—perfection —and reached down the mountain into our abyss.

God's Alpha, Beta, Gamma

God's ABC's are much different. His measuring stick is much different. His basic principles are much different. We must learn His basic and foundational principles if we are to build our house correctly. In Scripture, many have assumed that the letter of God's Old Testament law is the framework provided for a Christian's basic principles. However, Galatians 3:24-25 says the law of the Old Testament and rudiments of God were not meant to be for our *proving*, but rather for our *disproving*. The law's purpose is to teach us about the perfections of God and to reveal our need to depend upon His keeping of them, not our desire to reach them. The law was provided to be our schoolmaster to bring us to Christ—the word used in Galatians is *paidagōgos*. Galatians continues in saying that the Scripture's law served the purpose "to shut up all under sin in order that the promise on the ground of faith in Jesus Christ might be given to those who believe. But before the aforementioned faith came, under law we were constantly being guarded, being shut up with a view to the faith about to be revealed. So that the law became our guardian until Christ, in order that on the grounds of faith we might be justified; but this faith having come, no longer are we under the guardian."

Jewish ears would have heard this in a very specific way, for they themselves knew what a schoolmaster was. For them, Paul's words "referred to a slave who was assigned to a boy from about the age of six to sixteen. His job was to make sure the boy obeyed his parents' rules." [114] This accountability partner was to instruct the boy as a teacher and as school policy does in what is right. However, at graduation—our graduation from the law being Christ's death, resurrection, and ascension—the school policy was no longer binding to the graduate. Graduation had purchased the fulfillment of all the rules. Though the underlying absolutes of God's law—such as don't kill, don't deface school property with spray paint, and don't pull the fire alarm—still may affect the under-graduate, a graduate's position toward those rules are different. A person who loves Christ obeys the laws of God in love, and some of this includes the policies of the schoolmaster —the law. Nevertheless, many of the laws of God, like a school's regulations, were given for specific times in history, such as for the Jews and the priesthood.

Paul, in light of this, still did not defame the law, but called it holy, just, and good. [115] He said that it provided a guide to us as if we were under tutors (*epitropous*) and stewards (*oikonomous*) until the fullness of it was revealed in the set time of the Father. We were under a form of ABC's (*dedoulōmenoi*) of dos and don'ts, but when the fullness of the time (that is, the time appointed by the father) came, God sent forth his Son born of a woman, born under the law, to redeem they who were under the law that we might receive God's sonship. This rudimentary idea of "sonship" in Christ's life, death, resurrection, and ascension is what is foundational.

We find that those who place their trust in Christ's completion of the law will experience a much different ABC mindset. The culture of family and "sons" is much different than that of a slavery mentality that accompanies the ABC's of the world. Sons serve *from* love, not *for* love. The world's ethic of religion switches love's equal sign to after the work, not before you work. The world intends that work = love. In God's mindset, love is held in Jesus.

Some have applied this ethic of Christ-like love to the Ten Commandments and made the observation that the first two commandments are to love the Lord your God, and to worship no other God. It can be wagered that if these commandments are obeyed, then the other eight commandments follow suit—they are merely a result and fruit of the first two commands. This perfect fulfillment of love was procured in the person of Jesus. He perfectly loved the Father and modeled a life free of any form of idolatry. Our work now proceeds from Him, but it never serves to earn His favor. This is a different form of ABC's of the world—Christ's ABC's release us from bondage. Galatians 5:1 says, "Stand fast therefore in the liberty wherewith Christ has made us free, and be not entangled again with the yoke of bondage."

DIDACHE

The question now remains as to how a person is to live out their life in response to this new bedrock set of principles set forth in the person of Christ. Where do we search to find such an outline? It's clear in Scripture that the underlying principle of the world is religion, but how are we to learn sonship—family?

First, we must return to the elementals of the Garden in Genesis 1:26 when God said, "let us make man in our image." As discussed in Chapter One about melody, the Trinity's image is bound in Community, Reasoning, Organization, Scripture, and Signature Mission. Their unity is secured in how they *relate* to one another, how they *do things* with each other, how they *organize* themselves and their creation, how they *believe and learn* together, and how they *lead and serve*. Therefore, the basic principles of the Garden were service and selflessness. The fundamentals of Garden life were love, service, mercy, and security. It was set up in a fashion that both the man and woman could be safe in the environment of family, and it was established in a fashion that the ethic of unity could be sent out into all of creation.

Since through our sinful fall we have lost the full vision of this image, we need instruction and help into how to we are now to live. Certainly the Scriptures give this to us, but other helpful documents have served to capitalize on the basic tenets of the faith that we are to follow. For example, we have the early teachings of what is known as the *Didache*. The Didache, meaning "teaching," is the short name of a Christian manual compiled before 300AD. The full title is *The Teaching of the Twelve Apostles*. Some Christians thought the Didache was inspired, but the church rejected it when making the final decision about which books to include in the New Testament. The Didache contained instructions for Christian groups, and its statement of belief may be the first written catechism (system of belief). It has four parts: the first is the "Two Ways, the Way of Life and the Way of Death;" the second explains how to perform rituals such as baptism, fasting, and Communion; the third covers ministry and how to deal with traveling teachers; the fourth part is a reminder that Jesus is coming again, with quotations from several New Testament passages which exhort Christians to live godly lives and prepare for "that day." [116] Within the Didache the following sections are included:

Chapter 1: The Two Ways and the First Commandment (Honor your God alone)

Chapter 2: The 2nd Commandment: Grave Sin Forbidden

Chapter 3: Other Sins Forbidden

Chapter 4: Various Precepts

Chapter 5: The Way of Death

Chapter 6: False Teachers and Food Offered to Idols

Chapter 7: Baptism-in the Name of FSHS in Running Water

Chapter 8: Fasting and Prayer: Taught the Lord's Prayer and Guidelines for Fasting

Chapter 9: The Eucharist

Chapter 10: Prayer of Communion

Chapter 11: Concerning Teachers, Apostles, Prophets

Chapter 12: Receiving of Believers

Chapter 13: Support Prophets

Chapter 14: Christian Gathering

Chapter 15: Overseers and Church Government.

Chapter 16: Watchfulness for the Coming of the Lord

The Didache presents a foundational writing for the early church community. It discusses not only the beliefs and tenets of the Christian faith, but it also focuses more on the ability to live out those basic precepts. The first few chapters deal heavily with the idea of worshipping God alone and repenting of sin—an idea held in the 1st of the ten commandments. There are then chapters that deal with the nature of following God once the worship of Him is solely embraced. It is a life of sacrifice, exposure of false idols and teaching, and a commitment to new forms and patterns of relating to community—baptism and communion. We are to learn to listen to and support teachers and prophets who teach us the truth of God's word and follow their instruction and also turn from those who lead falsely, teach rudely, and proclaim lies. All in all, the Didache outlines the life of God's family and their relationship to each other and to the outside world. This aided believers in modeling all of their lives around the truth of God.

In a way, the Didache was and is a book of wisdom. As knowledge in Scripture is built up in a person's mind through learning and acquiring a set of ideas and information, wisdom orders the information, makes sense of it, and teaches the learner how to outlet the information into true fruitfulness. The Didache presents the truth in ideas, but also calls and outlines what the believer is to do with the truths presented.

C. H. Dodd, in his work *Gospel and Law*, made sense of this information by outlining seven major themes and tenets that he observed in the Didache:

1. THE NEW TESTAMENT CHRISTIAN IS ENJOINED TO REFORM HIS CONDUCT.

For instance, Paul writes to the Ephesians: 'Put off your old nature, which belongs to your former manner of life and is corrupt through deceitful lusts, and be renewed in the spirit of your minds, and put on the new nature, created after the likeness of God in true righteousness and holiness' (4:22-24; see also Rom. 12:1-2; 13:11-14).

2. THE TYPICAL VIRTUES OF THE NEW WAY OF LIFE ARE SET FORTH.

'But the fruit of the Spirit is love, joy, peace, patience, kindness, goodness, faithfulness, gentleness, self-control' (5:22-23; see also Col. 3:12).

3. THE PROPER CHRISTIAN RELATIONSHIPS WITHIN THE FAMILY, THE PRIMARY unit of the Christian community, are reviewed.

'Wives, be subject to your husbands, as to the Lord ... Husbands love your wives as Christ loved the church ... Children, obey your parents in the Lord, for this is right' (Eph. 5:22,25; 6:1; see also Col. 3:18-21; 1 Peter 3:1-7).

4. RIGHT RELATIONSHIPS WITHIN THE CHRISTIAN COMMUNITY ARE SET FORTH.

'Let love be genuine; hate what is evil, hold fast what is good; love one another with brotherly affection; outdo one another in showing honor' (Rom.12:9-10; see also Col. 3:13-16; Phil. 2:1-4).

5. A PATTERN OF BEHAVIOR TOWARD PAGAN NEIGHBORS IS DESCRIBED.

'Conduct yourselves wisely toward outsiders, making the most of the time. Let your speech always be gracious, seasoned with salt, so that you may know how you ought to answer everyone' (Col. 4:5-6; see also 1 Peter 2:12,18).

6. CORRECT RELATIONSHIPS WITH CONSTITUTED AUTHORITIES ARE DEFINED.

'Be subject for the Lord's sake to every human institution, whether it be to the emperor as supreme or to governors as sent by him to punish those who do wrong and to praise those who do right' (1 Peter 2:13-14; see also Rom. 13:1-7).

7. THERE IS A CALL TO WATCHFULNESS AND RESPONSIBILITY.

'Be sober, be watchful. Your adversary the devil prowls around like a roaring lion seeking someone to devour' (1 Peter 5:8; see also Eph. 6:10-18). [117]

Dodd's analysis and themed selections are helpful to us because we see in his observations the heart of true Christian experience. The Christian life is not about simple input, but it is about output and throughput, meaning that, as Christ deposits things into us and changes our hearts and desires, there should be a competency in us to output His Trinitarian character into our spheres of influence; allowing His Spirit to work through us. To do this, Biblical principles cannot only be seen as mere information, but they have to be linked to transformation.

Considering the analogy of a tree may help in allowing us to grasp this idea further. When thinking of a tree, we need to think of it in two parts: its root and its fruit. If you were to walk by a tree that had branches falling off of it, and its fruit and leaves were clearly withering and rotting, you would assume this tree to be in bad shape. You would most certainly not go up to the tree, take off a big, juicy, rotting apple and take a sumptuous bite. That would be foolish. You would, however, attempt to fix this tree. To fix this tree, you would not simply go about wrapping the rotted fruit up in Christmas wrapping paper and decorations and then declare the tree to be healed. This again would be foolish. To fix this tree, you're going to have to go down to what you don't see, into its roots. You're going to have to change its water source, its nutritional diet, and its soil.

As for all humanity, we do not possess roots, nor do we carry on our arms actual fruit. We do in like fashion have things that motivate us below the surface that others cannot see. We have a heart inside us that carries our desires, our thoughts, our aspirations, and our wants. The only way to see those heart beliefs is to watch a person's fruit or actions. I call them the five senses. You can get to know a person's heart by watching what they touch, listen to, put in their mouth and say out of their mouth, what they watch, and by smelling what their overall fragrance of living is! If a person is eating badly, drinking a lot, watching or listening to garbage, and laying their hands on things they should not touch, this indicates there is a bad source. Jesus tells us that sin does not come from outside of us, but rather it comes from what is in us. To fix the fruit of a person, it would prove foolish to merely send them to rehab, to forbid them to watch that movie, or to take away their alcohol. These might help for a little while, but a person with a bad heart will continue to find things to replace their lost filth.

To change a person, we can't wrap up their outward appearance in decorations and make them look all pretty. This is often the approach and result of the psychological sciences. But the point is that the Scriptures reaches further into a person than just behavior modification and positive reinforcement. Psychological principles are not the rudiments of God. The God of the Bible changes someone from the roots outward to the fruit. The fruit of a person's five senses begin to transform as the heart becomes like Christ. This is the heart of the Didache.

When the gospel and good news that Jesus saves us from our sin enters and rebirths our heart to love and cherish Him, the result is that our outsides change. The results come not only in knowing the truth, but in practicing it; not only possessing the sword in our sheath, but knowing how to wield it. When we begin to outsource the basic rudiments of God's teaching, it begins to impact our environments. Our environments include how we govern ourselves and our conduct, how we manage our families and communities, how we relate to people and authority, and how we relate to the past, present, and future. This is why Kevin Perotta tells us that we should incorporate the Didache into Pastoral Care. He suggests in rooting the Didache (Christian competency) into the *kerygma* (the proclamation of the gospel and its truth), we can teach all things from Scripture in the truest and most practical sense. [118] This allows the truth of the Bible to affect the deepest part of the human, for at the root of human behavior is a motive. To sufficiently disciple and pastor someone is to unearth their ABC's of worldly thinking, call them to repent, and teach them the new mode of operation under God's standards and rudiments.

THOUGHTS ON DISCIPLESHIP:

THEOLOGIES RUDIMENTS: AS BASIC AS DRIBBLING IS TO BASKETBALL, THE Apostles had an idea of what was basic to Christian experience. Their idea

The Tempo of Discipleship

and bedrock belief is that all of life and belief need to find its anchor in Christ before going anywhere. The same way the basics of rudiments and technique apply to music, there are foundations about Christ's personhood to be laid in a disciple's understanding before they will truly be able to freely create. The truths of the gospel should not only be taught, but environments should be provided in which beliefs can be tested. A disciple is one whose environment of home, work, and play are transformed by Biblical truth. These environments, influences, and surroundings then become playing fields on which to practice and act out the truths learned.

BIOGRAPHY: THE WORLD IS A FIERCE TEACHER IN ITS RUDIMENTS. IT IS constantly singing its song to us of selfishness, desire, and want. It rarely speaks to us of thinking about others' needs, about sacrifice, and about service. The rudiments of the world are taught and brought to us every day in something as simple as an iPhone. The phone teaches us to access what we want, when we want, who we want, how we want, and where we want. It is a forever portal that links us to the core of our selfish soul. Everything is at our fingertips, and we can have it now at the click of a finger. It's forming. It creates habits in us, and it trains our brains to be easily distracted in how we deal with life. We need to expose this "have it my way" mentality. It comes to us as naturally as the ABC's. We need to expose our entitlement and how we think we deserve this or that. The bottom line is that the ethic of the Bible teaches us that all we deserve is hell; anything God grants us beyond that is simply a bonus of His grace.

We must begin to think about doctrine, truth, and Christlikeness in terms of what we are becoming, rather than in terms of only what we are thinking. In Titus chapter 1, Paul very intentionally compares two life styles together to make a point; the life of an elder and the life of a rebellious person. He clearly explains that an exemplary Christian leader—one who oversees God's flock—is to be blameless, faithful to one wife, patient, honest, hospitable, self-controlled etc., and the list goes on and on. A rebellious person however is recognized by their meaningless talk, their brutish lies, their laziness, overindulgence, and detestable disobedience. Paul clearly states that these rebellious people claim to know God (theologically), but by their actions they deny God.

This may seem like a pretty simple thing. I mean, we all hate hypocrites right?—those who say one thing and do the opposite (I'm sure we're all feeling guilty at this moment). However, what Paul says next is surprising in what it teaches us about beauty. In the following chapter Paul begins in the first ten verses like this:

 But as for you, **teach what accords with sound doctrine.** Older men are to be sober-minded, dignified, self-controlled, sound in faith, in love, and in steadfastness. Older women likewise are to be reverent in behavior, not slanderers or slaves to much wine. They are to teach what is good, and so train the young women to love their husbands and children, to be self-controlled, pure, working at home, kind, and submissive to their own husbands, that the word of God may not be reviled. Likewise, urge the younger men to be self-controlled. Show yourself in all respects to be a model of good works, and in your teaching show integrity, dignity, and sound speech that cannot be condemned, so that an opponent may be put to shame, having nothing evil to say about us. Bondservants are to be submissive to their own masters in everything; they are to be well-pleasing, not argumentative, not pilfering, but showing all good faith, so that in everything **they may adorn the doctrine of God our Savior.**

OBSERVE CAREFULLY TWO THINGS. ONE, THAT THE MENTION OF SOUND doctrine is followed by Paul's exhortation to men, women and children, to maintain a height and standard of character (being). This is the result of sound theology. In promoting theology we need to keep our eyes on the fact that the goal of thinking rightly about God is to help us live rightly before God and man. Two, we are to adorn or make beautiful the doctrines of God (doing).

Paul links sound doctrine (orthodoxy) to what a man, women, and child ought to be in sound character (orthopraxis). Paul is not undervaluing sound theology here, but rather recognizing that everything we are and do comes from our theology. Perverse belief leads to perverted being and action, and vice versa. To conclude his train of thought, Paul makes one of the most beautiful statements in all of Scripture by saying; "in everything … adorn the doctrine of God our Savior."

The adorn, κοσμέω (kosmeō), means to make something beautiful by cosmetically preparing or ornamenting it for a purpose of honor. From this word we get the English word cosmetics, and it comes from the root word κόσμος (kosmos) where we get the word cosmos—referring to the whole of creation. Matthew uses this word referring to a house that is put in order; Timothy uses it to refer to the inward beauty of a woman. John uses it to describe the Church (Bride) awaiting Jesus (the Bridegroom) at the end of the world, and he uses it to describe God's prepared city and new kingdom.

Paul is connecting us to powerful imagery of true beauty. In a world where the word beautiful is thrown around and attached to things such as images, iPhones, and created things, we need to first recognize that true beauty is not first and foremost about the thing the artist creates or innovates, but it is primarily about the artist's being—who they are! Paul is trying to say that humans beautify things cosmetically in the same way God beautifies things in the cosmos. As God's creation is a beautiful portrayal of all that is in his mind regarding his nature, character, glory and image, our creativity and doing pours out of who we believe God to be. God defines beauty in creating a cosmos that reflects and points to Himself. Our goal in doing and creating should be the same. Theological doctrine and thought without the accompaniment of a Christlike character in our biography is like a Christmas tree without decorations. The tree alone is beautiful, but once adorned with ornament, it becomes a brilliant icon of celebration and generosity. He's also saying, a life of incorrect doctrine is like trying to throw tinsel on a tree that isn't there. Being and Doing cannot be separated.

Doxology: Orthodoxy, as mentioned above, means "right teaching" and orthopraxy means "correct practice." This means that every belief connects itself with a practice or action. This means that everything that we see through a person's five senses of behavior demonstrates the fruit of their theology. What a person believes about God and human existence surfaces through their emotions, through their ideas, and through their living. Discipleship of others and ourselves means that we are to learn from how our five senses operate. We are to be good listeners, observers, and students of what comes out of us. Everything we lay our eyes, hands, mouth, ears, and nose on tells volumes about our belief in God—or lack thereof.

Too often, our attention is directed at the action of a person. We focus on outward offenses and how they make us feel when really we should be looking along the offenses and outward displays of hurt and malice in order to see the source of such hate. It originates in the heart. Then our role is to focus on orthopathiea. Not only are the right beliefs and actions important, but so are the right feelings and affections about those beliefs. The heart, the affections, and the motives in Jewish thought, used over 800 times in Scripture, meant the "whole" of a person. To transform the appetites of a person by greater affections, as found in Christ, was like the glue that held belief and practice together. God is not just concerned that we know truth and obey it, but that we feel passionate about what we obey. This is worship! He wants our joy to be in His commands, not just our allegiance to them.

4

Pitch

How do you say the words "I love you?" When you think of yourself or someone else saying these words, do you picture a scowl, a shout of anger, a furrowed brow, or even a slumped-back disinterested husband leaning back in his Lazy Boy as he mutters the words to his wife through his teeth? No! Even when emotions are removed from the words *I love you*, as they are as I'm writing dry words on a page to you, you picture something specific in your imagination. When I say I love you on a hollow page—I do love you, by the way—you automatically picture something pleasant; you hear a sweet tone and pitch, and you imagine my expressions toward you to be calm, inviting, and caring.

The reason I say this is because words and communication are more than what we say. It's how we say the things we say that's important. If I were to say the words "I hate you" with a pleasant tone, a warm hug, and a smile on my face, the message would not compute with my approach. It would leave anyone on the receiving end puzzled and confused by what I actually mean. The reason for this is because words are merely containers for meaning. How we say the words determines how those containers are filled. We see this in English all the time.

For example, take this sentence: "I don't think she deserves that compliment." In shifting the emphasis, the stress, and the pitch to different words we change the meaning:

. . .

I DON'T THINK SHE DESERVES THAT COMPLIMENT.

Meaning: Somebody else thinks she deserves that compliment.

I **DON'T** THINK SHE DESERVES THAT COMPLIMENT.

Meaning: It's not true that I think she deserves that compliment.

I DON'T **THINK** SHE DESERVES THAT COMPLIMENT.

Meaning: That's not really what I mean, or I'm not sure if she deserves that compliment.

I DON'T THINK **SHE** DESERVES THAT COMPLIMENT.

Meaning: Somebody else deserves that compliment.

I DON'T THINK SHE **DESERVES** THAT COMPLIMENT.

Meaning: In my opinion it's wrong that she got that compliment.

I DON'T THINK SHE DESERVES **THAT** COMPLIMENT.

Meaning: She deserves another kind of compliment.

I DON'T THINK SHE DESERVES THAT **COMPLIMENT.**

Meaning: Maybe she deserves something else instead. [119]

The reason that the meaning changes depending on where I place the emphasis is that words are only containers for meaning. We change the meaning of words by accompanying our language with pitch, inflection, timbre, tone, velocity, and volume. We also play along with the audio drama of our words by accompanying them with gestures, body movement, posture, facial expressions, movement, positioning, etc. Research has shown that this is why only 8% of communication is the words we speak. The other 92% is all the other communicating we do through our mannerisms. Not understanding this may lead many people to think that the speaker or the one doing the talking is the only one communicating when, in all actuality, we are all always communicating all the time. Accompanying our talking, and even our silence, are gestures and posture that are speaking to people about how we believe and feel. So, I'm speaking through this book—one form of communication—you better sit up and look alive.

MUSIC AND PITCH

Though words are one example of this particular communication phenomenon, I believe music provides us with the best metaphor. Music teaches us the crucial importance of the things we say, as well as the container into which we put them. In a piece of music, composers do not write with words, they write with notes. Each note is like a musical word that has something to say. These notes are then measured. They are not measured in inches or feet as you would a room or floor plan, but they are measured in beats, fractions, and increments. Each measure in music is marked off by two bar lines on each side, and these provide the walls to the composer's proverbial "floor plan." The composer can put as many or as few notes between the bars as he/she wants. The idea is that the composer can measure those notes in feet, inches, centimeters, or millimeters, which the musical writer will call whole notes, $\frac{1}{2}$ notes, $\frac{1}{4}$ notes, $\frac{1}{8}$ notes, and 1/16 notes. What the song and composer intends to then communicate through the notes themselves will be influenced by the speed of the notes, their duration (how long they hold), and their rhythm. Faster rhythms communicate tension, stress, worry, excitement, and joy to the listener, whereas longer notes hold out and communicate contemplation, rest, intentionality, and pause.

Musical notes can also fluctuate between high and low, between loud and soft. Low to high is called *range* and loud to soft is called *dynamics* —decrescendos and crescendos. If the song has a wide range from low to high, it might have ecstatic sections of vibrant emotion and joy and delve to the depths of woe and sorrow. The dynamics paint the emotion of the song like tone of voice paints the meaning of speech. All of these things work together to communicate the actual meaning that is in the notes themselves.

The artist can also change the pitch, the timbre, and the intonation of a note simply in how they play it. When a note sounds, the sound waves spin fast or slow; the slower the spin in frequency, the lower the tone and the faster the spin, the higher the tone. A trumpet player can change pitch by increasing how fast they blow or by adjusting the tension in their lips. A piano player can play up high or down low, and the pitch changes. A piano player can then bang on the keys to create an abrasive tone and can also caress the keys as lovingly and lightly as air to create a pitch that fuels the soul with delight. Further, a guitar player can play the same notes and bend them, slide them, tap on them, pull on them, and the intonation, the inflection, and the accent upon each note changes.

All of this is the way an artist uses their language. It is vibrant. It contains notes and words, but these notes are communicated with pulse and with meaning. Dynamics proclaim emotion, whereas inflection, tone, and pitch teach the audience about intensity and interpretation. Music, in the truest of ways, captures within itself how words and ideas resonate with us. It captures not only the notes themselves, but tries to paint how those notes feel and should feel when they collide with our reasoning.

Impressive and overwhelming as this may sound, we have only talked about individual notes themselves, but consider when you place these words into sentences, paragraphs, and pages. One way to do this is by writing an entire song of pitch and emotion. Before even arriving at a completed song, writers also do this with each individual note. They can take one note all by itself and play it in a cluster of other notes, called a chord, which changes that particular note's voice. If they play it in a major chord (happy sounding), the note sounds cheery and playful. If that same note is surrounded by minor thirds, it is sounded in a minor key (sad and somber sounding) and it sounds dark, moody, and haunting. So by keeping the note the same and changing the environment of the note, it changes the meaning as well.

The same is true of words. If I were to say "I love you" in the environment and major resonance of a wedding, the feel of those words are delightful. If I were then to say the same words to you on your death bed before you pass into eternity, the environment would have a minor resonance to it and would deepen, darken, and construe those words to mean something far different—something far more final and something far different.

The Tempo of Discipleship

. . .

MUSIC OF GREEK

This aspect of musical expression may seem to teach us a little about words, but may not fully make its impact on our faith unless we think about all the ramifications. Let's take for example the language and verbal song of the Greek language—the predominant original language of the New Testament. Just like the English language, it contains words and containers that are changed by non-verbal communication, like various expressions of tone, pitch, range, and timbre.

Like English, Greek fluctuates in *persons*. The person of the language determines whether the subject in the passage is the speaker (first person), is being spoken to (second person), or is being spoken about (third person). The person of the passage determines, to some degree, how the language is to be interpreted. It tells us the posture of the subjects within the passage itself. It tells us whether the person is doing the talking or if someone might be talking behind his/her back. All of this is going to change the actual meaning of what's communicated.

What follows is also the tense. Dana and Mantey boldly say that "no element of the Greek language is of more importance to the student of the New Testament than the matter of tense." [120] The tense tells the reader about the nature of an action or a storyline moment. In Greek, we have several tenses. There is the present tense, which is generally a continual/ongoing or undefined action. For example, Revelation 3:20 portrays Jesus this way; "Behold, I stand at the door and **knock**." The tense shows us that this is something Jesus is currently doing. It is something right now! It would change the meaning of it if we were to misunderstand the tense and pitch of this passage by thinking this took place only in the past. This would lead us to conclude that Jesus *did* knock, but is done knocking. In this manner, tense is crucial to determining correct meaning and application.

Next is imperfect tense. This tense generally demonstrates a continuous or reoccurring action in the past. For example, in Mark 4:33, it says, "and with many such parables He *was speaking* the word to them." This is a continuous action by Jesus as He spoke to people during His time in ministry. If we translated this as if He were presently still somewhere in the world speaking to people, this would change the meaning. If we translated it, "and with many parables He is speaking to them," this change causes us to ask, "Who is 'them'?" We might wonder where and to whom He is speaking right now. This would cause us to travel far and wide trying to find a location to hear Jesus speak. Confusing.

There is also the aorist tense. The word *aoristos* derives from an alpha privative (i.e., negation) and the verb *horizô* ("to bind"), thus meaning "without boundaries." [121] In easy-to-understand terms, this is generally something that already happened, but its effects are continuing. It could be that Susie hit Joe in the nose with a baseball. However, *hit* could be used in the aorist tense to share that the effect—the broken and bloody nose—continues into the present moment. In John 3:16 it says, "For God so *loved* the world, that He gave His only Son." "Loved" is in the aorist, which tells us God's love happened in the past, and its effects are still present today. If this word was interpreted in past tense only, we might think that God's love ran out.

The opposite is also true. Future tense explains something that is still in the future. 1 Corinthians 6:3 says, "Do you know that we will judge angels?" This paints the context of our reign in the future, which is much different than calling us to do this now! Finally, among the main tenses, we have perfect tense, which is an action that has been completed in the past but becomes final in the present. John 19:22 says, "that which I have written, I have written." He's telling us that he did it, it's done, and we can't add to it. As we can see, meaning and tense are important. Our interpretation can send us propelling into truth or send us spiraling into lies and false application.

If all this is not enough to convince us of language's complexities, things like tenses can also be accompanied by a voice and/or mood, as well. A word can have an active voice, which means the subject performs the action; a middle voice, which means the subject performs the action unto itself; and the passive voice, which means that the action is being done *to* the subject, not *by* the subject. Combine this with mood, in which Greek has the indicative mood (certainty), subjunctive mood (probability), optative mood (wish/prayer), and the imperative mood (command), you get a musical meaning that's far deeper than a mere literal reading of a book.

PITCH AND REVISITING PERFORMANCE

All of this discussion about language, pitch, communication, and meaning may confuse some as to why I would include this in how we approach discipleship. Does this apply? I believe that the effectiveness of our discipleship is dependent upon how we embrace the idea of language and its pitch.

The primary source that we use in Christian discipleship is the Word of God. Because of the invention of the printing press, people like Martin Luther were able to harness the power of new technology and put the Bible in a written form that everyone could read. This powerful development has empowered the global church for centuries. But if we are not careful, it can remove a bit of our understanding of how to approach the text of Scripture itself.

Because the words of the Bible are contained on a page, we must realize that the other 92% of crucial communication is removed. The text only contains the actual words and containers themselves, but those words are filled with meaning, contents and implications. The difficulty is presented here when, and if, we read the Bible in a static fashion. If we read this way, we might miss the story which is filled with tense, mood, person, and voice. These fluctuations are what make the story of the Bible dynamic. It is what makes the contents of these linguistic devices deeply impactful into the meaning of words and into how we are to apply them.

Here is a little excursus on meaning that you may find humorous. When I teach about this in Bible study method and teaching/preaching classes, I speak a lot about how words, if they are read wrong, can be applied wrongly. If we misunderstand the Scripture, we can misapply it. I use a humorous example. I love to watch arena football, and as you watch, you'll notice that, unlike regular football, the field is surrounded by a "fence" or border. If you go out of bounds, you will inevitably run into the fence if you do not make the decision to jump over it. So, for a head coach to say to a player, "When you see those guys coming after you, jump over the railing," it is good advice in this context. However, let's say a person is walking on a bridge high above a canyon stream. If they were to take and apply this "good advice" but do it in his/her context, the person would jump over the railing and plummet to their death. Another example is me telling a student, "Study hard for that test tomorrow, I hope everything comes out o.k." Sounds good, right? What if I told it to someone going in for a colonoscopy the next day? The advice becomes a little odd.

The same is true about the Bible. If we read it wrongly and miss all its pitch and cues, we may misapply it or tell another disciple to apply it wrongly, and the results, albeit sometimes humorous, most likely will lead to disaster. Discipleship should take this act of exegesis and Biblical interpretation with all seriousness. It is a life or death issue. We must read the Bible as it was written. It was mentioned in Chapter 2 that the Bible was written in story. The reason for this is because story best relates to how life really moves. It's a journey. In the time the Bible was written, the people did not have global printing like we do, so they passed on their tradition through story. There is actually little evidence for silent reading in antiquity. [122] With not many scrolls in circulation, many transmissions would have felt more like performances than actual readings. These performances were lively, embodied dictations that were given by messengers or carriers, as they would carry the message of the Apostles to and from specified locations.

This is actually a positive thing, for the limited circulation of scrolls would have helped the Apostles in their communication. The teacher, in this way, could see themselves more as an artist rather than a pragmatist. Their speaking was not merely one of transmission of information, but it was given to be presented with human skin on—with breath and life. The dictation method enabled them not to solely communicate content, but also timbre, inflection, emotion, cues, emphases, and a plethora of other textual energy. All of these tastes and flavors were as important to communication as that of the actual words themselves. Not to mention how nonverbal communication like posture, tone of voice, facial expressions, etc., would have enhanced the meaning to the hearers.

Typically, in an oral culture, the presenter would memorize the presentation not only word for word, but tone for tone. In fact, it has been shown that in situations that are even slightly ambiguous, intonation will trump literal meaning. [123] The experience of translating, memorizing, and performing these works would place the messenger into an entirely different relationship with these texts than that of a silent reader and even quite distinct from the experience of hearers in an audience. [124] In taking on the persona/voice of the text, the messenger would better grasp it as a whole; they would attend to every detail and communicate it both emotively and kinesthetically.

This not only introduces a fresh way of approaching life and faith, but also a fresh way for approaching theological study and development within the lives of individuals and within the life of the local church. David Rhoads, a renowned expert in this area, suggests that a discipline seeking to complete and round out the other disciplines of academic study would be that of *performance criticism*. When someone is reading the Bible they would look at it more like story and drama, and not only read it, but act it out and see how that would influence the meaning. He suggests that performance is a shift in medium; it affects virtually all disciplines, traditional as well as recent. [125] It does not simply look at the Bible's history, which is important. It does not look merely at the literary or redacted disciplines of academic study, which are also important. Performance is concerned with the meaning of the text.

I remember when this impacted me greatly for the very first time. I was watching a group of people act out Jesus' temptation in the desert in Luke 4. Up until the point of this performance, I'll admit, many times when reading this story I have perceived Jesus as a hungry and weak individual. However, when I watched this passage acted out word for word, they portrayed Jesus in great strength and security. I found myself wondering, Why? And then I kept watching the drama. When Satan came to Jesus and offered him bread, power, and protection, each time Jesus spoke to Satan and opened with these words, "I am the Lord your God." I'm ashamed to admit this, but I have always read this through my individualistic American lenses and thought that Jesus was speaking those words to me, reminding me of who is my Lord. But the reality is, I was and am not in this little drama. Satan and Jesus are!

In the dramatic depiction, Jesus did not look to me and say those words, although they are also true for me. He pointed to Satan and reminded Satan: "I am the Lord, *your* God." The words themselves were also accompanied by pointing, positions and "gestures which carry considerable meaning," [126] as the character playing Jesus pointed boldly toward the Satanic character in the dramatic reading. Not only could we as the congregation picture what Jesus was saying, but we could picture what He was doing: "Verbs are the driving force of drama." [127] The actors posture here tells us what is truly going on.

Satan had become so proud that he believed the kingdoms and powers of the world were his to offer to Jesus. Jesus reminded him confidently that all authority was His (Christ's). Satan lied. He was trying to trick Jesus into worshipping him even though Jesus very clearly knew that all things were already His. There are many people who believe and interpret this story to show that Satan is in control of the world and Jesus had to, in some way, get it back (open-view theism), and their heretical thinking comes from simply interpreting this verse wrongly. They capture the meaning of the passage incorrectly because they misunderstand the performance. So did I! This passage is now seen in my view as it should be. Jesus, in the original language and the drama is bold, powerful, and in control, even in his weakest moment. Satan is not Christ's equal and powerful adversary, but he is Christ's servant.

Performance looks at and thinks through the story and how the characters actually lived it! The original hearers did not simply learn it as theory or ideas—a set of theologies. They experienced it in its expression, tone, mood, emotion, and real rhythm. Thus, the memorization and inflection upon all the various elements of the text should not be seen merely as a devotional exercise, but rather as something that actually informs the believer in their proper and correct approach to the Bible and to all the disciplines of study.

Pitch and Emphasis in Poetry

Now that we have put a lot of structure to our argument and we have looked at how our real life affects the Bible's telling as well as our interpretation of its correct meaning, let's put a bit of flesh on this and apply it to the very real environment of discipleship amidst the war of life and within its trenches. Let's first turn our attention to the nature of one of the most real and vibrant books of the Bible. This particular book contains a range and pitch that resounds a dynamic song that includes the full scope of human experience and emotion. Let's turn to the book of Psalms.

The Psalter is a collection of songs and poetry written by various authors throughout Israel's history. They sing of a real God and of real human experience. And to fully appreciate the nature of Psalms and how they really influence discipleship, we must know a bit of how they relate to one another and how they differ from one another. Just like literature has many genres and flavors, the book of Psalms possesses these as well.

For example, there are Wisdom Psalms like what we find in Psalm 1, which paints a very clear picture of how the knowledge of God interacts with the real moments of humanity. It highlights very clearly what is right and what is wrong, and it very boldly proclaims what good and bad will bring if they are followed. This is wisdom to us. This is when the Bible instructs us in how to think and live. It has the tone of practicality and application. On this level, the Bible seeks to instruct us, counsel us, and craft how we think.

There are also the Royal Psalms or Songs of Praise, which are predominantly found in Psalms 92 through 108. They speak of Yahweh's kingship, and they exalt His reign. They outline His control, His Majesty, and His beauty, and in a very real way, they function to explain to us what heaven looks like. There is not much room provided in these particular Psalms for human frailty. Humanity's issues are not the emphasis in these Psalms. What is on display in these Psalms is the grandeur, the perfection, and the awesomeness of God.

The human must not feel left behind however even in Psalms devoted to God. They must not read things such as the Royal Psalms and think, "That's great, but does God understand my life?" For this, there are the Prayers of Lament. For example, in Psalm 3, as David is fleeing from the hands of his son, Absalom, who wants to kill him, David writes, "Lord, how many are my foes! How many rise against me!" Later, in Psalm 7, we have a prayer of David, who has been falsely accused: "Lord, if I have done this ... then let my enemy pursue and overtake me," but if not, "arise, Lord, in your anger; rise up against the rage of my enemies." Psalm 22 starts with the one who feels forsaken. Psalm 42 begins with one who is thirsty, desperate, and needy. Psalm 57 finds David in hiding. Psalm 60 is written after a military defeat. It goes on and on. In this way, it seems that the Psalms do not fix life's problems but rather cause us to embrace their reality. The Psalms do not erase problems, but they show us how God interacts with us to get us through them—in such a way that He might be glorified.

Additively there are the highs of the Pilgrim Songs, sung during journeys to Jerusalem and Festivals. There are the lows of the Imprecatory Psalms, pleading with God to attack the enemy and destroy the foe. The bottom line is that the Psalms have range. They sound the full breadth of human experience, from ecstasy to tragedy.

The Psalter, God's Song book in the Bible, is full of songs that cover the whole range of human emotion. Don't believe me? Feel free to explore all the Songs God includes in his Top 150 List: Laments [128] (sorrow, questioning, doubt), Penitential [129] (confessing) and Imprecatory [130] (praying for judgment and calamity), Thanksgiving (*Todah*) Psalms [131], Salvation History [132], Songs of Trust [133], Hymns and Doxology

[134], Liturgical Covenant Songs [135], Royal (Kingly) Enthronement Psalms [136], Songs of Zion (Kingdom) [137], Temple Liturgies [138], Wisdom [139], and Torah Psalms [140](Law and Word). Not only do the Psalms help us wade through the FULL dynamic of human experience, but they teach us and require us to Praise (external expressive action) and Worship (internal contemplative act of adoration) God in the midst of everything.

The Tempo of Discipleship

Theology: Why is this important? How does this relate to story, performance, pitch, range, and music? The most important question to ask is what does music, story, and the drama of the Psalms teach us about real life? We should be asking our questions in the right order. If life is expected to be a flat-line of static concepts, theologies, and ideas, then the Bible does not have much to say. The Bible, however, recognizes that life is a series of darks and lights, pros and cons, times of confusion, and times of conclusion. This is why the dynamics of God's Word reach so far in their stretch. God wants to encompass all of human experience. Our theology should not exclude real world dynamics. He wants to teach us what the depth of pain feels like and what the height of ecstasy tastes like. He's not interested in a flat-line existence where everything is status quo. He wants stable, firm, steadfast, and bold disciples who can ride the rollercoaster of life with all the grace and finesse of a skilled musician. The musician does not avoid the different timbres, but plays through them and embraces them in order to find out how the whole song plays together to sing one magnificent opus.

Biography: I've heard the Christian experience likened to many things. I've heard it most prominently related to a series of valleys and mountaintops. The philosophy and assumption here is that we will have good times with God that are so rich they will feel much like looking out over a valley from atop a 14,000-foot mountain peak. These are moments of clarity and insight that make everything else in life worthwhile. The trouble with this view is that the valleys begin to be perceived as the most evil of times. We view them as times to be avoided. Rather, God says in Psalm 23 that "he leads us beside still waters ... he restores my soul ... he prepares a table for us in the *presence* of our enemies." Our Pastor, a while ago, showed us an image of antelope feeding next to the still waters in Africa. The still waters of fresh lakes and ponds are down in valley beds. This is where animals come to get their drink of still, fresh water. The only problem is that this is where the lions hang out waiting for lunch.

This is the context of God's valleys. When He is preparing our valleys, He's leading us to some of the freshest springs, even when our enemies are the most present. Rather than reject such an encounter as evil or horrible, we should embrace it as a grace from God. In these moments, we see His power, His protection, and His provision in ways that we never would from a mountain peak.

I've also heard Rick Warren speak about the road of a disciple. He describes it as twin train tracks running beside one another. The reason he says it this way is that during the time that his book *The Purpose Driven Life* was on the Times Best Seller List, selling so many copies that it was only bested by the sales of the Bible, his wife was simultaneously battling cancer. He explained how pain and praise always run in parallel. When there are times of great victory, on the other track runs a circumstance of great hurt. This profound analogy is definitely more true to real life, for it makes room for the good and bad in the plan of God.

DOXOLOGY: MUSIC PROVIDES AN EVEN MORE ROBUST ANALOGY OF WHAT discipleship is like. Valleys and peaks are good, but they can tend to isolate the person in the story from the story itself. It can become very "me" focused. The train tracks parable provides a better analogy, but it still focuses around the individual in that there is only one set of train tracks. The tracks are not seen as flowing into, out of, and through others. However, music is a better analogy for life's movement in that it first focuses our aim around the melody—Christ. We are not seeking to understand the events themselves, but we are seeking to be reshaped and reordered into the very image from which we originated. As Christ's melody plays, we all interact with His tune. It's about all of us in relationship to Him and to each other. A good note sounded in others directly impacts us. Conversely, the moments of dissonance and mistakes in another person's notes result in our note being affected, and vice versa.

Considering it this way also impacts how we perceive good and bad in our lives. Valleys and mountains and train tracks connote a "good" and "bad" thinking in our minds. Music has both running in unison and amplified harmony. The bad creates tension that amplifies the good, and the good provides the melody to which the "suffering" of the song sharpens, awakens, and evolves. If life is seen like this, we realize that at one moment a person's song may be playing a royal theme, or maybe a lament, or even a pilgrim song of journey and victory. Rather than quickly trying to rescue someone from lament for example, discipleship in this fashion embraces the lament and sorrow and finds God's song within it. It's a perspective shift. On the other hand, when a person's theme is singing sorrow, we can also sense the right moments to insert songs of royalty and praise in order to counsel the attitude and thoughts of the person toward victory and healing.

This, again, is why this book is called *The Tempo of Discipleship*. Discipleship is an art, and it has a very real timing to how it moves. It slows and it runs, and we need to be sensitive not to quench the spirit. When we quench the spirit, we interrupt what He might be doing, even in the discord, to try and play our own song. Sometimes, like in the life of Job, the song of discord is what God is singing. Job's story wasn't just about Job—that's what His friends thought. They thought in valley-and-peak thinking. Eliphaz questioned Job's reverence and integrity toward God during his suffering (4:6). Later, Eliphaz shows up to give good advice at the wrong time in 5:9: "the great things God does are too marvelous to understand." Good theology, but maybe presented with a hint of train track thinking, as Proverbs 25:20 says, "Whoever sings songs to a heavy heart is like one who takes off a garment on a cold day, and like vinegar on soda." Eliphaz was discipling Job through his crisis with good and sound theology, but his timing was off!

Music teaches us about the pitches of life. Life possesses great range, dynamic, and ability to move. We need to possess this same versatility. How and when things get applied is as important as what's being applied. This chapter addresses both. On one hand, pitch teaches us about how this very wide range of music is within God's words themselves and should be experienced that way in order to receive their full and correct impact. His words contain precise meaning and are infused throughout Scripture with intended thoughts and should be carefully handled. Like Job's friend Eliphaz, we should have sound theology and think in greater ways than only words—even though they are important. On the other hand, the delivery of our theology has to have a wisdom to it—a timing. If it's applied rightly and with the right meaning, it reaps the right harvest.

5

Something Old | Familiar | New

There she was! She had a smile that lit up the room, a laugh that was contagious, and a sweet personality that calmed and made even the hardest of people feel at ease. Her character's something many people admire, and one can see that women want to be like her, men want to be with her, and parents wish their kids were her. She exemplifies what the Bible speaks of as a "gentle and quiet spirit." When I first saw her, there was a royal ring to her step, not in the clothes that she wore, but simply in the way she carried herself. She was confident, poised, and beautiful. There was something different about this girl.

This describes my thoughts the moment I first met my wife, Katie. We met in college and soon became fast friends, for we shared a similar network and background. Over several months of spending time in our group of church friendships, I found myself simply observing this woman. She was fresh, new, different, and altogether intriguing. I can remember, after many months, finally asking this fair lady for her permission to take her out on a date. In my mind, I'll admit, I was one of those guys that knew I was going to marry her the day I laid eyes on her; but of course, I wasn't the creep who actually told her that. Rather, I laid low and simply watched, observed, and prayed for God to give me an opportunity to experience her before taking the chance to pursue her for a possible lifetime. When the time came for our first dinner together without the crowd of friends, in the back of my mind I was prepared for something great. I did not just want a moment with her, I wanted a *story*.

When I first pursued Katie, I viewed it as the beginning of a beautiful drama. I knew that if this story were to continue as I hoped it would—on into the future—that I wanted to give my future wife a story worth enjoying—one to remember and reminisce over as the years went by. As I began to pursue her, I always kept this thinking in the front of my mind. The first thing that I wanted her to remember is that I came to her on her terms, not my own.

This desire drove me to take things very slow. In fact, by the time I received her permission to take her out to dinner for the first time, I'd already been good friends with her for many months and had observed her in many ways. When the time came for our first moments together, I wanted to give her a first date that would be memorable. Thus, I planned a week of flowers to be delivered to her house. It was a very expensive ordeal, but one type of flower was taken to her home each day for a week. Each flower represented, to me and to her, a different aspect of her and our friendship that I valued and appreciated. For her purity and gentleness, I gave her the daisy, for her joy and passion, I gave her a red rose, and so forth. It was all in hopes of beginning a story in the right way.

The months went on and I spent many hours with her friends, her family, and being with her in many environments. As time passed, it became very clear that I had fallen in love with this woman, and I knew I wanted to tell her that I loved her—and this moment, too, needed to take up a special part in writing our story. I wanted it to be special, and so I planned a special night for the two of us. I transformed my living room into an Italian café, I cooked an Italian meal for us to enjoy together, and I composed a song in which I hid the lyrics "I love you!" at the end. Here are the lyrics:

The New Had Come

I'd never dreamed I'd reach
This place of endless peace
But like a dream I met you.
You restored part of me
God has used you to bring
Out all the qualities in me that I couldn't see.

The Tempo of Discipleship

I believe this is something real.
I believe it's time to tell You how I feel.

I am amazed at how you've changed me
I'm taken by Your ways.
I can't explain the joy I know that
The past is gone
The new has come
His mercy's come

When I look in your eyes
Few words come to mind
Your beauty leaves me speechless.
You have given me
The opportunity
To see the wonders of His love.
I can't imagine me now without you.
I hope that I can somehow keep you around.

Something in me has awakened
Something in me has expired.
I come alive when I'm with you
I've died to what I once knew.

Chorus:
I am amazed at how You've changed me
I'm taken by Your ways.
I can't explain the joy I know that
The past is gone
The new has come
His mercy's come
And I'm in love!!!!

When I performed the song for her, and reached the final line she fortunately echoed my love and said the words "I love you" in response, and the story continued on. I was sold, in love, and I was ready to move on into the future with her. I immediately in my mind moved to planning the proposal. I soon devised a plan with members of our church, Katie's family, and my family to continue our story in a way that we would both appreciate and remember, and I wanted everyone involved.

The ploy to surprise Katie began with me getting my whole church behind me in affirming that they were sending me to New York for a week to a worship conference. I told her I'd be there, I told my future in-laws I would not be there, and I began devising a plan to surprise Katie. Over about 3 months, I planned how I would do this. I felt a bit bad that I had everyone lie for me about my trip, and Katie's Dad explained he could barely handle it. But the plan was underway. As everything fell into place and the week arrived for my "secret" departure to New York, I waved goodbye to Katie and was off to the airport. Little did she know, I quickly left to meet with her parents, and we began planning the proposal.

Her parents and I devised a celebrative party for her to throw her off the trail, and on the day she came for the party, I had already set up a scavenger hunt around her parent's yard. On each tree, I placed a plaque which seemingly read as if it was from her parents and started something like this: "Katie, you have given us so much as our daughter … " The card went on to explain how her parents loved and appreciated her. She moved from card to card, one by one around the yard, clumsily carrying her flashlight in hand, as it was pitch black outside. Slowly, she came ever closer to the final tree. On it was the final plaque, similar to the others, but at the end of this one it read, "Katie, you have given us so much joy in being our daughter, and now it is time for us to give you away." At that moment, I lit the yard up with lights and came out from behind the bushes to propose.

It was a story! Over the next few months we planned our wedding and along the way I tried to create signposts of memories for us to share. To this day, on every anniversary, we remember our first moments together, and I give Katie a new charm to place upon a bracelet that I bought for her. Each year that passes adds another charm to our life in order to catalogue and remember our journey together. The story still goes on… Each year, those once new signposts along the road have turned familiar, and they've become tradition. They are rich, and they continue to mean more as we continue to journey into our life together.

The New, the Familiar, and the Old

I share this story with couples that I meet for pre-marital counseling to explain to them the importance of creating a story together. I tell the future husband that it is important that he gives his future bride a story to remember. He will not only find it anchors them throughout the ups and downs of their marriage, but it will be a story worth passing on to their kids, grandkids, and an entire legacy that is following behind.

The reality that I'm trying to convey here is that inevitably, stories always begin new, fresh, and with great excitement. The purpose for marking this newness happens with intentionality in order to preserve its richness as it moves from the present into the past. Over time, our moments of newness become familiar, and, depending on how we deal with this process, our moments or relationships will either grow old or it will grow richer. This is a natural cycle of life. Personally, the newness of many of our family traditions have worn off now, and we have even passed many of our signposts and become familiar with our journey, but over the years as we celebrate our first date with a charm, the first "I love you" with a song, the proposal with a dance, and our wedding in viewing our video as a family, our experiences grow deeper and more rich. Each passing year, as we recant our journey as a family, we take it in as an opportunity to re-experience the times of excitement, and the memories become sweeter. The profundity of these types of ideas contributes to the concept of how art, creativity, and music mark us in a similar fashion.

Notice how natural it was for me, and for many people, to mark relational signposts along the journey with a piece of art, a piece of creation, or a photograph that freezes that moment in time and forever cements it in our memory. It's as if we as humans desire the old to anchor us, the familiar to comfort us, and the new to motivate us—and all of it pours forth in some kind of expression of creativity and artful memory.

Familiar New Songs

When songs first come to us, it is similar to a new love story beginning. The songs and artists are rich, exciting, and adventurous. We skip through the new album with joy just to hear the newness of it—we are in love. We play the music over and over, we surround ourselves with the newness of it all, and we get enraptured in the new sounds. Inevitably however, soon that album becomes familiar, and not long after this does it then move onto our shelves and into the dust. At one time, an album that marked a very important time for us seems only to pass into the past to be remembered in memory and at timely moments.

This is the power of music. This is the power of the new, the familiar, and the old. Music and words have this ability to amplify this progression better than anything else. Paul Ricoeur says it well when he says, "people speak or sing (voice—to be heard). This gets written down (text—to be seen). Then the text is read or sung again, it becomes voice again, it may be spoken aloud, or spoken silently within, or it may shape our speaking in other ways. To understand a text is to make it our own. A text comes to us from the past but, once read, it has present force again, shaping what we think and say."[141] Music creates a continuous cycle of renewal, remembrance, and recommitment. It renews us when it is fresh. It helps us remember by creating signposts to which we can return. Sometimes, it helps us to recommit as we remember the joy we once had in the past. We resolve to rekindle it or keep it going, and as we enjoy it, it expands deeper within our soul.

This idea of story not only plays into how music shapes and solidifies us, but it factors into how we build memories and create moments of importance in all our living. Relating to discipleship is the idea of special movements being important and monumental in our historic timeline. The Bible's word for these intertwining moments that connect together to craft a work of art is "providence." The idea that past, present, and future are all important to how God is making and shaping us is crucial. God is writing a love story. The notes and lines of our life song connect and are not independent of each other. Nothing in our life song is wasted or lost. It is all used to make us who we are! It is a story that He's making in and through us.

God even created three different types of music that demonstrate this providence and story. Colossians 3:16 and Ephesians 5:19-20 call believers to sing psalms, hymns and spiritual songs (new songs) to one another in order that the body of Christ may receive admonishment and encouragement. Our singing is then linked with the Word dwelling richly within us. This is as if to say that the fruit of a mature and healthy Christian or community is a vitality in experiencing the personal touches and moments from God's hand in song. This is inevitably marked by how much singing is present along the course of the journey. I believe that the reason God gives us these types of songs is to create a vital timeline in order to sustain a loyal marriage of faith in our lives between us and our Creator. They mark the moments in our journey of love and memories with Him. The songs we sing are supposed to establish us in Christ's love like a house, the foundation being the old, the walls being the familiar, and the roof being the new. These three types of songs and music seem to serve three different functions, and all are needed in shaping a love story that will sustain and last.

In the next section, we will look at specifically how these song types mark God's special memories within His love story, but for the purpose of setting a framework in our understanding of what these three song types are, it might be good first to consider R. P. Martin's brief summation of each of these song genres; "'Psalms may refer to Christian odes patterned on the Old Testament Psalter. 'Hymns' would be longer compositions, and there is evidence that some actual specimens of these hymns may be found in the New Testament itself. 'Spiritual songs' refer to snatches of spontaneous praise which the inspiring Spirit placed on the lips of the enraptured worshipper...These 'inspired odes' would no doubt be of little value, and their contents would be quickly forgotten." [142] All of these songs serve a different function in marking God's journey and story amongst humanity, and to this consideration we will now turn.

12 Songs of Revelation

These three types of songs are found in heaven's economy. These different styles and forms help to build up the household of God as the people of God richly sing both in heaven and on earth. In the book of Revelation we can observe and explore in brief each song type and its contribution to the culture of the divine. In doing so, the hope is to demonstrate how heaven's economy is anchored around this cycle of new, familiar, and old:

> **Revelation 4:1-2, 9:** After this I looked, and behold, a door standing open in heaven! And the first voice, which I had heard speaking to me like a trumpet, said, 'Come up here, and I will show you what must take place after this.' At once I was in the Spirit, and behold, a throne stood in heaven, with one seated on the throne. And he who sat there had the appearance of jasper and carnelian ... And the four living creatures, each of them with six wings, are full of eyes all around and within, and day and night they never cease to

say, 'Holy, holy, holy, is the Lord God Almighty, who was and is and is to come!'

A ring of freshness is in this experience and in this song. There is newness in experience that our writer, John, has never experienced up until this point. John is one of Jesus' closest disciples. He walked with Jesus and saw Jesus ascend, but now he "beholds" the throne. He sees it. He feels it. He hears it. At the same time he hears the ancient song, "Holy, Holy, Holy, is the Lord God Almighty, who was and is and is to come." The creatures singing this resounding and repetitive chorus recant God's "foreverness." Through the ancient truth's audible resonance John hears it afresh for the first time. In a sense, he encounters the economy of heaven for the first time by first being introduced to its ancient foundation. It speaks fresh to him, for he's seeing its reality for the first time in a new reality. For the creatures, this song anchors them in what they've always known. It keeps them bold and steadfast before God's throne. Right out of the gate, we see how the ancient interacts in conversation with the new.

> **Revelation 4:10-11:** The twenty-four elders fall down before him who is seated on the throne and worship him who lives forever and ever. They cast their crowns before the throne, saying, 'Worthy are you, our Lord and God, to receive glory and honor and power, for you created all things, and by your will they existed and were created.'

The elders sing a song of remembrance, an ode and a hymn that dates all the way back to creation. It's as if the remembrance captured in this signpost makes them want to cast their crowns, their riches, and their accolades down before the Creator once again. This song is rich in theology and history, and it not only births emotions and response, but it teaches and instructs. Its words call the listener to the exact moment that the lyrics ring most true, the creation event. The chorus calls the listener to meditate on the creation of the universe. This song serves to "point out" and draw heaven's attention so they may be encouraged by a particular time and theme.

> **Revelation 5:9-10:** The lamb takes the Scroll and they sang a new song, saying, 'Worthy are you to take the scroll and to open its seals, for you were slain, and by your blood

The Tempo of Discipleship

you ransomed people for God from every tribe and language and people and nation, and you have made them a kingdom and priests to our God, and they shall reign on the earth.'

A fresh and new action by God here inspires a new and fresh response. The opening of the scroll is something God has been planning to do since the creation of the world, but up until this point its occurrence has remained future, even for those in heaven. Everyone in all of heaven has known that Christ can open the scroll. Everyone has always known He has the keys to do all things, but in this moment, this future moment, His ability is revealed fresh. Out comes a new song from a new revealing. It's as if they understand His reign beforehand in the storyline, but now they deeply know His reign in a fresh way in the now. The past anchors this present moment. God communicates an age-old truth that is consistent with His character and story, but it captivates His people in a new way. They sing a new song! It appears to be more spontaneous and less theological, but it serves its purpose of being an exuberant and spontaneous expression all the same.

> **Revelation 5:12-13:** Saying with a loud voice, 'Worthy is the Lamb that was slain to receive power, and riches, and wisdom, and strength, and honor, and glory, and blessing.' And every creature which is in heaven, and on the earth, and under the earth, and such as are in the sea, and all that are in them, heard him saying, 'Blessing, and honor, and glory, and power, be unto him that sits upon the throne, and unto the Lamb forever and ever.'

This is a song of familiarity! Perhaps we can see this as the "CliffsNotes" version of the Psalms. The language of the Psalms is here expressed in concise form. This Psalm exalts the simple truth and conclusion that all God's works resound in His forever honor.

> **Revelation 6:1:** And I saw when the Lamb opened one of the seals, and I heard, as it were the noise of thunder, one of the four beasts saying, Come and see.
>
> **Revelation 7:10:** And cried with a loud voice, saying, Salvation to our God who sits upon the throne, and unto the Lamb.

Revelation 7:12: Saying, Amen: Blessing, and glory, and wisdom, and thanksgiving, and honor, and power, and might, be unto our God forever and ever. Amen.

Revelation 11:15: And the seventh angel sounded; and there were great voices in heaven, saying, The kingdoms of this world are become the kingdoms of our Lord, and of his Christ; and he shall reign forever and ever.

The mixture continues as the past, the present, and the future converge. In one sense, God has always been sitting on the throne in that He's always been sovereignly in control. Regardless, the beasts, in a special way, now bid us to come and see. What's happening is a journey which has been growing in God's kingdom past and is now familiar, and the new birth of the next phase ushers in new music and possibilities.

Revelation 11:17-18: We give thanks to you, Lord God Almighty, who is and who was, for you have taken your great power and begun to reign. The nations raged, but your wrath came, and the time for the dead to be judged, and for rewarding your servants, the prophets and saints, and those who fear your name, both small and great, and for destroying the destroyers of the earth.

This song echoes the new and taps into Psalm 2, 110:5, 115:13, and Daniel 7:10 for its content. It rings out the past and the fulfillment of God's peace and justice coming to the earth.

Revelation 15:3-4: And I saw what appeared to be a sea of glass mingled with fire—and also those who had conquered the beast and its image and the number of its name, standing beside the sea of glass with harps of God in their hands. And they sing the song of Moses, the servant of God, and the song of the Lamb, saying,

'Great and amazing are your deeds, O Lord God the Almighty! Just and true are your ways, O King of the nations! Who will not fear, O Lord, and glorify your name? For you alone are holy. All nations will come and worship you, for your righteous acts have been revealed.'

The throng sings a hymn. This song is a memorable greatest hit from Jewish history, written by the prophet Moses. This age-old hymn had been written by Moses as God delivered them out of Egyptian slavery and ushered them out under the freedom of His Lordship. The very distant past, in some ways, resembles the very real present in this passage. God not only delivered His people in partiality, but now is delivering them again in finality. The two moments relate. This song of old becomes fresh once again in light of the new insight being given to those in heaven and given to John, here on earth. Though the song was composed in a very real point in history, God recalls the memories to create new moments of depth, understanding, and insight.

> **Revelation 19:1-2:** After this I heard what seemed to be the loud voice of a great multitude in heaven, crying out, 'Hallelujah!' Salvation and glory and power belong to our God, for his judgments are true and just; for he has judged the great prostitute who corrupted the earth with her immorality, and has avenged on her the blood of his servants.

> **Revelation 19:3-8:** Once more they cried out, 'Hallelujah!' The smoke from her goes up forever and ever. And the twenty-four elders and the four living creatures fell down and worshiped God who was seated on the throne, saying, 'Amen. Hallelujah!' And from the throne came a voice saying, Praise our God, all you his servants, you who fear him, small and great.

> Then I heard what seemed to be the voice of a great multitude, like the roar of many waters and like the sound of mighty peals of thunder, crying out,

> 'Hallelujah!' For the Lord our God the Almighty reigns. Let us rejoice and exult and give him the glory, for the marriage of the Lamb has come, and his Bride has made herself ready; it was granted her to clothe herself with fine linen, bright and pure.

This song rings of victory as the whole narrative of Scripture peaks and comes to a close with the defeat of the prostitute Babylon and the marking of a new age without false religion. This is a song that is altogether for the future. It has been sung in Scripture, but it has not yet been heard within the human timeline. We can wait for it in hope, but we cannot experience the fullness of all that it reveals.

THE OLD

So, let's pause for a moment and digest a bit of what we just observed here so we can bring it together to understand its importance. On one hand, we observe the singing of the Old Songs in Revelation's end time culture. Those in heaven are seen and heard re-vamping, re-arranging, and re-doing Moses' greatest worship hit from Exodus 15:1-20. This ancient hymn is what the heart of heaven is built upon. The reason it is sung is because the story of God delivering people out of slavery in Egypt through the Red Sea is one of the largest markers that foreshadows His deliverance of us from sin through Baptism. This song also points to His ultimate deliverance of us from death through the waters of heaven. If you'll notice the structure of Moses' hymn, it is extremely helpful.

In Moses' full composition, he forms a rhythm in his song as he remembers and recounts Israel's journey. For example, in Exodus 15:4-5 he exclaims, "Pharaoh's chariots and his host he cast into the sea, and his chosen officers were sunk in the Red Sea. The floods covered them; they went down into the depths like a stone." Then he immediately follows in the response in Verse 11, "Who is like you, O Lord, among the gods? Who is like you majestic in holiness, awesome in glorious deeds, doing wonders?" This new upheaval of faith in Moses produces a new call to rely upon God as he remembers the old and creates a method for it to enter his present: "You have led in your steadfast love the people whom you have redeemed, you have guided them by your strength."

This is why the throng sings the hymns in heaven. They are foundation songs. They do not merely reach back into the last few decades as does Charles Wesley's hymn, "Love Divine, All Love's Excelling", nor do they only reach as far back as St. Francis of Assisi's words in "All Creatures of Our God and King." It is true that modern hymns of the last two thousand years are part of our history, but God here reaches back into the very foundations of His redemption story.

This is why the hymns are so popular in new generations. This is why they should be wholeheartedly embraced, re-arranged, and sounded forth with new song zeal. We are as a global, universal, centurial, and historical church, raising up united voices to sing the whole story of God, not just our little piece of it. It places us like an ant beneath the breadth of the cosmos. It fills us with awe and wonder at the smallness of our existence in this grand chronicle of God.

THE FAMILIAR

Yet in Revelation, the heavenly chorus also sings the familiar. Emily R. Blink and Bert Polman coyly observe that this is the nature of the Psalter; "Psalms were as much 'house music' as they were 'church music' both for the Jews and for the early Christians." [143] Psalm singing may therefore be considered to have been a normal concomitant of the religious life of the family in the home. [144] The "Psalms, were and are a blessing to the people, to the praise of God ... the joy of liberty, the noise of good cheer, and the echo of gladness ... it softens anger, it gives release from anxiety, it alleviates sorrow; it is protection at night, instruction by day, a shield in time of fear, a feast of holiness, the image of tranquility, a pledge of peace and harmony, which produces one song" [145] Realistically, these anthems provided comfort for the early church.

The Psalms have real skin on. They have real pain and real experience wrapped up in their prose. They do not sugar-coat nor do they make light of pain, but they do not diminish ecstasy and the wonder of praising God either. They provide us with the recognizable, the common, and the resonance to real life. As discussed earlier, these Psalms invite us to participate in the narrative of God, for they do not deny the lenses through which we labor.

The Psalms are the means not the end to human experience. When we are traveling in the midst of our very real marriage with the God of the universe, the hymns preach to us over and over again, reminding us of the memories of our story—our beginning. But the truth is, sometimes we have been in this marriage to the Lamb for so long that the signposts that were once altogether vibrant with color and excitement have now become drab with the familiar. The Psalms enter these moments and provide us with language to recapture this story of old right from where we are. The Psalms do not deny reality, but they help us deal with it and process it in a way that causes us to move toward God in greater trust and love. These songs become real to us, they make new memories, and they give us new mile markers to hold up along our journey.

The NEW SONG

When the old enriches the familiar, it begins to do in us what it did in those who are in heaven. We see in Revelation that suddenly the chorus of heaven begins to see the same truths that existed in the Word since ages past, but they see it through a new, fresh set of lenses. It's as if they gaze at God's wisdom from a new angle and see into His house from a different vantage point. From one angle they see only the story of Moses, but when they peer through the window of the End Times, they now see that Moses' deliverance points to an even grander exodus—one they couldn't fully understand until now. It was and is the victory of heaven itself. This is the final say, the final story.

This is the new song. It's not only when God's truth goes out (the old), and not only when God's truth collides with human experience (the Psalms), but it is when the truth of God is embraced in a way that transforms (the new) —it's a fresh awakening to what was there in the first place. It's not as if a new song replaces the old or the familiar but only that it re-embraces the truths at a deeper level. Scripture provides the basis for all new songs in that its truth never grows aged, but it continues to be forever awakened by new realities.

Consider for a moment Psalm 96:1 that says, "Sing a new song to the Lord, sing unto the Lord all the earth." The idea of a new song here is linked to a day when the Lord will receive praise from all His people. In Ephesians 3:4-6, we are provided a link that explains what this fresh song is. Paul writes, "In reading this, then, you will be able to understand my insight into the mystery of Christ, which was not made known to people in other generations as it has now been revealed by the Spirit to God's holy apostles and prophets. This mystery is that through the gospel the Gentiles are heirs together with Israel [all the earth sings His praise], members together of one body, and sharers together in the promise in Christ Jesus."

The previous generations of Gentiles felt alienated from God, but the reality is that God's song of salvation is inclusive of them and Israel since the beginning. When this age old song, which was planned from eternity past, was realized in Christ, [146] all of a sudden it awakens a theme that had always been present, but now is sung in a different way. It is a fresh experience of the song always present, and Christ encourages us in Scripture to pour forth these fresh understandings as God unveils to us what has always been there in His Word.

This happens all the time in the Old Testament and not just through song. The way in which the ancients would respond to fresh encounters with God was by building pillars or altars. When Noah came out of the ark on to the renewed earth, he "built an altar unto the Lord; and took of every clean beast, and of every clean fowl, and offered burnt offerings on the altar." [147] It was a signpost of rescue. When Abraham received God's promise and blessing, his communal encounter with God came within a hostile scene, for the Canaanites were then in the land. On removing from Sichem, Abraham came "unto a mountain on the east of Bethel, and pitched his tent, having Bethel on the west and Hai on the east: and there he built an altar unto the Lord, and called upon the Name of the Lord." [148] His altar is a response to God's blessing revealed.

Isaac later came to Beer-sheba with God telling him not to fear. God promised to remember his promise to Abraham. [149] Then later, an angel appears to Jacob in a dream on the property of the Promised Land, and when Jacob wrestles with the angel on guard of the Garden and is victorious in his desire for God's continued promise, He builds an altar acknowledging God's mercy in keeping His promises integrally. [150] Continuing, when the people were in Exodus due to their rebellion, they built altars and raised pillars when victorious in battle, for God was still faithful. [151] God continued with His people faithfully even in instances when God battled their gods at the altar of Baal through Elijah, forever communicating something new about His power. [152]

God clearly states that these altars and pillars were built in places of importance. He says that they were built in, "places where I record my NAME." [153] These altars and their meaning goes far deeper than just singing. They were acts of service, creativity, work, production, and ideas that came as an overflow to what God revealed about Himself. Paul wants the word of Christ to dwell in us richly and "links that richness to a richness of expression." [154] Think about it! In the beginning, God did what? He created. He being so overwhelmed with His love, broke forth in an act of creativity. This is what a new song is. It's an eruption that wells up as a result of a new realization. These new realizations are surrounded by the truth's through which God has already revealed Himself.

These pillars, wells, and altars stand in places in our journey where we will travel again. Their newness eventually marks the familiar and then fades into our tradition. The Israelite people, for example, came upon Jacob's well as they traveled in the book of Numbers. This very real place of newness for Jacob had become an old anchor mark for Israel's memory as it caused them to remember their own love story with God. This goes to show that Israel's journey is not too different than our own. The land mass in which they traveled seemed large, but in all reality, their story is very small and repetitive. As they circled round and round in the land as they traveled—becoming faithless, heartless, and complaining along the way—they continually passed by these places that reminded them of the record of God's name. They once again were refreshed by how He once had wooed them, courted them, pursued them, and married them. These altars, old songs, familiar places—whatever you want to call them—are creative land markers of art that anchored God's people in His story, His name, and in His work in and around them.

Our Tendencies

There's much to be drawn from such insight into how old, familiar, and new songs interact. We humans carry the tendency in our tastes to lock into one of history's three types of songs. Some of us lock into the songs of old. They are rich in their fabric, but if this is solely where we stay in song, this can lead only to traditionalism, dead faith, and remembering the "good 'ole days." These songs remember how God used to work through people such as Moses but may lose sight of present and future hope. The Bible also speaks of the fruit of remaining only in the old song and expresses that old songs, when solely dwelled upon at the exclusion of other memories, can produce tragic results.

Genesis 4:23-24 captures this moment when Lamech said to his wives, "Adah and Zillah, hear my voice; you wives of Lamech, listen to what I say: I have killed a man for wounding me, a young man for striking me. If Cain's revenge is sevenfold, then Lamech's is seventy-sevenfold." Here Lamech makes confession for his sins. In Genesis 4, if you'll remember, Scripture tells us that Lamech's son was Jubal, and he "was the father of all who play the harp and flute." By pointing to the origin and nature of the "old song" in the line of Cain, and in relating it to his own situation in the above passage, Lamech provides warning for all generations to be on guard. A very real nature of some "old songs" and teachings present us with a counterfeit. Cain's song is not really a song at all. It can be linked to sin. Dante knew this. As he takes us through the circles of the Inferno in his work, we hear much noise but no music; however, Paradise is bursting with music, the "new song." [155] Those who remain in the old songs alone will either die in tradition, or they'll tune their ears only to the ancient song that Cain's line sings to us. Though Cain's story portrays half the message of the gospel, in fully portraying the fallen condition of humanity, it cannot be complete by itself.

On the other hand, some of us lock into the familiar. We get stuck in the present reality and our song sings much like the Psalmist. Though there is much hope in the Psalms, and much enriching theology, it is also filled with moments of shortsightedness—instances when the humanness of people clouds their vision and keeps them from embracing what is really there. In a very real sense, the writers get caught in the familiar. They get sucked into what is normal, routine, common, and sometimes even comfortable. This mode can lock us into habits if this is the sole way we sing our lifesong, just like that of old thinking.

Finally, if we only lock into new singing, this can expose us only to what is adventurous, popular, off-the-cuff, free, spontaneous, and fresh. As stated before, this is not bad, it is just not all there is. Without a foundation and walls, the roof serves no purpose. There soon becomes nothing of substance within the songs we are singing, for they lose sight of the platform from which they spring. Without reflecting on the foundational reality of sin's presence in the world we easily cheapen or forget entirely to sing about grace—the new song. Without remembering our moments of true deliverance, we have no true anchor point for our joy. We can become like people who are "tossed to and fro by the waves, carried about by every wind of doctrine, by the craftiness of man, and deceitful scheming." [156]

THE TEMPO OF DISCIPLESHIP

OUR THEOLOGY: OUR THEOLOGY IS ENRICHED BY THE HYMN. THIS speaks to how disciples grow and are rooted. Theology has to be "whole story" oriented and rooted in how the whole timeline of old developed. This means it has to encompass the whole history of Scripture and the whole history of God's timeline. Everything serves a place in the whole, and our understanding about God and the truths of God has to be anchored in good soil and a firm foundation. We cannot reject moments in history and dismiss them, but rather, to be a disciple, we must wholeheartedly commit ourselves to learning the past. This protects us and enriches us in two major ways. Firstly, it calls us to remember the story accurately. When we look through Scripture, we are reminded how God authors the story, not how we think He authors the story. We allow Him, like sandpaper, to file off our false thinking and rough edges in order that we might commit to what is really most true. Secondly, it helps us to remember our old story. Like Moses' song meditates on the Israelites former life in slavery and their victory in deliverance, and in like manner helped the people of Israel to learn from the past and not repeat it, in the same manner we, in recognizing the snares and pitfalls of bad theology and practice in the past, can spare ourselves slavery-like living in the present.

OUR BIOGRAPHY: OUR BIOGRAPHY IS TRAINED BY THE PSALMODY. THIS again provides rich encouragement to the disciple who treads within life's authentically difficult journey. The real tangible "stuff" that confronts us every day needs decoding and deciphering. The Psalms provide us with the language not to avoid real life but to use real life and re-word it in order that we may speak clearly about God's intended purposes in it. The Psalms position us to be authentic about how we are coping with things and to embrace hope. Like the Psalmist says, "why so downcast oh, my soul, put your hope in God." We grasp the tension and make it our own. We embrace the tension, but instead of listening to ourselves and cuddling depression, we use the hope of Christ to preach to ourselves in order to stand in faith.

OUR DOXOLOGY: DOXOLOGY CHANGES OUR OUTFLOW, NEW SONG, ACTS OF praise, worship, and service to those around us. Firstly, it impacts the way we sing. No longer are we strangers to the old, the familiar, and the new songs, but we must embrace them all that they may intertwine with each other. Secondly, this impacts how a disciple is trained to worship and service. We are formed by learning history and theology, but we make our impact by being authentic and familiar with the way of culture. We must find ways to preach the old song which sings of chains being broken and deliverance being gained, and we must also move on into speaking of a journey that transforms us by hope.

The result of such a transformation in approach are new songs. These are not just meant to be actual songs written by Christ's believers. Notice that the pattern of God begins in creation. When God was overwhelmed and elated in the love He had within Himself, He innovated infrastructure, agriculture, government and leadership, work and rest, marriage and family, economy, and even commanded Adam and Eve to expand the Garden's borders through technological, entrepreneurial, and imaginative advancement. A creative and inventive ethic is in the Garden as part of the image of God. This ethical theme carries through the Old Testament and on into the New. The very Triune Godhead should still impact us in every field and area of study, and in shaping a sanctified mind within us, should cause us to create new benchmarks, pillars, and fresh songs of praise unto Him within our spheres of influence. In this way, He still creates places "for His Name."

6

Musical Conversation

> *At His family table we sit, eat, and recline, and by the power of His presence we are drawn to respond. Will we remember His family and table—its scent, its ethic? Will we understand His environment and allow the nutrients of His supply to grow us, nourish us, and redefine us? If we hear Him, will we follow?*

Recently a surge in production has emerged in creating reality TV shows that relate to the creative arts. Some examples come to mind, such as the show for fashion buffs called *Project Runway*. This show challenges teams of contestants to produce a range of clothing items. These clothing items are judged and the best garment and overall designer wins. Another show called *Platinum Hit* was a short-running show with host Jewel that assembled songwriters to compete in composing various songs for different markets, styles, and genres. Further, there have been shows in kind like *Hell's Kitchen*, *The Voice*, *HGTV Design Star*, *Face-Off*, and on down into more innovative shows for the left-brain types like *The Apprentice* and *Shark Tank*.

The fascinating thing to watch in each one of these shows is the creative process. Every challenge, be it an artsy one or an economic one, births in these passionate innovators a flood of ideas and "a-ha moments." As they begin to work, their output is amazing. They draw, plot, design, and shop in only the few minutes they are allowed. Once they begin their craft or begin operating in their area of strength, the real burst of creative juices flow, but also the tension begins to flow. Tempers run hot, opinions about each other's work start to fly, and all kinds of interesting dynamics take place.

The most interesting thing I notice in viewing these programs, amidst all the intriguing dynamics of the creative process, is that a moment arrives when eventually a judge or expert comes to edit and critique the artist's work. The expert begins to ask questions, make suggestions, and shave off the rough edges in each innovator's thinking and approach. This interaction is always fun and informative to watch. Usually, the viewer sees the artist erupt in one of two ways. The critique of their work results in their pride flaring as they belligerently or rudely defend themselves, or they humbly listen and receive the insights that the judges offer. It's insightful for me to watch because many of the artists who go on to win are the ones who listen to the editing comments of the judge and are not defensive.

Toss the Capo

Musicians understand this process of editing. I'll give you an example from my experience. When playing in a band, the guitarist uses a little clamp on their guitar called a *capo*. This capo enables them to change the key of the guitar by moving it up and down the guitar's long neck. One day, when working with a band in practice, I, as the editor, was having some difficulty explaining this process of editing to the band members. All of the players were wonderful musicians, but when they played together, it sounded horrible. They overplayed and they stepped on each other's toes. This led to a mess of sound from all of these artists as they were all playing solos within the group itself without playing as a team.

Frustrated at this dynamic, I quickly grabbed the capo from one of the guitar players and threw it into the hands of the piano player. I told everyone in the band, "Now, the piano player has the capo. That means when we begin playing again, they are the ones that are going to do the soloing and the 'talking' on their instrument. I want all of you to support their playing." We fired up the song again, and everything changed. The guitarists began listening to the parts that the piano player was playing. Not only did they listen, but they even turned their bodies toward the piano player in acknowledgement of her prominence. Not only did this cause them to edit their own creativity, but they began to play off of the piano player in support. Something special began to happen as I tossed the capo from artist to artist. A conversation started to take place.

It was as if each player, instead of only trying to amplify themselves, began to lift up each other. As a result, a beautiful dynamic of call and response started to form. The sound was good! Though each artist could play rings around the other, they all decided to give a little and take a little in the appropriate spots, and a unison conversation began to happen.

Drum Circles and Conversation

This idea of editing and conversation has always been present in music. In Cuban music, its experienced in those playing what are known as the bata drums. These drums originally belonged to the kings. Until the last few decades in Cuba, the drums were only played for the presentation of newly crowned priests (*Iyawos*), to the community, and to *Aña* (pronounced an-yá), the *Orisha* or deity whose secret resides within the drum. The percussive relationship between the three drums is a conversation: a conversation with each other, with the singer and chorus, with the *Orishas*, and with *Olofi* (God). [157] When in a drum circle such as this, it is known that many times there is a lead drummer, or caller. This drum uses rhythm to call other drums who are supporting its rhythm and speech. As it calls, the others respond, and the art of conversation is formed. This is why the act of music, particularly in oral cultures, is a creative form of communication and community.

Another use of this idea can be observed in the use of the Europeans in their use of what they call *talking drums*. These drums can be played in such a way that actually mimics speech. In the first half of the eighteenth century, they used these drums to send detailed messages from one village to the next faster than could be carried by a person riding a horse. In the nineteenth century, Roger T. Clarke, a missionary, realized that "the signals represent the tones of the syllables of conventional phrases of a traditional and highly poetic character." [158] For example, consider the Chinese and the African languages, which are highly poetic and artful languages. They are also very tonal. When speaking these languages, the pitch is important in determining the meaning of a particular word. When one speaks these languages, inflection is added to create meaning. They also add rhythm with pause, speed of speech, volume, etc. This is all done in an effort to create a call and response, and this ironically is also the rhythm of heaven.

Initiative & General Revelation

This valuable discussion about call and response—editing and conversation—is deeply helpful in discussing the dynamics of music, and what they can teach us about discipleship and Christian living. As the outline of this book suggests, there is a significant rhythm within the way God calls His creation to respond to Him. God Gathers us to speak to us by His Word. When He teaches us His commands, and by His Reality challenges our reality, we are then called into response. This quite possibly is one of the only subtleties to reality TV that is actually true to Reality, because it tries to capture an aspect of how God associates with His people.

God always initiates the conversation. God's voice always calls, and it always edits. Constance Cherry says that, "God takes the initiative to invite us to worship." [159] When He speaks, a very real conversation is started as He diverts our stressful attitude away from where it's focused, and He gathers us together to give ear to His attempts to edit. God thunders His loud voice into our existence to gain our attention and the message is clear—He has something to say.

The way God speaks, calls, and edits His Creation is through His Word. When God voices these revisions, corrections, and calls to "rightness," He refers to His method of doing so as *revelation*. When a person hears the revelation of God and sees the revelation of God, they can interpret it into different tiers and levels of comprehension. The Bible says we can embrace these revelations of God simply as mere pieces of knowledge, or only as facts to be learned. We can embrace the Bible with understanding—the facts broken down in our brains into a fashion that we can make real sense out of them—or we can eventually move our knowledge and understanding into the realm of real wisdom and belief where we know when and how to act out what we know in the correct way and with the correct timing.

Theologians are helpful here in understanding how revelation works alongside how we perceive it. They teach us that there are two ways in Scripture that God speaks by way of revelation: through general and special revelation. First, general revelation is called such for two reasons. Number one is that it has general content, and number two is that it goes out to a general audience. God's most profound general revelation comes through His work of creation. When God created the heavens and the earth in Genesis Chapter 1, He did so not by thinking it, not by imagining it, not by reasoning it, but by *speaking* it. What was in the mind of God came out of Him through His words. In a very real way, the actual contents of God's thinking were breathed out of Him and resulted in the formation of oceans, mountains, animals, galaxies, and planets. This is why the Psalmist in 19:1 says, "the heavens declare the glory of God." This is why a man or woman abandoned on a desert island with no one to share Jesus with them is still without excuse in their knowledge of Him. Romans 1:19-22 says, "For what can be known about God is plain to them, because God has shown it to them. For His invisible attributes, namely, His eternal power and divine nature, have been clearly perceived, ever since the creation of the world, in the things that have been made. So they are without excuse. For although they knew God, they did not honor Him as God or give thanks to Him, but they became futile in their thinking, and their foolish hearts were darkened."

The general content of God's message, the message of His invisible nature, is spoken out generally and given for all audiences to understand Him. His general content has been clearly perceived since creation. God's creation not only speaks wonders, it also helps us to know that we know God. God clearly calls us through His revelation to see Him. This leaves even the atheist in a dumbfounded stupor, for they claim that God does not exist. The fact that even such a claim can even be made is clear stupidity, for in Psalm 14:1, God states, "The fool has said in his heart, 'There is no God.'" Their statement is one of foolishness and is a result of what Romans tells us is a suppression of the truth. The creation is just too ordered, and too planned, and too magnificent for such a dismissal of God to be made.

Let's just take some examples of what the height of this absolutely foolish suppression of general revelation might look like. Recently, studies have been done to magnify the weight and impact of God's general revelation, such as in finding a star by the name *Canis Majoris*, a red hyper-giant star in the constellation of Canis Major, which is over 3,900 light years away. Just to give some perspective, not only into how big this star is, but also how far away it is, let's say we are traveling at current rocket speed of 25,000mph toward this star. It would take someone 2,700 years to travel 1 light year. To travel 3,900 light years to reach *Canis Majoris*, it would take 10,530,000 years. Because of this vast distance that remains between us and this massive star, the star appears to be very small. However, upon arriving at this star, one would quickly see this is not the case. To give us a mental picture of just how big this star is, let's start with the familiar. If you were to place the Earth inside the Sun, it would fit into the Sun roughly one million times. If you take the Sun and fit it into *Canis Majoris*, it would roughly hold 9.2 billion Suns. That's roughly 4-kagillion earths—if that's even a number! To consider this majesty and artistry, and still not see the hand of the divine in it and behind it, is absolutely foolish and arrogant.

Now dial general revelation down into the very smallest aspects of creation into something like the human body. Let's consider, for instance, something that we all contain in our human bodies known as Laminin. Laminins are major proteins that function like little glue sticks within the body, holding cells together. Below is an image of the shape of this finite bond that is making sure all of humanity does not physically fall apart ... literally:

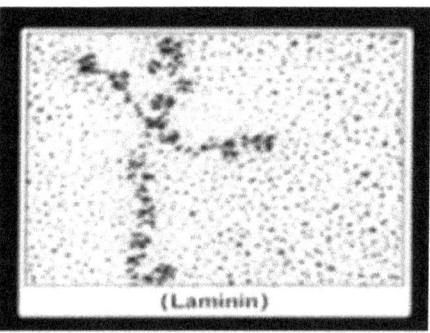

Fig. 5.1

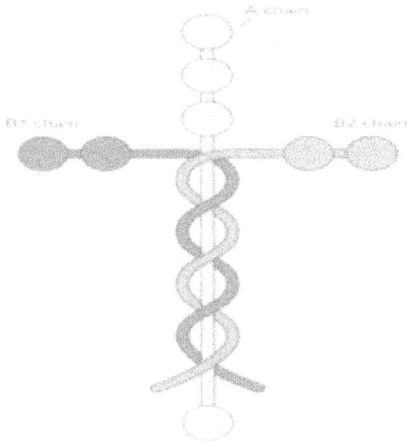

Fig. 5.2

The glue molecule that God designed to hold us together literally looks like the cross of Christ, further proof of the design of God in redemption and in revealing to us our need for Him by way of general revelation. Perhaps this little molecule could help us better understand Paul in Colossians when he writes about Jesus as the glue that fills and holds together all of creation. Colossians 1:17 says, "He is before all things, and in him all things **hold** together."

Gematria

If you will indulge my wonder for a moment on this issue, as I consider one more pet hobby of mine, this may be helpful in giving us insight into the weight of God's call through general revelation. This one is worth mentioning. We need to talk about *Gematria* when talking about general revelation. What is it, you ask? Let me show you.

In the Hebrew language, there are characters for letters but not for numbers. This means that each letter in the Hebrew alphabet is assigned a number. When a letter is seen in the Hebrew language it acts as numbers as well. Take a look at the chart below to see the Hebrew alphabet as paired with their numbers. You'll see that each letter of the Hebrew alphabet is also accompanied by a numeric value.

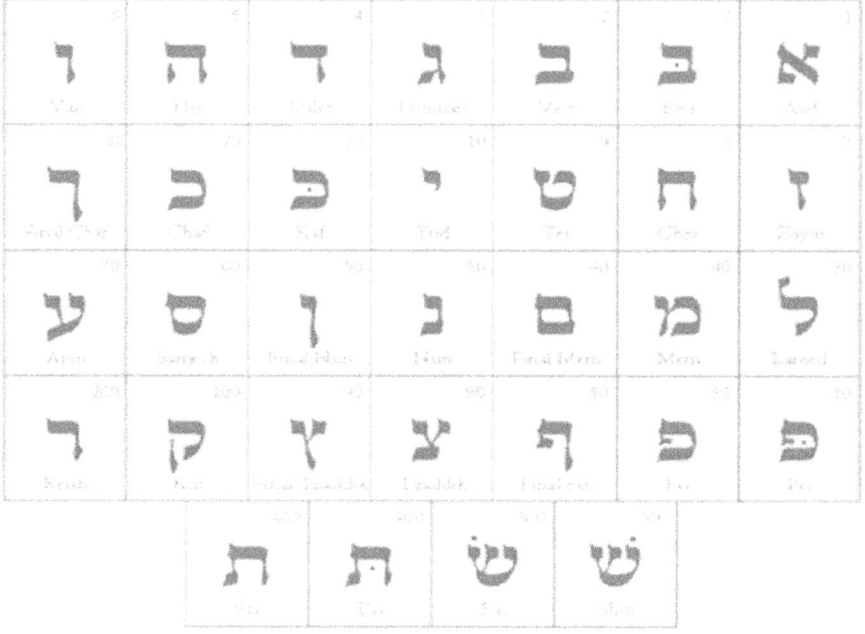

Fig. 5.3

The study of Gematria looks at the words in Scripture not only as words, but as pairings of numbers. This is what has led some crazy people to try to find Bible codes in Scripture in order to predict the future, which has ultimately led to a bunch of heresy and false teaching. Nevertheless, if we see the number system of God in the way it is meant to be seen—as His general revelation to express the truth of His detail and truthfulness in creation—we will be inspired, left in awe, and we will be more profoundly able to trust in this God who is alive and well.

As an example of how this works, let's apply Gematria to the names of the planets and constellations of the Universe, for they are the most splendid display of God's handiwork. Mark H. Lane, in his in-depth research of Gematria, has given us much to consider in this regard, not only in considering general revelation, but also considering how God's creation pairs with God's Word itself. [161]

Celestial Object	Position in Solar System	Position Among Planets	Product	Components of Spiritual Meaning	Spiritual Symbol
Sun	1		1	God is One (1)	Holy Spirit
Mercury	2	1	2	Witness (2) of God (1)	The Law
Venus	3	2	6	Witness (2) of Truth (3)	The Prophets
Earth	4	3	12	Measure (4) of Truth (3)	Measure of All
Moon	5	4	20	Division (2) of Testimony (10)	Religion
Mars	6	5	30	Division (2) of Peace (15)	Bloodshed
Ceres	7	6	42	Division (2) of Lawlessness (21)	Destruction
Jupiter	8	7	56	The Beginning (8) and the End (7)	Messiah
Saturn	9	8	72	New Man (8) of the Spirit (9)	Church Glorious
Uranus	10	9	90	Judgment (8) of Testimony (10)	Church in Decline
Neptune	11	10	110	Testimony (10) is Hidden (11)	Church in Hiding
Pluto	12	11	132	Mystery (11) Government (12)	World Government
Eris	13	12	156	Government (12) of Rebellion (13)	Church Not Present

Fig. 5.4

In his research contained in the above table we can see how Lane first applies the numbering system to the planets and their major orbiting moons in the Solar System, adding up the numerical product of their lettered names in using their correlating Hebrew numbers. In Fig. 5.4, his chart not only shows each position in the solar system and in relationship to other planets, but it shows the product of each planet's Gematria number after the Hebrew lettering/numbering system for each planet has been applied (that's the product number in the chart). The chart shows not only the Hebraic number for each planet its own right, but it then pairs the planet's final number (product) to words and ideas in Scripture that have the same Gematriaic number. We can see from the chart that the solar system not only is brilliant in its hugeness, but it also tells the story of the Gospel—God's handiwork. His revelation in Creation clearly speaks of His law, His prophets, His humans, evil's religion, destruction, and finally the Messiah, the church, the end, and the saints, appearing with Him in glory.

The above chart is fascinating, for it shows that the ordering, names, and meanings of God's universe are altogether providential and revelatory. At the base of their Hebrew meaning lie numbers that help to reveal what they truly point to and describe. Because of our distance in time and culture for the Hebraic way of thinking, we might miss such connections or even think them strange. In Jewish thinking however, this meaning would have been noticed and received, and would have resonated in a deeply impactful manner. This is why God referenced so many of the constellations in referring to His own intricate Majesty as He interacted with the people of the Old Testament. [162]

In a class I teach, I teach not only on the imagery of the universe, I also include some slides that break down the planets and a few major constellations into more minute detail in order to show how they more greatly relate to the numbering/lettering system in the Bible's language. It is not in our best interest, for sake of time, to explain in detail the slides and their full meanings, but as you look at them, pay attention to the general correlation between the scientific data and measurements and how these precise calculations portray and point to Biblical realities. The general idea of each slide is that they reveal the object (the constellation, star, planet etc.), and then show its Gematria number in some fashion (the product derived if the numbers Hebraically are added up), and then it displays the word they correlate to pertaining to words used in Scripture with the same number. I'm including only a few and I'm placing them in order of the planets first, and the constellations, so you can see the planetary flow of thought in the message that it teaches. Below are some of the slides:

Sun-1ˢᵗ Witness of God: The Holy Spirit

Milky Way 100,000 light yrs. across

Sun to Center of Milky Way 26,000 light yrs.
Sun is 333,000 times the mass of the Earth

Sun rotates every 25 earth days
Sun's gravity 28x's the Earth

1,000 = Tribe
100 = Flock of God
26,000 = The Gospel
333 = 3 x 111
3 = God/Truth
111 = Fear of the Lord
25 = Forgive Sins
28 = Christ In You

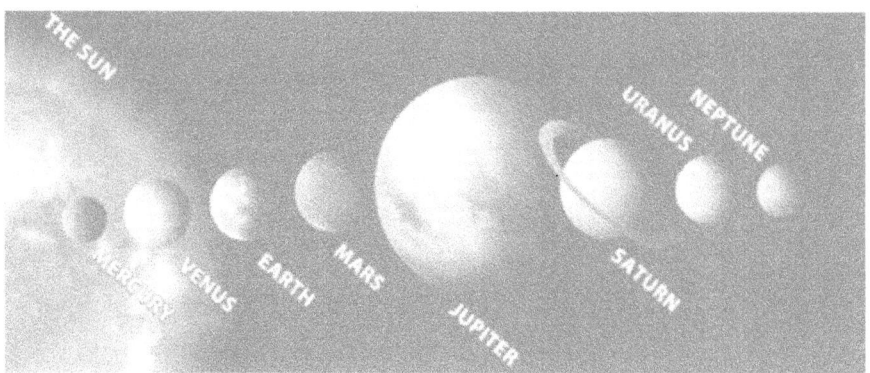

Mercury-2ⁿᵈ Witness of God: The Law

Duet. 29:10-13: The nation of Israel...under the law...by <u>oath.</u>
Rom. 3:31: The law has <u>authority...</u>
Gal. 3:22-24: The Law is <u>truth</u>...
Gal. 5:1: The law is a <u>heavy yoke</u>...
Gal. 4:9: Those who follow the law are in <u>bondage</u> and under a <u>curse.</u>

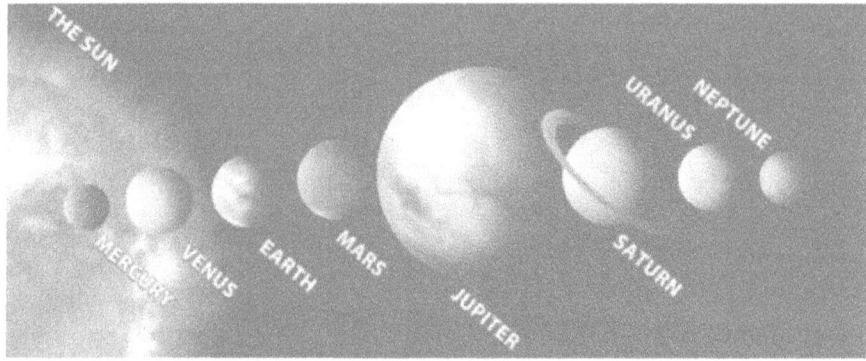

Mercury-Compare Dimensions

7 Mercury surfaces would cover earth   7= Oath | Fullness
3 Mercury distances from the sun = to earth's   3= Truth
18 Mercury's would fit inside earth   18= Bondage
88 Earth Days for Mercury to orbit the Sun   88= Saints Afflicted
59 days for Mercury to rotate 360 degrees   59 = Oppressor
0 is Mercury's axial tilt | Perfect alignment w/sun

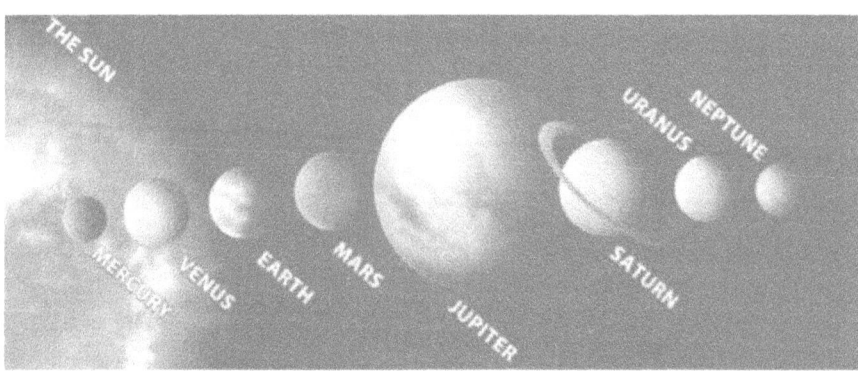

Venus-3rd Witness: The Prophets

2 Peter 1:19 "And we have <u>the prophet word</u> confirmed, which you will do well to heed as a light that shines in a dark place, <u>until the day dawns</u> and <u>the morning star</u> rises in your hearts."

* Venus is visible even after Dark.
* Connection between Venus and Prophecy

Venus-3rd Witness: The Prophets

Fact: Pure carbon dioxide atmosphere, another layer of sulfur and sulfuric acid. This causes a 90% reflection of the Sun's light. It has 92x's the pressure as earth making the surface heat +\- 462 degrees Celcius.

3rd object in the Solar System   3= Truth

Prophets Judgements: Burning sulfur (Gen. 19:24), Scorching heat (Rev. 16:9) Earthquakes (Rev. 6:12)

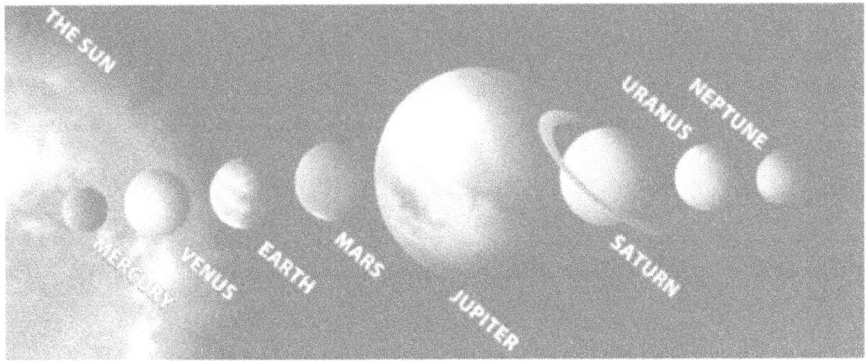

Venus-3rd Witness: The Prophets

1.11 surfaces to cover earth   111= Fear of the Lord
1.17 volume divided by earth   117= Religious NOT Redeemed
225 days for Venus to orbit the Sun   225= Weakness, Preservation
183 degree axial tilt   183= 3 (Truth) of 61 (Messiah)

<u>Morning Star:</u> Truth of Resurrection, resurrection of the saints, the Messiah, and the end.

<u>Evening Star:</u> Impatience, Rebellion Destroyed, Fear of the Lord.

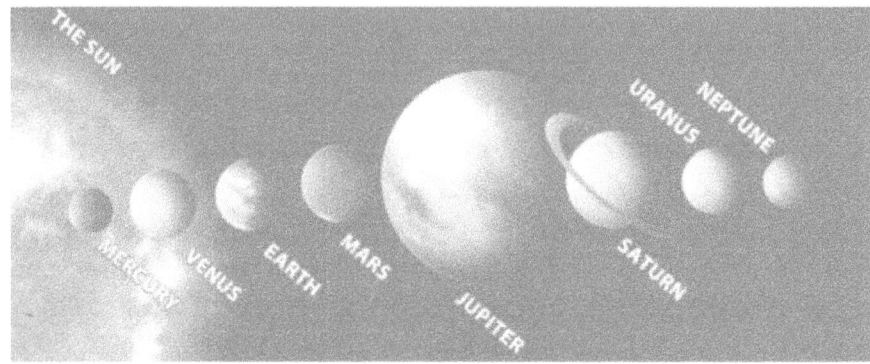

Earth-4th Witness: Measure of All

4th Object in Solar System
366 times it spins on its axis

103 Eccentricity of Orbit

4= Measure | Message
366= (3) Strength | (133) Brotherly Love
365= (5) Weakness | (73) Babylon
103= Name of God

Job 38:3-5 "Now, prepare yourself like a man: I will question you and you will answer me. Where were you when I laid the foundations of the Earth? Tell me if you have understanding. Who determined its measurements? Surely you know?

The Moon-To Steal

Surfaces to cover earth
Eccentricity of Orbit 1.1
Distance of earth divided by
Distance of Moon from the Sun
Moon rotates on its axis
Moon mass equal to earth

13= Rebellion
11= Hiding
389= 77th prime | False Prophet

27.3 days= Wicked Judged
81= Angelic Spirits

* Essence of religion: Hiding from God (dark side of the Moon)

The Moon-To Steal

Genesis 1:16 "Then God made two great lights: the greater (Sun) to rule the day, and the <u>lesser</u> (Moon) <u>to rule the night."</u>

* Night is a time of reflection on unseen world (Dan. 2:19, 7:2, 7, 13)
* Phrase "the lesser to rule the night" has a Gematria of 891. 9 (Spirit) X 99 (Perfection).

Ezekiel 28:11-19 "You were the <u>model of perfection, full of wisdom and perfect beauty...till wickedness was found in you....</u>
  Satan is the ruler of RELIGION—made in perfection and fallen

Jupiter- The Messiah (First Coming)

120 surface area related to Earth   120= Man of Peace
318 Mass related to Earth   318= Son of Man
5.2 Distance to the Sun relative to Earth 52= Gospel Worker
2.53 G-Forces to equal Earths   253= Mystery of Death
2.42 days to rotate   242= Light of the World

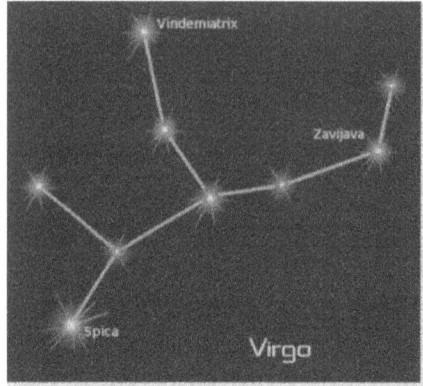

Virgo: Seed of the Women
- Women on her left Side.
- She's in the path of the Sun
- Spica (Heb. Tsemach) means "The Branch." (Is. 4:2 700 BC, Jer. 23:5,6 575 BC, Zec. 3:8 520 BC,

Reference to Messiah:
- Beautiful, glorious, line of David, servant, man, connection to Joshua (Yeshua), a king.

NOTE: Gematria of Isa. 4:2 is the 82nd Prime (8X421) 8 means "New or Holy" man.

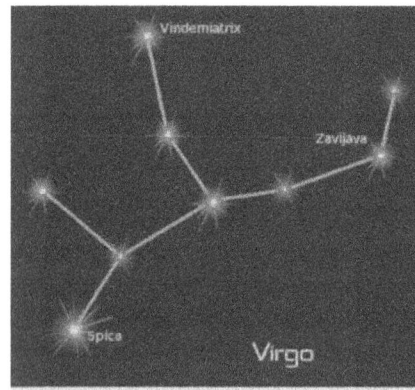

Spica: Tsemach
- Used only 4 times in Scripture
- Sheaf of Wheat in the Sign (Read Jh. 12:24)
- Pointed down to the ground

The Branch: Tsemach
- Resurrection of Christ (Isa. 11:1-4)

The Sun:
- Passes directly over Virgo
- Read (Luke 1:35)

The Tempo of Discipleship

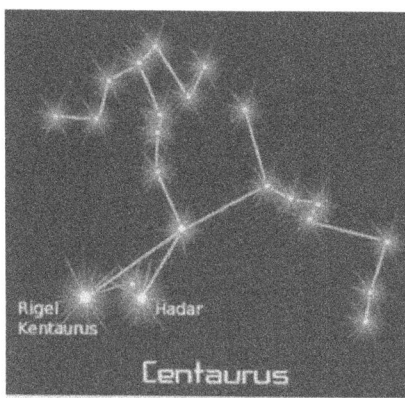

The Despised One

- ½ torso of a man, ½ horse

- The God-man.

- Spear in the upper left (Slain Offering)
  - READ ISA. 53:3

- The constellation contains 35 stars which means "The Suffering Servant"

- The Centaur looks as though he's charging to pierce LUPUS, or sacrificial offering, coming from LIBRA, the cross.

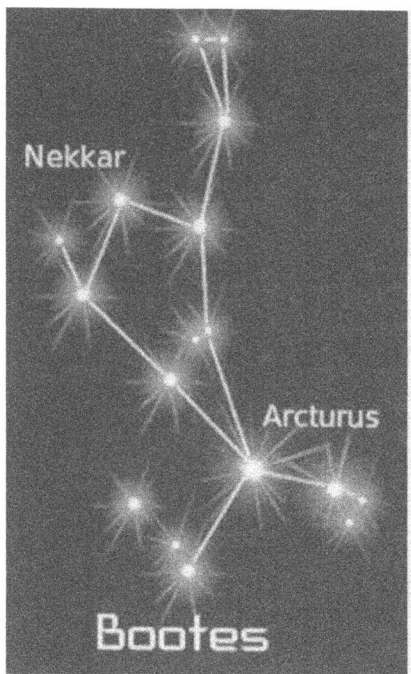

The Shepherd

- Shepherd standing up with staff in right hand.

- Arcturus (He Comes)
  - JOB 9:7-9

- Nekkar (The Pierced)

- Muphride (Who Seperates)
  - Mt. 13:24-30

- Merga (Who Bruises)

- Mizzar (Waist-Guarding)

I am the <u>Good Shepherd (Arcturus)</u>. The Good Shepherd lays down his life (Centaurus) for th sheep.

(Jhn. 10:11)

Fig. 5.5

The intention behind including this information is not so it can fully be explained in this book, but to allow the weight of general revelation to speak for itself. God's mystery in the planets is to speak of His rescue of all nations. God is deeply concerned for His flock and passionate about the heralding of the good news of the gospel. To explain the truth of His plan for forgiveness and reconciliation of humanity in Christ he includes the Sun. He reveals our separation from Him and need for Him in the Law (Mercury) and the Prophets (Venus), and through them He calls humanity to a measure of love, humility, and brokenness before Him (Earth). Though our sin has brought about our hiding in shame—plummeting us into original sin and evil oppression (Moon)—an ultimate Redeemer has always been promised to appear in a Son—a Virgin Son—Christ Jesus, the Messiah Himself (Jupiter). Christ is the seed of the woman and "The Branch" born into the line of David to be a servant King—a New Holy man (Virgo). Like a dying grain of wheat, he was hurled to the ground in a painful death only to rise again as imaged by the Sun passing directly over Spica. This God-man (Centaurus), who was pierced for our transgressions and bruised for our iniquities, "laid down His life for His sheep" that we might have life (Bootes).

Initiative and Special Revelation

Christianity is a revealed relationship! God does not want to be merely speculated about, He wants to be known! God has revealed Himself, unveiled Himself, and only foolishness can be found in our denial of Him. Only wisdom can be found in our believing in Him. God initiates this conversation, and He speaks to us not only generally but specifically. The Bible is a communicated language from God Himself. If creation truly paints His imagination in such a way that we can catch a glimpse of what He thinks about, then the Bible also speaks His dialect and helps us learn how to communicate with Him.

Special revelation is another way in which God reveals Himself to us. Special revelation and the method by which God wrote the Scriptures is most often spoken of as *verbal plenary inspiration.* "Verbal" meaning that God spoke, "plenary" meaning He spoke fully, absolutely, and comprehensively, and "inspired" meaning that He breathed through real humans to accomplish His penmanship. Like a body, God carried the mind and the voice, and He used humanity as His fingers and hands to pick up the pen of His sovereign notation. This is what enables the Bible's framework and plot to be so consistent across so many centuries and amongst so many authors.

Not only is this Word of God important in its nature of composition, but also in the point it's trying to make. The Bible tells us in Hebrews 11:2, "God, who at various times and in various ways spoke in times past to the fathers by the prophets, has in these last days spoken to us by His Son, whom He has appointed heir of all things, through whom also He made the worlds." What this passage is saying is that revelation is God entering into communication with our world of history, space, and time. "The plenitude of revelation has been given and fulfilled in the person of Jesus Christ," [162] Therefore, the truest revealing is not only through the Word of God, but through the actual person whom John calls the "Word" in John 1. Jesus is the Word. Without understanding the person of Jesus, it is impossible to understand that every Scripture in the Bible points to Him. We might think this elementary, but even the disciples did not get it. They missed it, and until Jesus explained it to them, they, like us, still seemed to forget it and divert from it.

The storyline of Scripture must first be known before true Scriptural understanding can take place. Jesus is the central theme and character, and Jesus is pure poetry and art to the human soul. J. Begbie says it this way, "the incarnation is in this sense the great Metaphor and as such is the true end of poetry." [163] God's conversation is most undoubtedly Jesus. Whereas the creation speaks of God generally, and allows writers like Paul in 1 Timothy to speak about God's common grace, unlimited atonement, and general revelation, God also speaks specifically in the person of Jesus which allows Paul to make an argument for electing grace, limited atonement, and specific revelation.

Paul teaches in I Timothy 4:10, "for to this end we toil and strive, because we have our hope set on the living God, who is the Savior of all people, especially of those who believe." In this verse, we see general and special revelation collide. God clearly makes it known that He has extended His grace to everyone—to all men. He allows us all to view His character, to breathe His air, and to experience the movie theatre of Creation that speaks loudly about His grace and His story of the gospel. This affordance, which God has so graciously allowed the whole human race, is not a kindness and a patience that we deserve. It is wholeheartedly a goodness that is given to everyone because of the sheer beauty of the cross. Though it's available however to *all* men, it particularly, and in limited fashion, saves only those who *especially* believe. The special revelation is that of Jesus Himself. He says that though all people benefit from His patience with humanity as displayed on the cross, only "His sheep hear His voice." [164] This is how Jesus is able to pray in Matthew 11:25, "thank you Father, Lord of heaven and earth, that you have hidden these things from wise and understanding and revealed them to little children." It's interesting here that Jesus connects the hiding and revealing of truth to the Lord of heaven and earth. It's as if Jesus affirms that creation can all clearly see His handiwork but yet remains in ignorance to its hidden mystery unless the Father reveals Jesus as the meaning to it all.

The Tempo of Response

What has been discussed above in very detailed fashion is the nature of God's call and God's initiative. The rhythm of the universe is conversational. God talks and we respond. He "revelates" and we resonate, or we simply tune out. He proclaims, we listen. This is why music has something profound to teach us about God's word and our response.

Everything in music interacts with itself. Notes play off other notes, just as musicians play with other musicians. One note or musician holds the capo and the others are not only required to hear it, but they are to undergird it and interact with it. This is where editing takes place. This is another word for what they Bible calls *repentance*. As God gathers us with His melody and speaks His Word to us, the first thing we are to do is listen. We are then to examine His challenge and conform every act of our creativity to his solo, for He's holding the capo. When we find that our playing has become too busy (sin), or that we are somehow overshadowing or trying to suppress His playing (pride), God edits us. He calls us to repent. He's like a reality judge standing over our innovating and spontaneity, reminding us of the challenge. He edits us, strips us, and calls us back, not to harm us, but to help us win the challenge. This process of editing and conversation is not just a puppet show where He pulls the strings and we dance.

This is a lively conversation. He allows us to move within His initiations. When God speaks, we can most certainly continue to play over Him and

The Tempo of Discipleship

attempt to suppress His melody and truth, but we will be sure to lose to our pride, or we can make the opposite mistake, as many contestants on reality shows have done. We can so overemphasize the editor's perspective in a way that we do not fully believe that He wants our input as well. God does not call us to merely undergird and support the coming up with of His ideas, or making His melodies, all the while losing our own perspective and flavor in our designs. He has also hidden the uniqueness of His image within us, and He wants our reaction and bi-play, not just a passive observer filling a pew waiting for God to do all the work. Instead of losing God or losing our uniqueness within His kingdom, we can interact with Him. We can speak to Him in prayer, and we can follow Him in mission in a way that's a conversation. He plays, and we respond. He sounds, and we find ways to intertwine.

THEOLOGY: THERE YOU HAVE IT. GOD *SPEAKS*. FOR A DISCIPLE TO LISTEN, their ears need to be trained to hear not only in 20-minute-quiet-time-intervals in the early morning, all the while sipping coffee in one hand and holding the Bible in the other. A disciple must see theology as a conversation in the real fabric of life. God is always speaking. A disciple's worldview must be shaped and encouraged this way if it is ever to apply hard and cold truths to vibrant "real life." It's as if theology has to have a right and left hand. In the right hand, we hold God's framework. It is the hand of power, and so that's where God's Word and Jesus are held. We hold His nature, His truth, His plans, His promises, and His purposes firmly without question. If we aren't equipped with this absolute, full, and plenary word when going into a postmodern, relativistic, and existential world that holds to all kinds of wishy-washy truths, then when we start to interact with how God is speaking, we will not have anywhere to ground the information. We will be tossed about on the sea like a raggedy old boat, ever-changing to fit the "new thing we hear God saying," all the while missing all our contradictions and errors in our own thinking.

But, in the left hand, we must also hold God's creation. It is His imagination. It inspires awe and inspiration. It puts blood, nerves, skin, and "touchy feely" stuff all over the framework of God's Word. Here, God's imagination becomes sensation. We can see Him, we can taste Him, we can feel Him, we can touch Him, and we can smell Him. Conversely, we can also sense how the world has perverted Him, suppressed Him, and sought to hide

Him. In this, we learn more deeply about the world of truth and lies that the Bible describes.

BIOGRAPHY: WE CAN, IN RESPONSE, CHOOSE TO PLAY OVER GOD, PLAY under Him, or interact with Him as we live. He assuredly holds the capo, and He is always editing and holding conversation with us. When He edits us, we'll either decide to play over Him by sinning, suppressing, or trying to stop His voice with our pride, or we'll condemn ourselves, shame ourselves, and grieve ourselves in our self-loathing (reverse pride). Pride and false humility are both sins because they both keep us from doing what God created us to do—bear His image. Our job is to interact and have conversation with Him. When the world stings and edits us, we are to find how God is allowing it to shape us. Everything is conversation. We need to seek the underlying melody of what God is doing in his providence and interact with it until we can find how to play and enjoy the music right along with Him.

DOXOLOGY: IT HAS BEEN SAID THAT DISCIPLES WORSHIP GOD, SERVE GOD, and honor God in both *gathering* and *scattering*. It would seem, then, in our living out the truths of God, that conversation should impact both environments. First, in the *gathering*, disciples are to be shaped and crafted in how the congregation meets. The environment should be *dialogical* (conversation). This comes down to many things in how the liturgy of the church is formed. For our purposes, let's consider the songs. Hymns have more of a teaching aspect in them, as well as a call. Praise choruses have more of a response nature to them. The trouble comes when we neglect one of them or try to replace one with the other. For example, we can force choruses into a role of revelation by placing them first in the service; they are thereby called on to function in a way that they are incapable of doing. Rather, songs should be looked at for what they are supposed to accomplish. The same comes down to the prayers and the giving of the Word. Everything should be done to promote the involvement of the disciples as they are being formed. When the Word is given, it should be given human touch with a response time, communion, prayer, ministry, etc. The people should be able to enter into and interact in the rhythms of God as He calls His people. Liturgists are to ponder deeply how they are crafting their people, not just in how they are "doing church," but on into the people themselves.

In the scattering, people are to be edited and called to repentance and innovation. God's word speaks the call, and people's lives should begin to reflect the interaction. Disciples are taught by God as they edit their home to reflect His artistry and leadership, as they edit their workplace to reflect His ethics, as they edit their entertainment to enjoy His rest, etc. Where people are out-of-sync with the conversation of God, they should be called to edit and repent, and where their lives are modeling the community, the reasoning, organization, beliefs, and mission of God, they should be called to innovate all the more in order to advance the kingdom. If disciples see everything as an opportunity to repent and create, then truly the tempo of discipleship should produce men and women who are influencing society at all its top levels, for we have the mind of Christ. [166]

7

Repetition and Remembrance

The brain is an interesting thing. Our little blob of grey "stuff" sits up in the top of our heads and with its left and right hemispheres, like electricity's positives and negatives, supplies the body with all the power and instruction it needs in order to rev up and run. Though the brain is one unit, it operates in two different halves—the left and the right. The left half of the brain is very logical and processes items in an item-by-item and step-by-step fashion. Marcel Kinsbourne admits this narrow logical style is able to best attend to "a few members in any one category" and notices "detail in small differences." [167] This part of the brain is very systematic, is always "on alert," and is able to isolate the smallest of details in order to accomplish specific purposes.

On the flip-side, the right half of the brain functions all-at-once and stretches in imagination with leaps and bounds. This part of the brain is able to take a wide variety of similar subjects and concepts together without paying much attention to detail or difference. [168] The right brain is like the internet in that it creates a web of connection that can detect similar ideas and can grey differences together that appear black and white.

In short, the left brain is rational and prescriptive (narrow), whereas the right brain is experiential and descriptive (diverse). Though people predominantly use one half of their brain more naturally than the other one, both hemispheres are vital and crucial. In different situations, each part of the brain provides a different perspective. The rhythm of these two sides as they work together can be likened to a car in how it functions. A car to function properly, has to engage the gas and the brakes. Whereas the gas propels the car forward toward the intended destination, the brake provides the car the ability to stop for danger and more carefully consider its motion so that it stays protected and safe. In this way, in human interaction, right-brain people are overwhelming "gas" pushers. Their imaginations can look past hindrances into possibilities. However, their left brain needs to operate as the "brakes" and help control them in case their dreaming and ideas get too far out beyond the realm of possibility. In this way the mind balances itself. It can imagine the plans, but to be effective, it also has to order the plans.

The brain, due to this interlinking creativity, contains an incredible ability to hold and store information in a variety of ways. A study conducted by Stockholm University revealed the power of the brain's *olfactory memory* (sense of smell). It stated that smells have the tendency to take someone further back in time than verbal or visual memory cues. When introduced to a smell memory cue, participants in the study, whose average age was 75, most frequently recalled memories from early childhood. [169] This is the power of the mind. The power of the right brain can take abstract and imaginative things such as smell and input them into the brain in an ordered way that makes sense and is easy to remember and store (the left brain's function).

Not only is the olfactory memory a powerful tool for memory, but studies have also shown that music possesses a powerful ability to capture memory because of its ability to include both sides of the brain. A study was done in Alzheimer's units and dementia wards using music as a tool for enacting memory. The findings showed that with music:

 Residents are happier and more social.

Relationships among staff, residents, and family deepen.

Everyone benefits from a calmer, more supportive social environment.

Staff regains valuable time previously lost to behavior management issues.

There is growing evidence that a personalized music program gives professionals one more tool in their effort to reduce reliance on anti-psychotic medications. [170]

Every time music or an olfactory sense is repeatedly experienced, it not only reawakens memories, but it slows the actual decay process of mental disease. By attaching present meaning continually with past experiences, the brain is forced to continue to make connections and, in this sense, continues to grow and maintain its strength. This explains why Alzheimer's patients who listen to music are happier, experience a better quality of life, and almost receive a medicating effect from the music. Music contains that ability not only to create a tool that helps people to imagine, but also to be effective in helping a person to order information in a way that builds and anchors good memory.

Music's Role

In seeing music's effect on the mind, it shows that empirical evidence about the brain is more complex than the simple distinction about left and right processing. [171] Music's powerful influence upon the brain demonstrates that there is some way in which music unites the two spheres and causes our brain to work in tandem. In a sense, music helps take very detailed and narrow theologies of *proclamation* (precise truths) and blends them together with the theology of *manifestation* (expression), thus causing both sides of the brain to collide. Music can help us to imagine the plans (expression), and it can also order the plans (precise truths).

This is what enables the content of lyrics and of poetry to remain stuck inside a person's head in an annoying hook. It plays over and over again, far deeper, longer, and more imaginatively than any information that comes simply out of a book. This is also what leads people like Jeremy Begbie, as noted earlier, to conclude that theology can be done through music and is best done by considering how music affects the transformation of the brain. It not only deploys content, but it calls for full expression of that content.

Before research and awareness came out discussing things of this nature, aged Reformer Martin Luther, in some fashion, noticed this in his approach to discipleship. During every church gathering, in which Martin Luther preached over 7,000 sermons, he sought also to compose hymns that outlined the truths of his messages. These compositions of his contained music and melodies that were familiar to the everyday person of that time. He realized that people may not leave remembering his sermons, but they would leave humming the tunes to the songs. He envisioned hiding the truths of his message in the lyrics themselves in order to create mnemonic devices for the people to take with them. This would help them remember. They would not only be able to sing the lyrics and theologies in precision, but also meditate on the words in expression, thus driving the meaning deeper and deeper.

This approach to music and how it interacts with the mind contains similar thinking to how the Jewish people would meditate on Scripture. Meditation has always constituted an important element of Jewish spiritual praxis. The earliest account, found in Genesis 24:63, depicts Isaac going out into the fields and meditating. [172] For the Jew, the practice of meditation did not resemble New Age and Buddhist practices of meditation in that the goal was to empty the mind with some mantra like "ohm." The Jewish idea of meditation is similar to preparing a field for planting.

When a farmer approaches a field for planting, it is filled with huge dirt clods that are too big and too un-fertile to create a healthy environment for seeds. To prepare the land to reap a great harvest, the farmer tills it over and over again. Finally, all the dirt clods are broken down into their smallest form, and seeds can grow and flourish.

In the Jewish mind, theologies like God's oneness, His mercy, glory, law, redemption, etc., are like giant dirt clods of truth. They present huge concepts that need to be broken down before they can be swallowed, or they'll cause someone to choke. For a seed of belief to truly implant itself in someone's life in order to begin to grow, it needs to be broken down into its simplest form. Then it reaps a harvest. The meditation of the Jews is not an "emptying of the mind" but a filling of the mind with God's truth. They break it down, think upon it, and carry it even upon their actual foreheads until the truth of it unravels all their false reasoning and assumptions.

In Luther's approach to musical meditation, he understood how music helps a person to relate to, break down, and, in a fun, musical way, repeat the same idea over and over again until the truths of it reach deeper levels of understanding. This is why he combined theology with music. He wanted people to be able to remember the messages and truths of precise theology (left brain), so he put them into right-brain creativity, which allowed the melody to hook the believer onto the ideas—singing them round and round, deeper and deeper, until their meaning produced a fertilized soul.

DO THIS IN REMEMBRANCE OF ME ...

This act of memorization and meditation, what the Bible calls *anamnesis* or remembrance, is carried heavily into Jesus' commission to His disciples. At the Last Supper in Luke 22:7-38, on the night of the Passover, Jesus broke bread, gave it to his disciples, and said, "this is my body broken for you, this is my blood, shed for you." In this instance, Jesus taught some very precise theologies about Himself and about how He was about to die, but He attached the meaning of the evening to very imaginative and physical elements (the bread and the wine). His act and instruction are combined with artful metaphor in a way that causes the analogy to stick and root deeper through meditation within disciples for generations to come. In the minds of those disciples, the breaking of this bread and spilling of this wine would have, and should have, opened their minds up to something much deeper than the elements themselves. It should have connected all the dots of Scripture and revealed Jesus' fulfillment and victory in every meal that had taken place in the history of the Bible up until that moment.

The meal should have first connected their thinking to the precise environment of the Garden of Eden. This is where creation started. This is where humanity started. We all started in a Garden surrounded by nourishment, supply, and food. God's original plan for man was that he was to work the garden and eat from it. Being in the garden was a symbol to Adam that God is his source of provision and all his nourishment. The food then was a promise of covenant blessing. It resembled the binding of God to his people for their wellbeing, filling, and sustenance.

The snake however entered the Garden in Genesis 3 and took this food, by way of the apple, and promised his kingdom to Adam and Eve through dishonest intentions. This food that was meant to display God's goodness to

Adam and Eve was the very same food that Satan hijacked and perverted in meaning, so that humanity's parents would fall into sin and judgment. On that day, the paradise of God that was given in food was given up in food. Cooper says, "Up to this moment, nothing had ever been done apart from the life and love of God. Now, suddenly a whole new world opened up. The seed of that forbidden fruit sprouted deep in human hearts, spreading out roots and branches that encompassed the whole of humanity's future, blossoming into pride and envy, murder and deceit. Every crime, personal and corporate, private and public, grew out of this common root, from sex trafficking to genocide, adultery to petty theft. Life with God was rejected and life without God, embraced. The bite from that fruit was truly the kiss of death." [173] This horror and atrocious fall forever filled food with a mixed message, a message of blessing and a message of judgment.

This theme continued in Genesis 18 as God visits Abraham through three men; as He confirms His promise to give Abraham and Sarah a son to restore the mess that Adam and Eve's sin had set in motion. During the meal, He shares that this son would lead to two things. The promised son was to make Abraham a very rich man in blessing and legacy—as many children as the stars in the sky. Secondly, and ultimately, this promise was to fulfill what God promised through Eve, that a Son (a Christ—Messiah) would come through Abraham's line and crush the head of the serpent who brought sin and death into the world through that forbidden fruit. Once again, over a meal came the promise of a blessing to God's people.

Abraham had Isaac and Ishmael, and soon Isaac had Jacob and Esau. The story tells us that Esau was born first and so, by birth order, was entitled to the father's inheritance. The line of blessing promised to Abraham was to come through Esau, but in Genesis 25:29-34, Esau came in hungry one day, and Jacob offered him a bowl of soup in exchange for the family inheritance. Esau snatched the bowl of soup in ravenous hunger, gave his inheritance away in that moment to Jacob, and forfeited the blessings of God all over again for a bowl full of food.

As Israel's history progressed, it brought along men like Joseph who were raised up for a particular time in human history. He was raised up when Egypt was experiencing a historic famine of food. Joseph, a man blessed by God in wisdom, saw fit to harvest what was left in order to thrive through the worst days ahead in the famine. Again, food becomes here a symbol of blessing and of judgement. Joseph was put in charge to steward and store

The Tempo of Discipleship

this provision for future famine long after this sign of blessing in provision from God came. God allowed famine to come upon the land. The use of food not only supplied blessing but also allowed God to display his judgment. Due to the famine and Joseph's faithful stewardship of the years of produce, everyone in all the land came to Egypt to live and survive.

This led to a change in hands in Egyptian leadership, which caused slavery to come upon God's people for 400 years. We all know the story from there. God raised up Moses and called him to go to the Pharaoh speaking the words, "Let my people go," and after 400 years of slavery and nine plagues, Pharaoh still refused to oblige. On the tenth and final plague, God promised to take the first-born son of every family in the land as a sign of judgment on the Pharaoh's stubborn disobedience. This plague was to impact everyone unless they obeyed one condition. If the people were to take a lamb, kill it, and smear its blood over the door posts of their homes, the angel would accept the death of the lamb in the place of the first born son. That night, as the angel passed over the houses smeared with blood, God extended grace in light of the lamb and entered the homes to take the lives of the sons of those without this sign. The whole land once again experienced God's dichotomy in food. Some families killed dinner and were spared, and some refused to take God's provision and were judged in the death of their first born.

This led to the glorious freeing of the Israelite slaves as they followed God into the desert toward the Promised Land. God had beaten their evil king. God had proven His kingship over His people once again, and as the people traveled toward the Promised Land, God provided for His people. In the desert, God provided manna—a bread and meal from heaven—for them to eat. [174]

After the desert, things continued to transpire in Israelite history as it progressed into the times of Jesus. The Israelites were carried into slavery once again by Babylon, in which Nebuchadnezzar changed the names of God's people to reflect the worship of his God, and he offered men like Daniel a place at his table. Interestingly enough, Daniel didn't mind his name being changed, and was even offered a position in the King's school of diviners, witches, tarot card readers, and new age psychics, which he accepted, but the one thing he wouldn't take was the King's offer that Daniel would share in the meals of the King's table. The reason why can be further seen as the Bible's story progresses even on into Esther.

The King's table under Nebuchadnezzar and on into the time of Esther under King Xerxes was a deeply pagan event. The King would throw huge feasts, tainted with sex, drugs, and rock 'n roll. Food was linked to the idea of sin, un-cleanliness, revelry, and partying among those who gladly took Satan's apples. Once again, the judgment that echoes the Garden is undone by God's redemption. Esther came into the center of all the revelry to plead for God's people, who were about to experience genocide from this demonic kingship. She cooked the King and his evil side-kick Haman a meal, all the while pleading for her people. The king relented and the *tables* of history were turned—literally. The people of Israel were saved from the tyranny around a meal. They celebrated the victory with a feast, a meal called Purim—a tradition still observed in Jewish tradition today.

Memory is for Remembering Jesus

When Jesus enters human history in human flesh and was birthed in Bethlehem (which means "the house of bread") and grew up only to be tempted in the desert to sin by Satan's false offers of provision like Adam had (through an offering of food), [175] it is more than just coincidence. In beginning His ministry and referring to Himself as the Bread of Life; [176] feeding the 5,000 with bread and fish—linking him to Elijah in 1 Kings 17 when he was fed by ravens—and showing up in Matthew 26:26 on the feast of Passover to offer communion "in remembrance" of Himself, the meaning in the event of the meal becomes more profound than a simple dinner. The dinner is attached to all of Holy history, not only to remembering the past but also to remembering His promises for the future.

The future church began and grew around a meal, [177] and ultimately the whole of human history ends in Jesus' second coming when, in Revelation 19:6-9, after all the judgments of the earth had been completed, Jesus hosts the feast and Marriage Supper of the Lamb. This will be the ultimate sign of blessing and of judgment. Those who are invited to the banquet are blessed, and those who eat elsewhere are not.

In this manner, *anamnesis*, the art of remembering, is attached to a set of left-brain and hard line theologies, and explodes in tangible creative elements (bread and wine) with meaning in imaginative story and art that tantalizes the right-brain cortex. It's as if it resounds like a repetitive lyric each time the elements speak the message. The reminder drills deeper and deeper within us. This must be what enables people in heaven to sing the very simple words of "Holy, Holy, Holy, is the Lord God Almighty," over and over again. This act of repetition does not cause the brain to tune out and lose track of its footing, but rather, it engages the mind in remembrance. Each time the lyric passes, it delves deeper into the person's understanding of the word *Holy*. If the mind is engaged in thinking about very real and left-brain theologies, and yet is revolving over and over in singing the same chorus, it's as if the theologies provide the tiller to the singer's soul, churning up new meaning as the same rows in the field are plowed over and over.

Just like any skill, remembering and repetition go together. Repeating an act often, such as singing or partaking in communion, helps a person to remember deeper and stretch further in understanding and application.

Our Response

In Chapter 5, it was mentioned that God's Word is in the Scripture and in the creation, bringing with it a call, and we are to respond. God's *tempo of discipleship* is that He gathers us, teaches us, and then calls us to respond to His call. Typically, this is why focused times of communion, singing, ministry times, prayer, meditation, and "altar calls" occur at the time of response after a sermon, after a bible study or small group, or after a telling of the Gospel message. Our hearts naturally respond to information with imagination. Once God has spoken to us through His words, we take time in our finite brains to blow those truths up into all their ramifications. We need the time to imagine our home lives, our marriages and parenting, our church, our workplaces, our culture, our entertainment, our government, and the individuals who are closest to us. We must ask ourselves, "How do these truths intersect and transform real life?" Then we sing, we meditate, and we allow the imagination to work as it challenges every part of us to change, to shape, to mold, and to grow. These concrete truths, like huge dirt clods in a field, begin to mull over in our brain and bring clarity. Just like in music, there is the "signifier and the signified," [178] as the music itself points to a greater imaginative truth of God. All things in life are not simply things in themselves, but they point to and preach about the greater realities that are found in Christ. Training ourselves to see these things is the greatest application. When the communion time comes, and we repetitively remember the blessing of Christ upon all that we imagine, we are engaging the artful signifier in order to ponder Christ's real reality. We remember His intentions for all that He created, and we ponder the brokenness that we created. We ponder relationships we have, beliefs we hold, and purposes we cherish. We analyze places where we've remembered the story of God and have aligned to it, or where we've forgotten the story of God and we need realigning. It brings us to places of forgiveness and repentance; it brings us to be honest with ourselves and each other, and, in a very real way, it causes us to allow Jesus to remove sin-barriers that have kept us and Him apart. Our blockages to Him are exposed and removed, bringing us ever so much closer to each other and to Him.

THE TEMPO OF DISCIPLESHIP

THEOLOGY: TRUE MIND TRANSFORMATION HAS TO BE DONE IN THE RIGHT and the left brain. For example, as concerning our discussion on meals, "people are saved through the gospel message [left brain content], but meals will create natural opportunities to share that message in a context that resonates powerfully with what we are saying [right brain expression]." [179] This is not to say that the gospel message is not enough, it's to say that the gospel message was never meant to be a set of truths only to be shared, but also a set of truths to be walked out and lived in artful expression. The gospel is audio (heard) and video (visualized). It's a message and a people. The context around a meal creates an atmosphere of family that not only speaks in words about the nature of being in the kingdom of God, but the environment it creates is the truest to the actual nature of what it means to be "in Christ." This is how the gospel transforms. It has to go beyond the classroom, and it has to extend into our character and competency (our ability to use it).

The word *belief* in Scripture carries this implication. In Romans 10:9, we are told we are saved when we believe in Christ. This word, *pisteuō*, implies that we intellectually learn the facts and events of Jesus's life, but that we must also trust them. Entrusting ourselves to them is an action. In the simplest form, we could say it like this: "We know what we believe by watching what we do." Concepts have to collide with real character and real environments of expression. If they don't, then belief never happens.

. . .

The Tempo of Discipleship

Biography: Coupled with a disciple's theology in knowing truth and living truth is the aspect that these truths are grown over time in remembrance and repetition. It's almost as if the more we remember, the more it causes us to reexamine, re-question, and reaffirm what we know to be true. It stabilizes us, roots us, and secures us in our deep level of constant reaffirmations. Further, combined with repetition, it destabilizes us in causing us to break down and build up the information afresh. It's like exercise. Remembering how to bench press, for example—the technique, the form, and the muscle memory—helps secure us and stabilize us. In repeatedly lifting the weights over and over, we break the muscles down, building them up afresh and shaping ourselves in greater strength. Spiritually, we can see this in the communion meal. We are opened to Christ's past bearing down upon us, and this stabilizes us—we are anchored in His work. The very same Eucharistic repetition also destabilizes and opens us repeatedly to Christ's past and to be opens us to an anticipated future in Him—continually experiencing a recharging of God's promise of a new hope. [180] The spiritual muscle in continually being exercised continues its development of our soul.

Where this plays out in discipleship is that right and left brain regions—remembrance and repetition—cannot be disconnected. If the imaginative story of God is disconnected from repetitive events like church, prayer, quiet times, and meals, then they merely die and wither in their effects. Vice versa, if modes and rhythms of memory are not repeated over and over, then spiritual Alzheimer's will set in and cause the disciple to lose a grip on anything and everything that they believe.

Doxology: How music and memory interact with one another teaches us great wisdom. They teach us how to praise God. In how we live out our faith, we should examine how we are truly formed by how we think and how we act. We are formed by the theologies we believe and by how we imaginatively express them. This is how we become like the image of God and truly become disciples and worshippers of Him.

The doxology of acting out the truths of remembering and repetition comes when we blend the theology and biography sections of discipleship together (to be discussed more in Chapter 8). In brief, what this means is that being a disciple has to include moments in the day that build up the mind in content. We need moments of reading, learning, input, and education—this has to be part of a Godly person's regiment and discipline. However, moments of creativity, art, imagination, invention, innovation, output, and expression have to combine with education. As with Alzheimer's patients, the content is in the brain, but until it is expressed in repetition, it is not remembered.

8

Transposition

Have you ever been to a church service where the leader of the music kicks in with the opening song, and you're ready to sing along and belt out praise to God, only to find that when they sound their first pitch, you try to match it and discover that your voice cracks like a teenage boy in puberty? The music leader is singing so high you cannot hit the note if you tried. The opposite is true, a female leader may begin to sing, and when the entire chorus of men join in, they are singing so low it sounds like they have nasal congestion. Can you relate? This happens when the musicians set the song in a key that is too high or low, and it complicates a person's ability to make sense of the melody. In this scenario, one of three things happens: the musicians in the room will harmonize the pitch in a range they can sing, the non-musicians in the room will try to sing along as their voices crack, break, strain, drone, and put them into fits as they try to find the melody, or the individual will simply quit singing altogether.

Speaking as a person who leads the musical praise in my setting, this is the hardest and most frustrating thing to balance. Finding a key that everyone can sing in comfortably in a room full of men, women, children, non-musicians, and musicians can prove impossible. When you are the one in the audience on the other hand, watching this mess occur, it can be quite humorous. I always love watching these cross-over faux music leaders with their swoopy bangs, skinny jeans, chain wallets, and rocker tattoos, as they attempt to get the congregation to join in as they sound out their teenage, girly voices. They'll sing so high it makes everyone's nose bleed. I often think about people watching this phenomenon who are not "churched" and wonder how odd this must all seem to them.

Nevertheless, this is a real challenge of music. It's not just a challenge in worship, but in all kinds of music. Musicians come with all kinds of ranges to their voice (highs and lows), and when they perform, sing, or write a song, a key must be found that works for their voice. For those of you who are not musicians, let me explain very briefly how the science of this concept works so that you can follow my train of thought in the rest of this chapter.

Simply put, songs are made up of notes (as we have discussed), just like sentences are made up of words. Certain words belong in certain sentences, otherwise they don't make sense. For example, if I were to say, "Hold still and smile while your dog takes our picture," you might look at me funny. However, if I were to say, "Hold still and smile while your Grandma takes our picture," you'd respond nicely. Word choice is important.

In music, this same idea is present. The musical alphabet is housed in what are called scales, and these scales lay the foundation for the chords and songs that are created. Scales are a cluster of notes (or letters) that can be grouped together to express ideas (songs). Below is an example of a scale in the key of G:

G A B C D E F# G

So I don't lose you non-musicians, I won't go into in-depth detail as to why this G-scale makes sense, because that's not the point. I'll just simply say this is a major scale and it makes sense. All the notes above belong in this scale and it creates a *key*. If I play any of these notes, it will make sense to someone listening. If I play a note outside the key like an Ab, it's going to sound a bit weird. Not only is each individual note in the above illustration of the G scale in the key of G, but every individual note receives a corresponding number as seen in this example below:

G A B C D E F# G

The Tempo of Discipleship

I ii iii IV V vi vii° I

Each number tells the musician that, if they build a chord (a group of notes such as GBD) off a particular note, it will be called a I chord, a ii chord, etc., depending on which note a person starts using to begin their grouping of notes (I won't take time to explain all the roman numerals ... just trust me).

The problem in a singer's range appears when the person singing tries to hit the notes in the key in which the performers are playing. If those G's are too high, or the B's are too low, then some people's range will not be able to sing it. How we solve this problem in music is we are forced to do something called *transposition*.

In science, transposition means taking a piece of DNA from one spot and moving it to another; in Math, it means to take a symbol or number on one side of the equal sign and move it to the other side of the equal sign. In music, it's very similar. For example, if G is too low for me and my congregation, I want to raise the key up to another key. So if my "I" chord is G in the key of G, my "I" chord in the next key up in A would be an A chord. See below:

G A B C D E F# G

I ii iii IV V vi vii° I

A B C# D E F# G# A

I ii iii IV V vi vii° I

Transposition is the process of taking one musical note and putting it into another key. But, of course, when you do it, you can not just change that one note, you have to change all the notes to form to that new key (this is a general rule). This is what enables a person singing in the nosebleeds during musical worship on Sundays to simply take it down a key or two and make it singable for the congregation.

KOINE INCARNATION

This idea of transposition is profoundly helpful for thinking about discipleship, as well as helping us grasp key theological concepts. In order for God's people to respond to Christ and His culture of heaven, Christ underwent a process that is something similar to that of transposition.

The first thing that God transferred from heaven into humanity was His very words. To do this, He needed to sing in a key that we, in our simple non-deity minds, can understand. This is why most of the New Testament, for example, is written in what is called *koine* Greek. It is a simple language and a language of the people. When Paul transmitted most of His writings to the people and taught them the very words of God, it was important that it came to them in a key that they could sing it in and understand it in. In an absolutely radical way, the language and dialect of how God believes, teaches, speaks to, and relates within Himself became readily available to our way of hearing it.

Not only did this happen in the actual keystrokes of Paul's penmanship, but God did this in His very nature. Theologians call this the *incarnation*. God, the Triune spirit-being, [181] took on flesh and translated and transposed Himself into our likeness. He became flesh and gave us a very real understanding of what He is like in a nature that we can understand. Think of it this way, if I were to take the note of B from the key of G and put it into the key of A (where there is also still a B) there's a commonality created between both keys. God, in like fashion, came to earth as God and man and created a commonality between the key of heaven and earth. What I mean by this musical mumbo-jumbo is that in heaven, there is a certain key, and God took a common note from that key and put it into our song. This ensured that the God-man Jesus was both God and man. He was fully in the key of G and fully in the key of A at the same time (B is in both keys—in G its the 3rd note, and in A its the 2nd note). He resonates and functions fully in both without losing anything. Music helps us understand the feasibility of the God-man (fully man and fully God).

C. S. Lewis, in a bit of a different fashion, looks at this issue through a slightly different lens. His insights can benefit our discussion greatly. His perspective is particularly helpful in this area in discussing how he has come to understand the wide application for the idea of transposition. One day when Lewis was out and about, he captured, out of the corner of his eye, a glimmer of sunshine peering through a crack in an old wooden barn. As he approached the light, the light shining directly in his eye caused him to look

The Tempo of Discipleship

away. He quickly stepped to the side of the light and got a whole new picture of how to look at the light. Though he could not see the sun behind the barn, nor could he stare directly at it, he could look along the beam and understand the sun's existence. On the other side of that barn was a real sun, a real glory, a heaven if you will, but this strand of light, if looked along, could reveal the real thing.

This is how C. S. Lewis would have been able to see and understand the God-man and the rest of this world's existence. We cannot see God, for His image is too potent, but in looking *along* human flesh in Jesus, we get to see the Father's image in full. This is mimicked all over creation: in the fire, we see God's passion; in the eagle, we see protection; in the mountains, we see his majesty; in the oceans, we see his unsearchableness; in the wind, we catch glimpses of his spirit; in the bread and the wine of communion, we catch an image of sacrifice. God created all things in a language we can understand and in a language that we can look *along*. This grace of God helps us to understand a bit more about what an object, a piece of art, or an image points to and preaches about in our realm.

Before moving on, I have to include an excerpt from Lewis's book, *Weight of Glory*, that finishes this idea for us:

> Let us construct a fable. Let us picture a woman thrown into a dungeon. There she bears and rears a son. He grows up seeing nothing but the dungeon walls, the straw on the floor, and a little patch of the sky seen through the grating, which is too high up to show anything except sky. This unfortunate woman was an artist, and when they imprisoned her she managed to bring with her a drawing pad and a box of pencils. As she never loses the hope of deliverance, she is constantly teaching her son about that outer world which he has never seen. She does it largely by drawing him pictures. With her pencil she attempts to show him what fields, rivers, mountains, cities, and waves on a beach are like. He is a dutiful boy and he does his best to believe her when she tells him that that outer world is far more interesting and glorious than anything in the dungeon. At times he succeeds. On the whole he gets on tolerably well until, one day, he says something that gives his mother pause. For a minute or two they are at cross-purposes. Finally it dawns on her that he

> has, all these years, lived under a misconception. 'But,' she gasps, 'you didn't think that the real world was full of lines drawn in lead pencil?' 'What?' says the boy. 'No pencil marks there?' And instantly his whole notion of the outer world becomes a blank. For the lines, by which alone he was imagining it, have now been denied of it. He has no idea of that which will exclude and dispense with the lines, that of which the lines were merely a transposition—the waving treetops, the light dancing on the weir, the coloured three-dimensional realities which are not enclosed in lines but define their own shapes at every moment with a delicacy and multiplicity which no drawing could ever achieve. The child will get the idea that the real world is somehow less visible than his mothers pictures. In reality it lacks lines because it is incomparably more visible. [182]

This is also true of us! "We know not what we shall be" [1 John 3:2]. In some respects we know the shadows of what we clearly see on earth through all creation, but we shall be more and see more, not less, once the full kingdom is finally revealed. Our natural experiences (sensory, emotional, imaginative) are only like the drawing, like penciled lines on flat paper. When they vanish in the risen life, they will vanish only as pencil lines vanish from the real landscape. They will vanish like a candle flame, not put out, but made invisible because someone has thrown up the blinds, thrown open the shutters, and let in the blaze of the risen sun.

We can put it in whatever terms we please. We can say that by Transposition our humanity, senses and all, can be made the vehicle of beatitude, or we can say that the heavenly bounties by Transposition are embodied during this life in our temporal experience. The second way is the best. It is the present life which is the diminution, the symbol, the etiolated, the (as it were) "vegetarian" substitute. If flesh and blood cannot inherit the Kingdom [1 Corinthians 15:50], that is not because they are too solid, too gross, too distinct, too "illustrious with being." They are too flimsy, too transitory, too phantasmal.

Our world and our culture are too flimsy, and we can't hit the high notes of God's kingdom, so He transposed His values into statements we could read and provided us with His mind in creativity we could see. He gave us His Spirit in an air we breathe but cannot see, and He gave us His Son, Jesus, in a human form in whom we can touch and believe. This idea of transposition is vitally important to understanding how the Word of God comes to us and also how we are to begin to understand the personhood of Jesus. We are to take and transpose this into all of our living. We do this by viewing the things around us as objects that help us in looking along flimsy realities in order to see the real—the truthful Reality.

BIBLE STUDY METHOD

To understand where I'm going with this, please allow me to discuss a bit of my understanding of how we approach the Word of God. In this book, I'm trying to paint how music is a dramatic picture of God's hand, similarly gathers us, teaches us, calls us to respond, and then sends us. This is the rhythm of God. He gathers, He teaches, and then, where we find ourselves at this point in the book, we respond. Part of our response is being able to correctly understand and apply what God has taught us to our life and culture—this is transposition.

To transpose the truths of the Scripture into our cultural context and life with precision and accuracy, we must consider briefly our method of approach to studying the Bible. When it comes to Bible study methods, there are predominantly three disciplines of study that we must understand. There are whole seminary classes devoted to these three disciplines, so in describing these three systems in this work, I'm going to borrow some language from Andy Stanley to simplify our approach here. He discusses that a proper approach to studying Scripture is that we must first take a big idea that concerns or intrigues us (**our hook**) and approach the Bible in this area of study in which we want more insight. We might pick a topic such as dating or the grace of God. Once we have what we're looking for, we approach **the book** of Scripture and **look** into what it teaches in order that we may then change our thinking regarding the particular topic. This ensures that we apply the Scripture's paradigm to our lives in "**the took.**" He talks about the Hook, the Book, the Look, and the Took. [183] His approach is sound in many ways, but I do not like that he begins with the hook or idea first. This implies that we come up with the idea and then go to Scripture for the definition. This can lead to a deadly practice of what I call *overstanding* the Scripture. Subtly, we can begin to define and assemble the topics and themes of Scripture together in ways that we think are most important. We can then miss the themes that it emphasizes within itself. I'd like to simplify and correct this approach a bit by introducing a sound bible study method that begins with the Look, determines the Hook, and then moves into the Took. I'll show you how starting with the look will help in understanding the themes that the Scripture creates and emphasizes within itself. Approaching it like this will allow for us to summarize its main ideas (the hook) and apply them in sound transposition into our real lives (the took).

In theological terms, the disciplines that correspond to our approach are known by their more theological titles as Biblical Theology, which is the one that performs the "Look," Systematic Theology, which gathers the "Hook," and Christian Theology/Practical Theology, which expresses the "Took." Like I mentioned before, there are whole college degree programs dedicated to each of these approaches and methods, and many people will often fight for one of them as superior to the others. I, on the other hand, believe they all must work together to achieve sound Biblical interpretation and transposition. I'm more apt to borrow from Vern S. Poythress's idea of Symphonic Theology. [184] He suggests that we harmonize all of these disciplines in a way that helps us study Scripture in all its Majesty. Regardless, I'm going to take what we can learn in all these areas of study and boil them down to some simple *koine* ideas so we can all apply and understand them.

THE LOOK: BIBLICAL THEOLOGY

In its simplest form, Biblical Theology helps us to look into Scripture. Whether we like it or not, when we first pick up the Bible, we approach it with our own set of lenses—our worldview. We carry our own set of expectations, backgrounds, cultural distinctives, beliefs, sins, emphases, and presuppositions concerning what we will find in God's Word, and these color EVERYTHING we see in Scripture. This is why it is important to first ask the Bible what it actually says and not tell it first what we think it means. This is the difference between understanding Scripture and *overstanding* it. When we look at it through our lenses first, we *overstand* Scripture. We stand over it and we become its authority. We then either add to it things we wish were in there or we subtract from it things we wish were not.

The trouble with this approach is it's all based in human pride. If we first approach the Bible with *overstanding*, we are saying we're smarter than God, and if that's true, we're all in a world of hurt. Biblical Theology protects our approach. It causes us to historically look *into* Scripture by first allowing it to describe to us what it sees. We ask questions of what we are reading like Why, How, When, What, Where, etc. We seek to ask ourselves, "What was going on in their culture? What is being emphasized and why? How would the original audience have heard this? What is the author's purpose in this writing? Does this change how I understand it?"

Biblical Theology not only looks *into* Scripture, but then it looks *across* Scripture. It looks "not just to what the Bible teaches, but also to how the Bible arranges, or organizes its theology." [185] This helps us see major themes and minor themes as they're carried and connected across the storyline of God's narrative. Like any book, the Bible emphasizes things of major importance. First and foremost it emphasizes God as the main character, not us. It helps us to consider the things that were and are important through this way of learning.

I've included a diagram below that gives us a picture of all three steps in our interpretive journey and we will use this as a visual stamp to help us picture what we're trying to achieve with sound interpretive methods. Biblical Theology, as seen in the image below, is the first step. You'll see in the image that the Biblical culture comes first. We are to first enter the world of the Bible before we ever allow it to enter ours. This is the order if we are to draw the right conclusions.

Fig. 7.1 [186]

The Hook: Systematic Theology

After we have let the Bible define its own themes for us, we can begin to put these ideas into what Bryan Chapell, in his book *Christ Centered Preaching*, calls "Big Ideas." [187] This is where systematics in Theology are helpful and crucial, for it helps us take big ideas—the hooks or the main thoughts and themes—and trace them across Scripture. As shown in Fig. 7:1, Duvall and Hays call it the Principlizing Bridge. [188] They discuss that each passage contains major principles to teach us—hooks or Big Ideas. Our job is to mine them out (Biblical Theology) and to bring out the nuggets of gold below the surface (Systematic Theology).

Whereas Biblical Theology looks into Scripture and across Scripture, Systematic Theology completes the journey by tracing the big hooks *across* Scripture and then allows for looking *into* other sources for clarification and robust understanding. For example, when 1 John 4:8 says, "God is love," there appears, on the surface, to be no secret as to what this means. However, using Biblical Theology to look into the book as a whole, we note that the author is John, Christ's beloved disciple. Our investigation also tells us that the book of 1 John is written to a bunch of people being taken apart by false teachers. John's encouragement to them is to remember that they are God's children and that He is their Father. He encourages them that focusing on this love will keep them from falling into intimidation and fear of the false teaching and attacks. This Big Idea is suddenly enriched by our Biblical Theology. Now the context is that love is warfare, its home is family, and its spokesman is God through John.

Now, Systematics can take this idea and move it thoroughly *across* Scripture to broaden this theme of love as it fits into the whole narrative of God's unfolding revelation. Systematics can now helpfully consider John's relationship with Jesus as a basis for understanding love; it can look at the idea of covenant in the Old Testament. It can even look at family love as presented in Scripture. This blows the concept of love into something we can start to understand. Its principles start to come alive. It comes alive in the boundaries that Biblical Theology provides. Only now are we equipped to look at what other people say about love, for we are under Scripture's authority, and we now know what to search for and what to leave out. Maybe we now consult Augustine's writings on the Trinity, where he discusses the Father as the Lover, the Son as the Beloved, and the Spirit as the Love between them. This might blow up our idea of love even further.

The idea is that Systematics should gather its Big Ideas from the Scripture, not from what the human mind or circumstance dictates.

THE TOOK: CHRISTIAN THEOLOGY

Where Biblical Theology looks into and across Scripture, Systematic Theology looks across Scripture and into other helpful sources. Christian/Practical Theology, in rounding out this process, looks *across* big ideas and looks *out* and *across* current culture to confront the world's ideas and context with the realities of Biblical truth. A resource I'd recommend is *Christian Theology* by Millard Erickson. He does a brilliant job not only in taking the major hooks of the Bible apart, but then beginning to look out into the culture while allowing the truths of the Bible to interact with the other ideas that culture is proposing are true. Once again, I'll include:

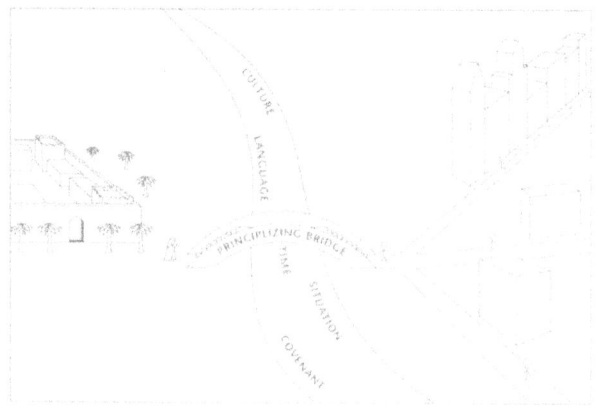

Fig. 7.1

WHAT CHRISTIAN THEOLOGY DOES IS HELP US TO MEASURE HOW WIDE THE river is between the Bible's ancient culture and our present culture, and then it helps us to apply what we know to today. Biblical Theology helps us to analyze the Bible's culture (to the left of the image), Systematic Theology helps us mine out the major principles, ideas, and hooks in the passage (the bridge), and now Christian Theology helps us to exegete our context.

To put it in another light, a big threat to those building the Tower of Babel in Genesis was that they were becoming too sufficient in and of themselves, wanting their own fame to be seen rather than God's glory and perfection. Because of their heart motive to exalt themselves, we see in the story that the displeasure of God is soundly awakened. Considering this story's presentation of the struggle between God and man is the task of Biblical Theology. A Big Idea that emerges very quickly out of this approach is the central focus upon the people's pride, technological snobbery, and self-sufficiency. In measuring the river between their struggles then and our struggles now, we may find that we are not exactly like them, as we are not a people united in a universal language anymore, resulting in our attempting to build a tower to reach the sky, but we certainly have technologies that exalt our glory by hooking us up with global communication (e.g., Facebook). We certainly feel more self-sufficient with Google. The iPhone certainly helps in bringing the world together again in one common "language" to exalt our own creative inventions. In a quick way, we can apply Scripture to culture by looking at similarities and unearthing places in our own selves that reveal this same pride, technological snobbery, and self-sufficiency in us.

Another example is the idolatry of the Old Testament. We see in the Old Testament that the sacrifice of children on altars to sex gods was a prolific problem (sound like abortion?). We see hero worship, cheating, and infidelity; we see the worshipping of shiny stuff like golden calves, the giving of money for absolution, the sacrificing of animals for forgiveness, and so on and so forth. Today, we see this Big Idea carry into our culture with

> ... the E! network which holds out idols in the form of celebrities showing off fabulous lifestyles, walking red carpets, and partying in jet-set cities. We worship as we buy into the lie that they have it all—money, status and happiness—our hearts swelling with desire when we see their plasticine bodies and glittering wealth. 'Deliver us,' we think as we imagine that if only we had what they have, we'd be happy. We worship as we feel the pain of their divorces and drug addictions, weeping to see the temple of our idols in such a sad state of disarray. How could our gods of wealth and power disappoint us? How long will they be so far off? Networks like ESPN offer twenty-four-hour worship of

athleticism, sports teams, and with them, wealth, masculinity, and victory. Pornography is a temple of worship where the actors make a sacrifice of their bodies and dignity for money and fame, and the consumers make a sacrifice of their hearts, their marriages, and their cash for a god that titillates and pleases, if only for an instant. [189]

The truth is, the Bible's world and Big Ideas are not so far from our hearts today. Our identities are still shaped by idols, "by what we ultimately love or what we love as ultimate." [190]

The question we might ask then in Biblical Theology is, "What does the text mean?" We are mining out the actual context of the story itself. The question we then ask in Systematic Theology is, "What's the Big Idea?" This Big Idea helps us to zero in on what God Himself is emphasizing, as opposed to with what we believe He's dealing. The question we ask then in Christian Theology is, "Where is the culture trying to direct our love today?" In asking the question in this way, we can expose our heart's deepest motives, apply the healing salve of God's big idea, and seek to remedy in our culture the sins of what transpires before us. This is the Look (Biblical Theology—into and across Scripture), the Hook (Systematic Theology—across Scripture and into other sources), and the Took (Christian Theology—across ideas and out into culture).

TRANSPOSITION

Now that we have adequately formed a sound process for transposing the Bible's notes and key into our time and language with the correct meaning and equal emphasis, it begins to transform our living today. Our creativity can follow suit with proper application and true contextualization. "Cultivating creativity is an exercise in contextualization. We're truly contextualized when the culture of our church is shaped and formed from the roots of the community, rather than outsourcing it from someplace else." [191] Our creativity in and throughout the world now has a gold lining of truth that guards and guides us into principled safety. We are now free to look along everything within our world and created surroundings in order to find where God has hidden His truth, His message, and His mission.

As we have used the analogy of music and the incarnation previously, once truth is transposed into a key where we can sing it and into a God-man language we can understand, we can relate to it. Music has always, to some extent, picked up on modern cultural and societal values and norms, and it helps us to engage with the configurations and patterns of the world in which we live. Music is fully contextual and also full-bodied. Music represents this full cycle of how God gathers us, teaches us, and transposes us out into environments in ways that help us make the most sense. Music represents how change and transposition can be ordered and done even amidst utter chaos. Music takes themes and thoughts that are particularly hard to nail down and translates them into our ears so that they become a profound "message sent, to a message received." [192] This is what transposition teaches us. It's not just a message sent, it has to be a message received. Reception means that truth weaves itself into the very fabric of who we are and plays itself out in a resounding audio that we can hear and understand. This is the final step in not only allowing God to gather us and teach us, but in allowing Him to lead and send us.

The Tempo of Discipleship

Theology: Discipleship has to be Biblical. This may sound like a trite statement, but the meaning of it has to reach into our understanding of Biblical Theology. We cannot just learn the truths that Scripture teaches, but we have to enter into its world. Disciples need to be shown how the Word of God is not a fuel source for quiet times, but that it is a dynamic drama that is still unfolding, in which we all play a part. We are not removed from the world of the Bible, but its world describes our world. The shades of war and peace, idolatry and worship, slavery and freedom, covenant and contract, truth and lies, love and hate, beginning and end are themes that pervade Scripture and Scripture is not shy about them. This is what helps us to trust God in our own story!

If God's writers, for example the disciples, share with us their moments of failure and faint-hearted faith, their times of denying Jesus, like John in his gospel, and would dare paint a picture of a jealous, stupid, and naïve crew of disciples who just never could quite understand what Jesus was getting at, then we can trust them. Obviously, the writers were not writing to highlight their own fame. They clearly maximized their very real blunders in comparison to God's glory and perfection in Jesus. Good thinking about the Bible has to embrace the Bible as it's written. It does not overshadow all the real misunderstandings and foolishness that perpetuate humanity. Rather, it accents them, draws out human failure, and lays them beside the Holiness of God. We are forced to see the real us and the real Him.

BIOGRAPHY: DISCIPLESHIP HAS TO BE SYSTEMATIC. WE ARE TO RELATE TO God's story, but this means we must also learn to bite off the big chunks of His truth in order to chew them up and digest them for ourselves. If left to our own story and our own Big Ideas about what we think it all means, we are going to undoubtedly shift the focus away from the Big Ideas of Scripture onto our own Systematic opinion of where we think the emphasis of life should be.

Oh, don't we shift! We place the big idea on social agenda and politics, gay rights, being green, free-range organic, do-what-you-want-when-you-want-and-how-you-want philosophy, prosperity and poverty, health and wealth, pull yourself up by your own boot straps type thinking, fame and fortune, sex and celebrity, and yada, yada, yada. It goes on. These are our basic principles. All of this is our own Systematic Theology and desperate attempt to form a construct that will make earth into our little piece of heaven.

It doesn't work. Discipleship has to lay emphasis on the *didache*—the first principles of God. Love your neighbor, love your enemy, pray for your leader, lead your wife, submit to your husband, obey your parents, tell the truth, purity in all areas, etc. This is God's ethic. These themes are huge throughout the Bible. We have to understand them in order to be able to apply and live them out.

DOXOLOGY: DISCIPLESHIP HAS TO BE TRANSPOSITIONAL. UNDERSTANDING then means we not only learn about God, but we transpose His truth into real situations, like a song-writer. These truths and teachings of God have to be turned into a language that we and those around us can catch and comprehend. It's simple. Sometimes we try to make it so complicated. When arguing with people, we will jet into philosophy and start arguing confused logic with confused logic, and pretty soon everyone is confused. But the gospel is simple. **G**od created us to be with Him (Gen. 1-2); **O**ur sins separated us from God (Gen. 3); **S**ins cannot be removed by good deeds (Gen.4-Malachi); **P**aying the price for sin, Jesus died and rose again (Matthew-John); **E**veryone who believes in Jesus alone will have eternal life (Acts-Jude); **L**ife eternal means living for and living with Jesus in His kingdom forever (Revelation). That's easy. That's the GOSPEL. [193] A simple, yet deep understanding of this over-arching theme in Scripture can go a long way into planting these simple lights of truth into the very depths of the world's darkness.

9

Ryhthms

The journey begins as we join His rhythm; how He moves, how He lives, and how He works must captivate and encapsulate our time and space. He plugs us into His image and begins to improvise a unique tune in and through us. His composition moves high and low, with sound and in silence, but the ever steady hand of God will faithfully guide us.

Scientists measure it in light years, the Greeks in sundials and astronomical *merkhets*, the Mayans in calendars, and in the West with clocks and wrist watches. It's time. Every person in human history has been born within time. From the moment life begins to the second it runs out, every human gets this gift all in the same measure. Each human life is allotted 24 hours a day and 7 days a week. C. S. Lewis said the future is something which everyone reaches at the rate of 60 minutes an hour, whatever he does, whoever he is. [194] What this means is that no one receives more time by asking for it. We all are allotted the same amount to steward, for better or for worse. The only thing that distinguishes highly effective people from the rest of the pack is how one manages and uses time.

Time is woven into the very fabric of the universe. Even music unfolds in time. In pondering how time's interaction with music can enrich us in our approach to discipleship, let's again quickly explain some musical ideas in a way that is common in some form to everyone. If I were to try to figure out the distance between two walls in a room, I would take out a measuring tape and measure it in order to count the inches, the feet, the yards, or the meters between each. In calculating the distance in feet, for example, I'm saying that if I were to walk between walls, it would take me so many steps to reach from one side to the other. If I take large steps, it may take a few leaps; if I take small steps, it may take a few hundred motions.

Music is no different. Instead of walls, music has bar lines, and contained between two bars lines, which mark the beginning and ending of musical phrase, is what is called a *measure*. This moment or section in the time of a song contains thoughts, phrases, and musical sentences intended to say something that contributes to the whole of the song. Each measure is then dictated in length by a number of notes (steps) in which it will take to play from one bar to the next. In Figure 8.1 below, it can be seen that music, like the ruler, is very mathematical in how it takes these steps.

Every note value below equals four full beats or counts. If I were to take one leap from bar line to bar line, it would be called a whole note (it takes the whole measure, covering the whole distance). If I take two large steps and hold them out, each for two counts, then that's a half-note (2 + 2 = 4). This continues on down into something like thirty-second notes. Though I have 32 of them, if I were to add them up, they would still add up to four whole counts. What's important to observe here is not a full understanding of the musical terms used, but to observe that there are different lengths, durations, and note types within music that still add up to the same number of beats.

The Tempo of Discipleship

Symbol	Name	Number per measure (4/4)	Rest
𝅝	whole note	𝅝 1 per measure	𝄻
𝅗𝅥	half note	𝅗𝅥 𝅗𝅥 2 per measure	𝄼
𝅘𝅥	quarter note	𝅘𝅥 𝅘𝅥 𝅘𝅥 𝅘𝅥 4 per measure	𝄽
𝅘𝅥𝅮	eighth note	𝅘𝅥𝅮𝅘𝅥𝅮𝅘𝅥𝅮𝅘𝅥𝅮 𝅘𝅥𝅮𝅘𝅥𝅮𝅘𝅥𝅮𝅘𝅥𝅮 8 per measure	𝄾
𝅘𝅥𝅯	sixteenth note	𝅘𝅥𝅯𝅘𝅥𝅯𝅘𝅥𝅯𝅘𝅥𝅯 𝅘𝅥𝅯𝅘𝅥𝅯𝅘𝅥𝅯𝅘𝅥𝅯 𝅘𝅥𝅯𝅘𝅥𝅯𝅘𝅥𝅯𝅘𝅥𝅯 𝅘𝅥𝅯𝅘𝅥𝅯𝅘𝅥𝅯𝅘𝅥𝅯 16 per measure	𝄿

Fig. 8.1

Noticing the different note lengths is important because they are all divisions of time. Some play long, some play short, but they all form the music. Music's term for how these steps are measured is called *time signatures*. For example, the signature 4/4 tells someone that four steps take place between bar lines—divided in many different ways as long as the sum of all the notes is 4. The signature 3/4 denotes three beats, 5/8 is five beats, and 9/8 denotes nine beats. This is how music measures time.

MUSICIANS AND RHYTHM

When things really get creative is when musicians start to hold conversation within these places in time. Drummers, in particular, play a significant role in keeping this time for the rest of the band. They provide the speed (fast or slow) and tempo of the time, and the other musicians talk and play within that time. These conversations will cause different instrumentalists to use a series of long notes or short notes to create emphases, beat, and what in music is called *rhythm*. As musicians interact, they create pulses that intertwine, forming something that the audience can feel and experience. Depending on the different cultural tones involved within the musical interaction, various languages begin to speak through various styles—Latin, Rock, Jazz, Hip-Hop, Classical, etc. The patterns of respiration and pulse that are felt within music are reflective of how styles are formed, but also how cultures interact. Thus musical rhythm captures much more than audio conversation, it transmits and forms identity. [195]

One example of how rhythm forms culture and identity is the example of the *clave*. The clave pattern originated in sub-Saharan African music traditions, but the pattern is also found in the African and Haitian drumming, Afro-Brazilian music, and Afro-Uruguayan music (Candombe). The clave rhythmic pattern is used as a tool for temporal organization in Afro-Cuban music, such as rumba, conga de comparsa, son, son montuno, mambo, salsa, Latin jazz, songo, and timba. Just as a keystone holds an arch in place, the clave pattern holds the rhythm together in Afro-Cuban music. [197] This has led many to believe that the *clave matrix* is a comprehensive system for organizing music. [198] The clave's pulse can be measured in what is known as 3:2 son clave or 2:3 son clave (there is also rumba clave, not discussed here). This feel, though stylized in tribal music, exported itself and became popularized in all of Western music being called the "BoDiddley" beat—famous now in how it's used in Rock, Hip-Hop, and Country. It is now the standard underlying pattern for much of the world's music. As seen in Figure 8:2, groups of notes organize the time into long and short lengths in order to create something that is playable and enjoyable to a person's ear.

The clave pattern gave framework to tribal music, but has come to the Western ear through ports like New Orleans and New York via popular music like Jazz. The clave has now been adopted as a rhythmic motif or ostinato (repeating pulse), or simply a form of rhythmic decoration.

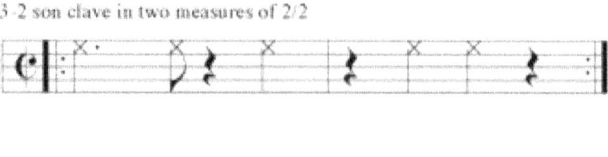

Fig. 8:2

THE CLAVE MERELY PROVIDES ONE EXAMPLE OF HOW TIME BEGINS TO BE ordered in fragments, sections, and moments of different lengths, importance, and durations, all of which form the song. The deeply profound lesson for all of us in this is that God's approach to how He created music is also the same approach that He took in designing the fabric of the human timeline of history.

GOD, RHYTHMS, AND TIME

The purpose in mentioning and describing how music forms its own conversation, tempo, and rhythm within the time in which it operates is that life and faith in the journey of a disciple are altogether similar. Scripture has a lot to say about time. Though the Bible describes God as having no bounds within time, [199] and as holding all time in His hands [200] (as if to imply that He inhabits some place altogether beyond our time dimension [201]), and as encompassing time as the altogether Beginning and the End, [202] the Scripture clearly demonstrates that God created the time signature and bounds for this story of humanity in which we all play and converse. Within this time signature of history, God created various moments of different lengths—some deep and lasting in impact, others incremental and small in lingering memory. Although the rhythm of history is deeply connected in that it plays the same song, its rhythm changes as it moves from beat to beat.

Considering this will help us relate to God's methods for creating His music; which are His people. The Bible, written by God, seems to affirm two kinds of time that bear significant importance upon our discussion about how musical rhythm relates to how disciples are formed and created. Aristotle generalized these two types of rhythm, one being organic (relating to the body and its heartbeat) and the other spiritual (related to the human consciousness of order in the cosmos). [203] The Greeks understood these two concepts of time and rhythm as *chronos* time and *kairos* time. *Chronos* time is what is defined as linear time, or sequential and chronological time. When we look back through the events of our *chronos* timeline, we see that each event has built upon the other and has formed history. This *chronos* time progression is a moment-by-moment movement that progresses along a line of record.

Matthew 2:7 affirms this aspect of time when it says, "then Herod called for the wise men and learned from them the exact time [*chronos*] when the star had appeared." Clearly, what can be seen is there was an exact way, even in Herod's mind, to measure quantitative time pertaining to when events start and end. Even into today, we call out *chronos* time every time we say yesterday, today, tomorrow, five minutes ago, 5 o'clock, and so on. We are simply acknowledging that history continues to move.

The universe also moves in what is called *kairos* time. This is what is more easily understood as cyclical time, seasonal time, or circular time. We can see how the season of Fall comes in the wake of Summer, and Winter comes before Spring, and so forth. The way the universe is set up is in a period of climbs and falls that not only come fairly consistently, but return the next year in the very same manner. Carried within this idea of seasonal time is the idea that there are instances when we cease to be conscious of time because we're caught up in moments. Seasons represent this because though they move along, they accomplish "critical moments from God's point of view—'a right and proper time ... in which God has accomplished a new dimension of reality.'" [204] These periods of time not only move past us, but they continually return, ever deepening us. *Kairos*, then, refers to unique occasions—times that hold the possibility for profound impact. [205]

We have all heard the phrase "it's as if time stood still;" emerging not only when the time moves, but also when time is filled with meaning and/or space becomes a profound memory. It's when time centers on a point for a moment even as it's traveling, and it seems to accomplish something different as we're experiencing it. Seasons are examples of this on a broad level. Photographs capture these on smaller human levels, with special days, births, and anniversaries. Into established spiritual levels, occurrences such as Christ's incarnation, the Virgin Birth, and the Crucifixion and Ascension create anchor points in the human timeline of great significance. It's as if time itself provides a container which enables something profoundly "other" and supernatural to fill it with greater meaning and remembrance.

DISCIPLES ARE FORMED BY RHYTHM

The Tempo of Discipleship

The Bible speaks of God's perspective on time as being when all things are in order for something momentous to occur (*kairos*), and it also speaks of our human perspective on time, the date and hour for the occurrence of an event (*chronos*). [206] The difference is pointed out in the Bible in the Second Letter of Peter, which says that a thousand years of *chronos* time is, from God's *kairos* time perspective, like a day (see 2 Peter 3:8 and Psalm 90:4). The impact this has on the life and formation of disciples is profound if we deeply consider how God's view and manipulation of time works.

One of the greatest examples of how this time works together is found in Numbers 28-29. The Israelite people had come out of slavery into the desert and were, in this section of Numbers, about to enter into the Promised Land of Canaan. One can only imagine the broken mindset that the Israelites had formed in being enslaved for 400 years, and when God brought them out into freedom under His leadership, it's almost like He had to rehabilitate them to think freely again. Due to this, it required new leadership, new laws, a new framework, and a new schedule. It is as if God brought them into the rehab clinic, sat them down, and said, "I know your heart is broken, beaten, and discouraged—you're drunk and drugged with oppression. Here in my clinic, we are going to provide you with a schedule. You'll have a time to rise and a time to go to sleep. You'll have food and shelter and a daily regimen of medication. All of this will help you gain back a feeling of safety and control in your life, so you can feel valuable again and so you can remember who and whose you are."

God's plan for medication and rehab began in Numbers 28:1-8, where God prescribed the people to provide daily offerings. These offerings were to be brought in prescribed amounts of food and in the sacrifice of animals as specified by the Lord. It was as if the Lord was calling His people daily to a regimen of not only doing something, but to "hear His voice" [207] in their offerings. Each day, His new presence among them would be remembered, His leadership over them would be embraced, His sacrifice to free them would be demonstrated, and His mercies would be newly encountered. [208]

Then, God moved to the weekly Sabbath offerings in verses 9-10. If the six days of the work week were to provide God's people a chance to work and remember through sacrifice, the Sabbath day provided a day to rest. Not only was it God's rhythm for work to stop and for rest to happen (to be discussed more in Chapter 11), but on the Sabbath the sacrifices were doubled. It was as if God were saying through the sacrifices, "I need you to remember me daily, but also weekly, I need you to trust in my work on your behalf in a far greater way. My sacrifice is what spares you. Remember! Doubly remember it, and find rest in the fact that it is I who freed you, and it is I who will continue to free you."

God then proceeds in verses 11-15 to institute monthly offerings that were to establish a larger pattern and rhythm for the people. Then on into Numbers 28:16 through chapter 29, God establishes Special Occasions throughout the Jewish calendar year to continue their rehabilitation further. The Passover Feast occasion came in the Spring—remembering God's deliverance of Israel out of Egypt; the Feast of Weeks in May and June—remembering God giving the Law at Mount Sinai (our Pentecost); the Feast of Trumpets—a day of celebration, war, and victory in September; the Day of Atonement (Yom Kippur) celebrated in September—to remember God's payment for sin as the blood is poured on the mercy seat of the Ark of the Covenant; and the Feast of Booths following soon after, celebrating God's protection of Israel as they traveled in the desert toward the Promised Land.

What can be observed here in Israel's history and travels is that, as their sojourn toward the Promised Land continued on, God set up strategic seasons, anchor points, and places for the supernatural to interact with the natural in order to ensure that Israel did not forget their own story.

Anyone reading the book of Numbers can quickly see how Israel seemed to complain about everything at every turn. It's as if they freshly and naturally forgot the goodness of God in each passing moment. Therefore, God shepherded them by creating rhythms of worship within their days, their weeks, their months, and their years that would begin to form His people into following Him. This example found in Numbers provides a profound illustration of how God's *chronos* and *kairos* time work in tandem. Time not only moves in one direction between points, but it cycles, deepens, and fills, as well. These same rhythms need to be present in the forming of a disciple.

Sacred Space and Sacred Time

James K. A. Smith, referenced earlier in this book, in his book *Desiring the Kingdom*, provides some helpful insight into how the concept of time can be broken down and applied in a disciple's life. He breaks it down in looking at

The Tempo of Discipleship

how people practice what he calls both *thick* and *thin* rhythms. Thin rhythms are habits and practices that we find ourselves doing every day. Most people participate in some form of daily routine. We hit the snooze on the alarm clock, we stumble toward the shower, and we clean up, brush our teeth, get dressed, and get in our car to commute to work or to school. We have lunch hours, meetings, and then we go on home to get ready for bed. This is a person's daily rhythms, which are thin. As time goes by, we pass the time with these habits. Though they are thin, and not necessarily connected to spiritual truths, they nonetheless form us, creating in us disciplines, patterns, and rhythms. A rhythm that is thick, on the other hand, is very much the same in how we observe it, but it is one that may already be connected with a deeper purpose, enrichment, and meaning, such as a quiet time, church, small group, Sabbath rest, etc.

All of these rhythms are important and should be considered in a person's day to day schedule and liturgy, as well as in their *chronos* moments. Not only do these rhythms occur daily, but they spin weekly, monthly, yearly, in decades, in centuries, etc. In order to help people transform in their desires, their desires need to connect to their rhythms in time and space. Their daily patterns of environment, and the spaces they occupy, must also be paired to spiritual habits.

This is when spiritual time and spiritual space collide. When we go about our day, our week, our month, and our year, incremental instances can be connected with spiritual practices in order to transform spaces in time into *kairos* encounters. Thus, a traveling commute filled with worship music, seminary theological classes on tape, Bible memorization, or prayers on behalf of friends and family can become an eternal moment of growth and development. A time of taking a shower can become a place of thanksgiving for the purity that comes from God, or a chance to remember our Baptism. A time of brushing our teeth can serve as a reminder for us pray to God for our family and express our love to them, or to ponder the gift of God's life to us and in us. Though these simple rhythms are just "spaces in our time," they become supernatural when connected to spiritual realities. In this sense, the whole of a person's life becomes a liturgy. The very schedule a person keeps in their day planner becomes a tool by which they are formed.

In this light, everything in life is not divisible into sacred and secular, but everything is sacred. Everything then is sacramental (defined here as important and significant). Things don't become sacramental until connected with spiritual realities. Everything then, from sex to alcohol, to brushing our teeth and taking a shower, were all created as GOOD. If the good intentions of God are sought in moments and things in Creation, then everything can be enjoyed as sacramental if it is used as worship and in the way intended by the Creator. True maturity knows how to enjoy God's *everything* rather than abstain from it. Abstaining should only happen when it is evil or if a person holds an area of weak faith.

In a very real sense, not only are things transformed, but spaces are as well. Holy and sacred spaces in the Old Testament were things protected from the unfit and the impure (e.g., Levites in Numbers 1:53 were given to protect the purity of the temple). In the New Testament, God calls the human heart the Holy Temple and the place where purity and holiness should dwell. [209] The human heart is really shown in the Bible to be the true place and target of God's rhythmic work. His intention is to transform how the human heart uses each and every thing in all of creation as a way to honor and glorify Him. This is when normal spaces like an office building, a car, a restaurant, a church building, a home, and a town square are transformed into places that hold the Kingdom of God (*karios* time). It's when the hearts of God's people enter and connect everything to a spiritual reality and use all things to draw attention unto the glory of Christ—this is what creates sacred space (standing on Holy Ground).

Rhythms Train our Habits and our Desires

Not only does our view of time and space change in how we participate, but the practices themselves begin to train our habits. Let's consider the rhythms of Numbers 28-29 for a moment. When the Israelite people observed daily remembrance and time for God in sacrifice (what we might call a quiet time), they were forced every morning to remind themselves anew of God's goodness. When they stopped every week to remember God's work in Creation, and how it ended on the Sabbath rest of God on the seventh day, they were forced to cease and remember their rest in God; the Sabbath being the last day of Creation but the first of intention for man. [210] This continued into monthly and annual reminders and observances that created habits of discipline, which began to mold and shape the people's desires toward God Himself.

The Tempo of Discipleship

The way this shapes us is deeply profound. God speaks through this text of present time and space. [211] In doing so, He's not merely shaping our thoughts, but our desires as well. [212] These rhythms train not only our thinking, but they train the second sight or our subconscious, in which we do most of our operation. Smith explains how, when we walk through a city for example, we predominantly do not decide our way through it, but we feel our way through it. Our patterns so shape us that we can literally begin to go from place A to place B without much thinking involved. We simply train the whole of our being to merely respond in a specific way. This is what enables us to drive from home to work and not remember how we got there. It's just engrained in us. In this way, doctrine and the training of our minds are more akin to a map of knowing a city, whereas imagination is more akin to know-how, reflex, and intuition about how to get from place to place. [213]

Thus, we must teach doctrine and right teaching in theology (the map of the city) but must realize that people find their way around life through intuition, feeling, desire, reflex, and know-how. This assumes that a person does not merely lead with only their head, but also with their heart and hands. [214] This means that daily habits, rituals, disciplines, and routines are more important than meets the eye. Habits are like little doctrines and road maps that help us to measure our day, and after perpetual use, they move into our affections and simply begin to direct our steps in the same way that cruise control directs a car. We don't think about the importance of much of what we do anymore, we just simply do it—we cruise. True transformation happens when Scriptural truths are connected and paired with Spiritual realities in these moments of cruising in order that, as we do it, we are targeting the shaping of our spirit, not our flesh. Rather than just merely coping and sailing through life, we bring up sleeping practices in our life that we have become numb to, in order to retrain them the right way and then put them back on the shelf of our subconscious book rack.

Each moment in time or space should have this goal. As stated before, "being a disciple of Jesus is not primarily a matter of getting the right ideas and doctrines and beliefs into your head in order to guarantee proper behavior; rather, it's a matter of being the kind of person who loves rightly." [215] When we say that to be human is to love and to desire the kingdom, we are suggesting that this vision of the kingdom's good life becomes inscribed and infused in our habits and dispositions and thus woven into our precognitive (second) nature. [216] This paints a picture of what the true end goal of God was in passages like Numbers 28-29. He used the preset rhythms of days, weeks, months, and years within His framework and time signature to create moments (long and short, thick and thin) of deeply spiritual connection in order to teach His people the significance of how to love Him and each other rightly in every moment.

What a Drummer's Rhythm Teaches Us About Habits

Drummers are a fabulous example for how all of these things work together and are learned. A drummer begins learning rhythm by first tuning into a steady beat, as kept by a metronome—a time keeper. The drummer then begins learning a beat within the time and space provided by the metronome. As the drummer starts to play the rhythm, they begin doing so one arm and leg at a time.

First, the drummer will begin a complex drum pattern in disciplining the right arm to play its part. The drummer will practice this one hand over and over until the rhythm can be set to cruise control in their passive thinking, meaning they can move it into the back of their mind in order to begin focusing on another hand. The goal is to move one hand into the back of the mind (his passive attention—intuition) so it functions on its own out of sheer habit. Now the drummer can turn his active attention toward the left hand. Once they complete the interaction between right and left hand, they can move that to their passive attention in order to bring in the right foot. All of this is done until the drummer can achieve what is called four-way independence. Four-way independence is when a drummer can play four different parts, one in each limb, and weave them all together to form a complex beat, like the one found in Figure 8.3.

Fig. 8.3

It's not so much that the drummer is actively thinking about all four parts, but is more passively feeling how each part works together and then playing creatively, spontaneously, and naturally. This is why a good drummer is referred to as having a good "feel" in music. This feel enables a drummer to then go into a concert-type venue and be able to interact freely with the band and the crowd. It's not that the drummer is multi-tasking and doing six things at once, they have simply trained movements into their habits. This enables them not to focus upon their own playing, but rather on how to love, interact with, and build up the rest of the band and onlooking audience.

What this teaches us is that each rhythm in our timeline presents us with a chance to train a new arm and leg. We do not tackle every limb at once, but one at a time. We may first start with training ourselves in a particular spiritual discipline such as prayer, Bible study, fasting, etc., and once that is engrained into our pattern, we begin to introduce a new one. We might also begin with removing a cancerous sin from our lives such as an addiction, a stumbling block, or a bad attitude. Once removed, we shift to another. After a while, an integrated life of sacred space and time is woven into our framework. As we involve ourselves in the thick and thin of life, we find ways to connect everything to a spiritual reality, which results in transforming all our environments—from work to play—into Holy habitation in which God can live in and through our hearts as we present and advance the Kingdom of God.

The Tempo of Discipleship

Theology: Let's ask ourselves a question about music and theology by pondering the following quotation: "If music's aim is not to send a message, but to open a space in which both musician and listener share in that experience, it is at least 'reasonable' to ask about how that dynamic could open human sensibility to the presence of a triune and sharing God?" [217] What this means is that the goal of theology is not merely to transmit a message of content, nor is that the nature of music. The nature of theology is to ingrain itself into how we perceive every moment so that a space for God may be opened up in our awareness and daily receptivity. The awareness is that every *chronos* moment in our daily, weekly, monthly, and yearly rhythms is a container in which God is always depositing His deeper *kairos* kingdom intentions. Because of this reality, theology cannot be merely a set of principles, but it also has to be a set of practices. This is where music presents deep truths to teach us about the tempo of how a disciple is formed, taught, and created. The disciple is not merely indoctrinated with a set of truths and arguments, but those arguments are to be given with the goal of causing the disciple to show and feel greater love.

These acts of love and affection are the true output of good theology. Therefore, theology should embrace all of life and focus on "the good, the true and the beautiful" [218] within it. This thought seems simple, but it is complex in application. We are not to say "don't touch" to anything in all of creation, but rather we are to say "touch rightly." In everything that has been profaned by Satan, we can drill down to the original intentions in that person, place, or thing and discover God's goodness and beauty within it. In all the layers of perversion that the world has piled on, God's beauty is residing along it and underneath it. If, like an onion, theology can strip back the guise and mask of Satan's twisted lies, and help us to embrace things that seem even the most disgusting in order to once again embrace all of Creation in its original shape, form, and intention, then theology has served its purpose.

BIOGRAPHY: THE DISCIPLE'S LIFE IS AN ENVIRONMENT OF FORMATION. A sailboat may provide us with a proper analogy that may help us is to consider the weight of this statement. A sailboat is created not to move on its own, but with sails that are to interact with the weather in order to produce motion. By positioning a sailboat rightly on the water and with the right mast and sails erected, the boat is set up to catch the wind as it blows. In this way, a disciple is like a sailboat. A person does not move, have being, or do anything in and of itself. Without the wind, the boat stands still.

The disciple's life is made up of environments and disciplines within those situations that provide the sailboat with its sails. If a disciple harnesses each and every moment by positioning themselves with rhythms that are ready to catch the wind, then they are free to see God move them and work in and through them. Bible study, fasting, prayer, evangelism, fellowship, memorization, love, etc., are thick rhythms that, if done over and over again in faithfulness, will position a person's heart to catch God's movement with humility. If a disciple remembers God as they brush their teeth, learns about God as they drive their car, shares God at the coffee shop, meets with God's family in small group and church, eats with God and family at dinner, and sings with God as the kids dance around before bedtime, the disciple is continually positioning themselves to catch God's wind.

Doxology: This ultimately forms the disciple. It not only forms the disciple in thinking, but it begins to craft the disciple in their "second sight"—their subconscious. Whereas a person in the flesh begins to form habits of dealing with life in fleshly ways, ones they are not even aware of, the disciple of Christ begins to train the Spirit in the same way. The world provides our flesh with vehicles of formation such as pornography, entertainment, educational institutions, work ethics, relativistic government values, and structures that form us subconsciously. Before we know it, we're selfish, bitter, hateful, unloving, and we use everyone around us for our own desires. The Spirit also provides vehicles of formation, such as liturgies within church services, small groups, ministry, prayer and worship, and so forth, and subconsciously, before we know it, we're loving, kind, joyful, and desirous of God and everyone around. This all comes about through habits within God's family, He trains us how to think, and everything we do is a liturgy. "An education, then, is a constellation of practices, rituals, and routines that inculcates a particular vision of the good life by inscribing or infusing that vision into the heart by means of material, embodied practices." [219]

This bears great weight on how we consider every piece and fragment of our lives. God gave the people of Israel daily habits, weekly habits, monthly habits, and yearly habits. Today, I believe this rhythm is not to be legalistic for us as we incorporate it into our lives, but it should be spirit-filled and principally freeing to us. Daily acts of sacrifices should be encouraged, where one lays down their time, their talents, and their finances to serve others and to enrich themselves and others. Though the Sabbath is not binding in the New Testament covenant, the Sabbath ethic was in the Garden before Adam and Eve fell. This shows us that a day of rest is helpful for us in remembering the every-instance rest that is found in Jesus. [220] On up, monthly rhythms such as birthdays, anniversaries, and special holidays can be crafted into our lives and traditions with more than just festivity in mind; they can be created with intention to be filled with eternal meaning and significance. Seasons such as Advent, Christmas, Epiphany, Lent, Easter, Pentecost, and the Christian calendar and events within the year can be helpful times to place extra focus and emphasis upon the *kairos* moments of Jesus' life, death, resurrection, and ascension. These are the greatest rhythms of human history.

Numbers 28-29 provides a great framework for discipleship and worship, but it does not imply law and regiment. God's calendar and schedule for the Jewish people was to help them arrange their time with a conscious awareness of His fingerprint upon all of time and upon everything in creation. The goal was that this awareness would become so ingrained that His people would expose acts of the flesh and therefore repent in their hearts in order to follow the Spirit. Our daily rhythms function today in much the same manner.

10

Form and Improvisation

Before beginning to paint a picture, an artist starts by sketching the outline. In her mind, she holds the image in its fullness. She can see the depths of color, the textures, and the contours of everything in her work. She can feel its emotion, and in a sense she can enter into its story and imagination. The first step begins with painting the foundation, the outline, and the form. Only then does the artist begin to add color, paint strokes, and personality to the painting. With each stroke of the following brush, as it whisks over the canvas, it eventually completely covers the outline itself, possibly never to be seen again. However, the framework remains, like the rebar beneath concrete streets, in that it holds everything together in a manner that makes the work strong, vibrant, and able to hold all its beauty.

Every art form holds true to this shape and ethic. The musician is included in this. They too hang their creativity on hooks of form and structure in order to create space for vibrant creativity. Jazz and Blues musicians, often known for their intense and colorful presentation, underneath all their looseness hold to what is called *a ternary* form of A B A. This means that the two A sections contain the same chords and form and switch in the middle with the B section. The Rock or Hip-Hop musician may follow a tradition of *sectional* form (like verse, chorus, verse, bridge) in which the verses build the thoughts, the chorus expresses the thoughts, and the bridge unites the thoughts and explains the point of the tune. Furthermore, hymn writers use a more *strophic* form in that every verse is the same, and yet each verse lyrically builds on the next. These forms, although not comprehensive, serve as the rebar around which the artist can begin to improvise, move, and change in freedom even as the base stays solidly the same. This is what enables the Blues greats like BB King and Jazz greats like Dizzy Gillespie, John Coltrane, and Roy Haynes to improvise with such precision. They are at the mercy of their form. Without the form, their playing sounds like gibberish. With the form, their improvisation comes to life. In the simplicity, the complexity can flourish.

This artistry that humanity uses can also be first observed in the artistry of God. Proverbs 24:3-5 tells us the manner in which God fashioned the whole of the created universe: "By wisdom a house is built, and through understanding it is established; through knowledge its rooms are filled with rare and beautiful treasures. A wise man has great power, and a man of knowledge increases strength." God hovered over the waters of Creation with a plan in His mind. He not only held understanding of what was to be established, but His wisdom provided the insight with how to go about building it in a manner that would sustain it. He laid the foundations of the earth first. He built the framework, He drew the sketch, and He defined the details. He crafted every detail down to the mathematical calculations of the framework—the shape of every tree, the scientific method, the rules of logic and ethics, etc. When He spoke, it came into being and it became His outline. He outlined the skies, the lands, and the seas, and then by His knowledge, He creatively filled them with every color on His painter's palette.

God's simplicity works together with His complexity. God's form enabled His improvisation and creativity. In this way, every work of our hands holds its most foundational set of rudiments and fundamentals, and only once we have learned them can we begin to create.

God Sends us

We have thus far discussed how God gathers us in his song and calls us to participate in His culture. When we have gathered, He speaks His truth to us and lays the framework for how we are to think and live. After His Words are given, we are left to respond, either to rebel and ignore His instruction, or like a composition, allow Him to strip us away in repentance until we leave all our own sinful melodies aside in order to join Him. After all this, God sends us. He sends us into the rhythms of life to be formed and to form others with a new perspective, a new outlook, and a new approach. In sending us, generally people embrace two basic frameworks for how to tackle life. First, people may embrace a philosophy of simplicity and form or secondly, one of complexity and improvisation. If an either/or approach is taken in living life solely in one of these categories, then tragedy follows. However, if like God, we embrace the harmony of both of these seemingly opposing views, we will find in the midst a truer understanding of who God is.

Camp #1: The Simple and the Regulative

The song writer's form is the verse and the chorus, the painter's form comes from the outline and sketch, and the disciple's form and prescription comes from the Scriptures. 2 Timothy 3:16 and 17 says that, "All Scripture is God-breathed and is profitable for teaching, correcting, rebuking, and training and righteousness, so that the man of God may be thoroughly equipped for every good work." This is the purpose for the Word of God. It's to provide humanity with the very language and thoughts of God in a way that is easy and simple to understand. This form makes our task of following God very simple. There are 3,573 promises in the Bible (more or less), and it records one plan of God and one purpose, which is Christ. Simple! Clinging to this one person of Christ makes life simple, and holding to these promises provides security and assurance in a profound and holistic way.

S. W. Carruthers says, "The whole counsel of God concerning all things necessary for His own glory, man's salvation, faith, and life, is either expressly set down in Scripture, or by good and necessary consequence may be deduced from Scripture: unto which nothing at ANY time is to be added, whether by new revelations of the Spirit or traditions of men." [221] Simple! God's framework is complete, it's untouchable, it's laid out, and it is not to be called into question.

Therefore, a simple and minimalist person in their thinking may (and I'm being general) equate everything outside of Scripture as being contrary to God's way of thinking. They'll reason that the true source is God, and He has a prescribed a way of doing things, and if we do not follow it, the logic would follow that, at some level, we're being influenced by some other form or thinking. Albeit, in this mode of thought, a person may be embracing the words of the world and its traditions, or even tapping into the voice of the one who authors false light, [222] lies, [223] deception and disobedience, [224] and confusion [225]—Satan himself being the accuser and deceiver of the brethren. [226]

Satan's end game is always sin, and sin always complicates things. A simple person may look at any complexity, any form of improvisation, as stepping outside the bounds of God's perfect plan. It is true that this is the nature of sin. It complicates things. I can even think to when I discipline my kids, I stress this simple principle to them that sin is complicated. If relationships are getting messy, lives are getting fuzzy, and situations are becoming cloudy, I always call my children to look for where sin is lurking because it always complicates things.

What eventually emerges from this view of the world and of humanity is that we are to go about creating and forming disciples *regulatively*. To look at what I mean, let's (for our purposes here) take the environment of a traditional church service for instance, in how it attempts to form disciples. In a church service, holding to the regulative principle, they will only follow what God has said explicitly in Scripture. Whereas some may fall into Ezekiel 8, where he lists all the ways people worship God in a form that was unacceptable—going to paganism, demonism, and other practices for their worship—the regulative principle adherents will cut this possibility out completely. They will only observe what is specifically in Scripture. This means that the Bible tells us to preach the Word, [227] baptize and observe the Lord's Table, [228] pray, [229] give financially, [230] and sing songs. [231] This is what is prescribed and anything apart from this receives the warning, "Stop!"

Positively, this view does not seek to overcomplicate things beyond God's Word, and it really tries to govern all of life and worship by God's Word. This is a true strength of this view. It also tries with all its might to honor the Bible and uphold the fullness of its counsel. This is also a strength. This perspective also really tries to create a distinction between God's people (the Church) and the world. This distinction for regulative believers is one that calls believers to Holiness. This attempt is courageous, for it not only attempts to provide a place of sanctity for believers, but also encourages an

The Tempo of Discipleship

environment of purity, distinction, and safety for people who are lost and beaten up in the world's system.

However, a weakness to this thinking emerges in that it separates "gathered" and "scattered" worship. This means that the regulative people begin to apply principles to their services that cannot function in real life. The hour of the worship service becomes drastically different from the rest of life, and we should know that "there are no separated-out worship services; there is only the glorious and glorifying life lived with and unto God." [232] What happens when we apply these rules of a service, which is a little over one hour long, to the whole of our life's rhythms, is that we become confused with what to do with the rest of the majority of our life. Because of this, the regulative form is not sufficient to answer all of our specific questions in real life, such as, "When should I have a quiet time? When should I go to church—Sunday morning or Sunday night? How should I dress—jeans or slacks? How do I lead in my home with music—do I sing Hymns or Hillsong—brush teeth early or late?"

Most importantly, the regulative principle ignores, to some degree, how the New Testament speaks about the heart. In the Old Testament, God highly regulates worship. The Temple is a place of purity, holiness, and devotion. It was not to be profaned, and God's law was very specific about everything. The priests were given strict rules, the people were provided with strict rules, and God's presence was valued above all. God's language in the New Covenant, however, significantly completes the focus of the Old Testament truths.

Fast forwarding into the New Testament, Paul tells us that the new Temple is our heart. We are now the Temple of God, meaning that the purity, holiness, and devotion that was once symbolized in the temple is now personified within us—we are the inhabitants of the Holy Spirit. Yes, God does regulate the actions of our heart very intensely. He provides us with rules in His law that protect His presence and value in us above all other things. Proverbs 4:23 says, "guard your heart above all else, it is the wellspring of life." Jesus is very clear in this, that what's inside us motivates what we do outside us. The reason He says this is that out of our hearts overflows everything that is within us. Everything in our heart has the ability to come out of us and affect all we taste, touch, smell, feel, and hear. Therefore, if sin is allowed to stay active in us, it colors everything we do—our worship. Any dormant sin in us begins to lead us to worship falsely. Regulating the environment will not change the heart. Only God can do that.

This is why, when Jesus came on the scene in the four Gospels, He did not seem too concerned with what was going on in the Synagogues and places of meeting. They had their worship, their teaching, and their services, which Jesus attended. However, when Jesus began His ministry, He railed against the hearts of men. He didn't address the services so much because they were only reflections of what was in a man's heart. His logic follows that if we are going to regulate things, and make things truly Biblical and Godly on planet earth, we must start with the heart itself. This is the arena upon which God places the most emphasis. The idea then becomes not to address our outward stuff as if to rule and regulate it to death in hopes of changing it. Rather, we are to drill down to the motivations and the heart of what causes us to choose things in the first place—this means that sin needs to be dealt with inside of us.

Case #2: Improvisation in the Normative Principle

The Normative Principle, like the Regulative Principle, also presents its strengths and weaknesses. In sticking with the corporate church worship services as our example as to how this outputs itself, a worship service within this mode of thinking believes that it must include all the elements which Scripture commands and may include others so long as they are not prohibited by Scripture. [233] This means that if a disciple was to walk into a Normative service, the service would include preaching, prayer, giving, singing, and the like, but may also include other things such as digital media, modern technology in all shapes and forms, and various artful additives.

This view now appears to be complicating things, making things more versatile and possibly unstable, for it appears to be suggesting that simplicity and Scripture has lost its way. The normative person would suggest nonetheless, though sin complicates things, God's complexity and improvisation is different in nature. God's work does not complicate things, but it is most certainly complex. For example, in Psalm 139, we have one of the most famous passages quoted in the entire Bible in verse 14: "I praise you, for I am fearfully and wonderfully made." In the context, David is peering out into the heavens and marveling at the complexity of God's

The Tempo of Discipleship

creation. He sees the heights of the heavens and he ponders the depths of Sheol, and in it he's brought to ponder how God created him. Though most people quote this to state how valuable and precious they are to God, this is not the full intent of this passage, nor is it the main idea. The main idea is not that David is marveling at how precious he is, but more at how complex he is. It may be helpful to switch around the words in this passage in order to help us better understand the tone of what he's saying. As he's looking up and pondering the complexity of God, he says, "I praise you, for as I look out over Creation, it fills me with fear and with wonder." This normative person's viewpoint would be that, though the framework of the universe is very simple in that it's based on very minute laws, its complexity is one that speaks of a great improvised solo that is far greater than any Jazz musician could play.

The strength of this view is that it sees the Bible not as *prescriptive* but *descriptive* and as a set of principles. God gives us defined principles of living and worshipping, but He gives us the ability to play our own song within that framework with improvised finesse. "Rather than prescriptive, in that the aim is to limit future interpretation (presenting a score which must be faithfully adhered to) but to provide a tool for analysis independent of or before future interpretations or developments." [234] The idea is not to do away with the source, the piece of music, or the Bible, but to understand that, though the score of it is defined, the different human instruments are going to act on their principles in ways unique to them.

This not only allows for the Bible to be the source for all truth, but it allows for freedom in bringing the Bible into real life. In this manner, it helps guide the Great Commission as it spreads to all nations. It allows the worship of God and the truth of God to answer its own questions within a tribal context, an urban context, a country context, or a international context. It allows for the principles to stay the same, but the application to remain flexible. What is meant by freedom and flexibility here is that freedom is mediated through and in relation to constraint (form). "'Constraint' here refers not essentially to 'confinement' but to 'specificity' or a 'particular shape.'"[235] "In the case of a musical instrumental improviser, when the text and the analytical step of reading music (the form) is removed, the tactile relation between the performer and the instrument becomes especially close and sensitive." [236] It's not as if the sheet music is done away with, for it governs everything the musician does, even after he's finished looking at it. The form, engrained in his thinking, allows the musician to outlet truths into real experience and playing, which creates a true connection and love between him and his craft.

Another strength is that the normative view treats gathered and scattered worship the same. It recognizes that real life has form, but it also has areas of grey, where "matter of fact" is not so clear and clean-cut as we would like it to be. This allows for life to assume more than one shape. Normative does a better job at trying to target all matters as relating to the heart. The things we are exposed to in life are not what are important, it's the motives with which we do them or avoid them. This assumes that all of life will hand us more than one shape and form, and that we are to, in our heart, use everything in the shape, manner, and form that God describes to us. This more adequately targets the heart in that the heart must first understand God's form in order to improvise upon it. Though this is different very slightly from the Regulative Principle, it makes all the difference. When improvisation occurs in the regulative mindset, it's questioned rather than welcomed. The Normative Principle welcomes the creativity, but guards the heart to ensure that the right creativity pours forth.

This view also presents a few challenges in that it can deemphasize tradition, form, and shape, particularly in a gathered worship service where disciples are formed. Unfortunately, this view can lose its source, its framework, and its foundation in the story of God and can begin to create a song altogether its own. No longer does the disciple or the church reflect God, but they begin to attach their images to things that are worldly and even demonic. This has happened to many church goers who begin saying, "I don't need the church, I can worship God by myself in my home or out in creation." That's a worldly form that has resulted from years of leaving the truths of Scripture. The rejection of Scripture's form has led to deformity.

The normative principle, in leaving places for freedom, can allow for people to misinterpret that freedom. This is what happened in the Corinthian church when people were arguing over what to eat and not eat. Food became an issue because the Regulative Principle guys were saying, "You can't eat it, see, it says it in Leviticus," and the Normative Principle guys had run off the deep end and were not only saying that enjoying God's feast was okay, but they were going and eating in the pagan temples and participating in the worship of false gods, as well. In this, they took their freedoms too far and became enslaved once again. All too often, the "normatives" can move to a place of misunderstanding freedom as what one *wants* to do and not understanding freedom as God understands it—what one *ought* to do.

SIMPLE OR COMPLEX?

My reason in bringing this up in relation to discipleship and music's approach is because I believe rather than thinking in either or, we need a both/and approach toward common ground on this issue. I've seen many people try to pick a side in regards to the two types of thinking above, and that's why I called these two groups "camps." People, churches, and whole denominations have used this issue as a reason to stay divided, and I really believe that if both sides would discuss the issue using music as a philosophical medium, we'd see a model for forming Christians that is better balanced and more fully rounded.

The fact is that the form and the simple parts of God's nature promote constancy, trust, and a place where His people can anchor their faith. God is unchanging. He does not shift like the world's shadows, and He is not secretive about His likes and His dislikes. The simplicity of God allows us the security to approach Him through His word and not find ourselves constantly guessing as to "what He wants." In relation to form and regularity, we can see that God used this approach in how He created the universe, and His approach to creating the design for the Temple was no different. Moving into the New Testament, Jesus did not ignore these forms and frameworks, but rather He explained that the order of the cosmos, the temple, and the laws of the Priesthood were originally meant to be carried out in the human heart. All these structures foreshadowed the coming spontaneous solo reality of the true painting of the priesthood of believers. In Ephesians 2:14-15, it shows Paul discussing the nature of how the temple and priestly system of the Old Testament was broken and fragmented. The Temple ultimately created a divide between the Jew and the Gentile, the profane and the pure, the inside and the outside. This was not God's perfect design for His creation; the Temple was to provide a shadow of what Jesus Himself would come to undo in His life, death, and resurrection. The verse in Ephesians says, "For He Himself is our peace, who has made us both one and has broken down in His flesh the dividing wall of hostility by abolishing the law of commandments as expressed in ordinances, that He might create in Himself one new man in place of the two, so making peace." Notice that Jesus didn't abolish all the commandments, just the priestly ordinances.

The reason for this is that Jesus meant for the veil of the Temple that divided His presence from His people to be torn.[237] His aim was to live in the human heart and make it His home. This is why 1 Peter 2:9 says, "But you are a chosen race, a royal priesthood, a holy nation, a people for his own possession, that you may proclaim the excellencies of him who called you out of darkness into his marvelous light." This verse shares that the priesthood had come to the human heart. The regulations, the restrictions of purity and holiness, had moved into the human soul. Today, Jesus, in His word, does not shrink back from calling us to holiness as we live as His people. His commands are ruthless and perfect, and this is why His grace has to be equally glorious. Grace is patience with our un-holiness. Jesus covers our mistakes like the blood of the animals covered those who approached the temple. Jesus lives inside of us, but through His grace, He not only perfects us in making us holy at any cost, He also shows mercy when He holds back the judgment our mistakes so readily deserve.

In God moving into our heart, He brought with Him a dichotomy. On one side, He's made us perfect, and on the other side He's making us perfect. He's aggressive and He's passive at the same time. Yet, His focus upon our heart should be what gains our attention here. He regulates it and focuses on it because He knows everything flows out of it. He knows that not one thing in the world has control upon us unless the heart itself gives it that profane control. So, when Jesus got up and preached the Sermon on the Mount, he sounded like a Regulative Principle guy. He was dogmatically at war with our hearts. He was dogmatically simple with His requirements, and He was fundamentally sound in His guidelines.

But in the same manner, God's improvisation, creativity, and complexity is always present in some form in everything He did, does, and will do. Therefore, it is in our fabric. Improvisation brings with it the possibility of risk, love, and opportunity. God is also the God of the impossible, the "Out of the Box" God, and moment by moment He is full of surprises. This is what enables him to observe the law but also see through the principles to the heart of the law. It is love.

This is what enabled Jesus, in John 8, to receive the women caught in adultery. The Pharisees were not "fair-you-see" and applied the Scripture to her sin in judgment. It was true, her sin was vile and of great offense. But Jesus knew in His heart that the principle purpose of the law was to love, not regulate and condemn, and so He turned to the Pharisees and said, "He who is without judgment cast the first stone." The Pharisees were caught in their own stew. Their application of truth to the situation could not embrace the situation's complexity. When they'd drifted away, Jesus turned to the women and said, "go and sin no more."

Jesus' Normative Principle could see the woman's heart, and He adjusted the situation to fit her need. He could see that she was repentant in her heart, and that, at that moment, she needed a soft rebuke and encouragement, not an eviction notice. However, Jesus also observes the Regulative Principle to discipleship when He addresses her heart. Though the situation needed a different approach and Jesus flexed, her heart still needed hard truth and real repentance. The fact was that her heart was still caught in sin, and it needed to respond to the pure regulations of Scripture. Jesus did not neglect one or the other—the normative or the regulative—but rather He embraced both.

THE BOTH/AND TEMPO OF DISCIPLESHIP

The regulative and normative principle of worship, as normally applied in a worship service setting within a church building, really provides us with a construct for how we see all of life. It is good to embrace simplicity, form, and the bare-bones nature of things. Form promotes security, and it helps us to understand God with our little ant-like brains. When God created the heavens and the earth, His manner of doing it was very simple; He spoke and there was sky, land, and sea. He spoke again, and he filled sky, land, and sea. Simple! There's no need to complicate such a situation when God very plainly describes how it happened. In speaking this way, God also brought with His voice a very regulative way of governing the earth. In creating planets and stars, He also created gravity, laws of thermodynamics, mathematical precision, and natural laws to which the creation was subject. Therefore, there are real absolutes. There are real ways God governs His creation and world as seen through the rhythms of gathering, speaking, responding, and sending. His word not only brought with it incredible structure and simplicity, but the depth of that organization, when pondered, gets as complex as anyone can want to go.

Though the laws govern creation, the palette of creation, for instance, is made up of numerous colors, of which there is no end. They can ever be mixed together, refashioned, repositioned, textured, and dimensioned to create *forever* creativity. There's incredible improvisation and creativity that God leaves to us. Part of his commission to Adam was entrepreneurial. Before the Fall, God gave Adam dominion over the earth, to expand it, cultivate it, and make it livable. This was implying that Adam would invent new technologies and methodologies for efficiency and that Adam would harness all the resources he had from God to create his own works of art. When the Triune God was so overwhelmed with HIMSELF, and HIS love, He didn't need to create humanity—He was full with joy! It was His fullness of joy that overflowed into creativity. He had to give His joy away— He had to share it! This very improvisational and normative inventing aspect to God is in us.

The Tempo of Discipleship

Theology: Theologians call it the *essentials* and the *adiaphora* (non-essentials); we'll call it the open- and closed-handed issues. Things like the Fall, the life, death, resurrection, ascension, and return of Jesus are essential. If anyone were to question these regulative essentials to our faith, we say, "They are closed-handed." We don't ask, "Is there more than one god?" We don't spend our time debunking whether Jesus rose or not. These are solved. The Bible and its evidence clearly solve them. However, in relation to many things, such as the spiritual gifts, Old Earth vs. Young Earth, PreTrib vs. PostTrib, Covenant Theology vs. Dispensational Theology, Election and Choice, and so on and so forth, there are often differing perspectives that, when brought together, often show that the Bible leaves many grey areas.

It has always been fascinating as I find myself in debates over these open-handed issues. Normally, what I observe is that both sides usually present a half-truth. I've found that many times issues resolve in both/and, not an either/or. So what would you say if I said the earth can be young and old at the same time? [238] What would you say if God's work could be Dispensational and Covenantal at the same time? [239] What would you say to a God who elects absolutely but allows for choice in our decisions? [240] The fact is, most issues allow for a harmonizing rather than a dividing. There are some issues that provide hills that are worth dying on, and there are hills that are also worth conversing upon.

We must, in our discipleship, look for the form and the improvisation. We must learn to be able to tell the difference. We must be able to apply hard truths in loving ways. Instead of asking all the time what is the most "true," we should ask ourselves what is the most "loving," like in the instance in Corinth when they got all divided over food. Paul, in essence, says it is right and wrong to eat the food provided by the pagans. He shares that all food is from God and can be enjoyed—this is right. However, Paul says, if it causes your weaker brother to stumble, then it is wrong to eat in the same respect—the most loving thing to do is abstain. The truth factor is that food is always okay to eat. The love factor is that food may not be appropriate to eat if it hurts God's child in the process.

The reason God leaves these grey areas for us is because His priority is love and faith. He wants to provide enough foundation in His over 3,000 promises in order that we might be confident trusting Him. His death on the cross, by which He proved His commitment to His promises, proves His faithfulness in looking out for us. He also wants to leave enough room for improvisation for us because He wants relationship among us. He wants relationship that's not static, but dynamic. He wants to plan with us, He wants us to come to Him, and He wants areas of "I don't know" to cause us to trust Him, to love Him, and to have faith in Him.

BIOGRAPHY: IN OUR LIVING OUT THIS BALANCE OF FORM AND FUNCTION, WE must carry and hold fast to the firm truths of Jesus in the Bible. We must take seriously His commands. We must hear His call to Holiness with a resounding, "Now!" We must mortify the flesh. We must crucify impurity, and we must guard our hearts with the spirit of a warrior. We must fear God and live every moment *coram deo*—before the face of God. We must realize the zeal with which He crafts, disciplines, and trains our hearts to love, honor, worship, and please Him. We must grip the essentials and closed-hand truths of God with all our might. However, when this mentality exists on its own, it produces insecurity, fear of failure, shame, and terrifying condemnation, for we can never measure up to this fully. We're going to fall. We're like the woman before the Pharisees. We get caught in adultery.

We must get in touch with the real soft skin of life! We must be willing to put human faces and names to real truths. We need paper and people theology. We must be willing to apply the principles of Scripture in ways that preserve the dignity, uniqueness, and personality of those with whom we're dealing. Though we hold fast to the truths of Jesus, we must learn to improvise. We must learn to be aware of our circumstances, our situations, our quirks, and our temperaments in order to apply truths in the right way and at the right time. Proverbs 25:11 in the NLT says, "timely advice is lovely, like golden apples in a silver basket." It also says in 25:20 that "Whoever sings songs to a heavy heart is like one who takes off a garment on a cold day, and like vinegar on soda." Therefore, there is timing and a real sensitivity to how to apply God's principles to real life.

I remember once reading an article that discussed preaching, and it observed how embracing this both/and perspective changes how we communicate and live. The article called it the difference between mining and sifting. The article said that a preacher must mine the Scriptures in order to be faithful to them but must also sift the audience to understand how to best communicate with them so they can understand it. What this means for real life is simple! We must mine the truths with regulative intensity, but we must sift out those around us and apply the Bible's principles with normative sensitivity. Understanding the music's form is one thing, but playing a solo that works within the song is a whole new art.

Doxology: We must live and disciple in simplicity and complexity. This factors into everything. We are to be both/and people. I end by sharing an illustration.

An event planner is a brilliant both/and person. They plan an event down to the finest regulative principle. They know all the rules, they know the caterers, they know the venues, and they also know the people with whom they are working. When their guests show up to their event, they have everything from the moment they arrive to the moment they leave planned thoroughly. In this manner, once the guests arrive, they are free to focus upon the people who are there. They are not worried about where the drinks are coming from, who is parking their car, or whether or not there are bathrooms; they freely assume this is already planned. Nor is the event planner frantically moving about trying to order everything into place, either. If the planner does their job, they've delegated and planned for everything in advance. This enables them to fully invest into the party. They move freely, they love freely, and they are able to place the emphasis where it should be: love!

We should plan our lives, our churches, our marriages, our homes, our work, and our play with the same mentality as this event planner. We must work as an artist! Some of us are going to naturally work the details, and some of us are going to naturally work the fun, but all are needed. When God event-planned the universe, He did it with painstaking detail (scientists, oceanographers, geologists, psychologists, and mathematicians are still trying to figure it out). The details are endless, and yet this form ensures that we can live freely and place our focus on love, risk, and improvisation. When God spoke the world into being, it was a painting, a very geometric and astronomically correct painting. That's because God thinks in fun and creativity, but also in form and function. His creation, when it came out, naturally contained both.

The human heart contains both too. We are made in His image. What is really at stake if we live only by the Regulative Principle or only by the Normative Principle, is God's glory. If we only follow one, then we will lose a piece of God's image and nature. If we hold only to the regulative, we can become too restricted and therefore, we will become like the older brother in the story of the Prodigal Son. He was a religious legalist. If we hold only to the normative, we will become too "free," causing us to fall into all kinds of confusing sin like the Prodigal Son himself, whose fake freedom landed him in bondage. He became a rebellious pagan. We, as humans, should revel in the fact that we need guidelines and boundaries that are carefully defined, like the laws of God, so that we can play and live freely, energetically, and most satisfied within them. There's no use stepping outside God's lines because outside His framework lies only death. Our greatest joy is found playing the music of life within and by His rules, for in playing His game in His way, we are most like ourselves.

11

Transience

Life does not take place in a fish tank. It does not take place in a controlled experiment. It most certainly does not take place within a statistical analysis spreadsheet. The context of life is a journey—it's transient. Cultures change when rural communities move to urban hubs. Trade grows when economies rise and fall. Attitudes fluctuate when introduced to praise and to pain.

One of the best places to find the idea of life being a journey is to study the Book of Numbers. God records the travels of a motley crew of Israelites as they travel out of their 400-year bondage in Egypt. In the story, they are distrusting, rebellious, polytheistic, hypocritical, compromised, immoral, and on the verge of anarchy. When God frees them, it's a glorious day indeed, but the real mess is only about to start. Their hearts were severely damaged from legacies born and raised in slavery, bitterness, and oppression. God not only had a mess on his hands with these people, but he was going to have to handcraft a journey for them in order to reawaken them from their numbing slumber.

The first third of the Book of Numbers records God as he leads the people to the base of Mt. Sinai. The second third of the book records God as he leads the people through the desert toward the Promised Land, and the last third of the book records the journey of Israel standing on the verge of entering God's Promised Land. As they travel, their journey is filled with false idol worship, thirst and hunger, complaining and victory, serpent bites, and quail meat coming out their noses. They encountered sorcerers and magicians, kings and armies. They experienced great moments of celebration and real moments of disappointment. Leadership rose and fell, families were ordered and assembled, and families were cast into chaos. Emotions ran high with fear and anxiety, and they ran low with mourning in death and grieving in tragedy.

The point of the book has many facets, but the one we need to highlight here is that the journey of human life, under the leadership and Lordship of God can feel at times like a long car ride with two kids in the back screaming "Are we there yet?" It's not pretty. Messes are made, threats are hurled, songs are sung, and through the stress, there is rest along the way. It's an ever-winding, up and down rollercoaster of moments that need managing.

Music's Journey

Music provides us with a very meaningful and useful tool in how to approach this mess with great hope and joy. Analyzing life using any other tool leaves something to be desired. If we are to analyze life scientifically, it doesn't fit the criteria; if we are to analyze life solely through statistical numbering, it comes up short. If the context of life is a journey, then it seems fitting to analyze it as such, and music provides us with a system fit for ordering a journey.

As a classical piece begins, it begins in intensity. The notes are rhythmic, fast, intense, and precise, and they capture the audience in their story. They move dynamically as they crescendo louder and decrescendo toward silence in their exposition. The spirit is gripping and motivating and culminates at that one held resounding note, "Baaaahm." In classical music, the author writes the elongated note to be held out in power with what is called a *fermata*. This sign tells the whole band to emphasize it, hold it, and pause the song on this one glorious chord.

Like the coming of spring, the flutes enter with a sweet melody, undergirded by the violins. The music is slow and sweet. It develops patterns of lifts and falls, ins and outs, loud and soft. This section then is concluded, only to be lifted out into a transposed key that takes the song in an entirely different direction. The notes go up, and the instruments change from soft and sweet to low and powerful. The French horns wail, and the percussion slams. Though this section is different, it repeats. It speaks the same phrase over and over, but it has a first, second, and third ending; each ending is just a little different than the next, but each builds off the one before it.

Finally, the song returns to the key it started in, only to sound in a new way with a slightly different focus. It wavers and moves and bangs all around until the final glorious moment comes when the song slows to a climactic end. The music is marked by a *ritardando*, and all the notes slow to a halt. Their majesty is brilliant, and the exclamation point to this song has arrived. The composer sweats and beats the air until he breathes his last breath of energy; as the band goes silent, the crowd goes wild, and the curtain closes.

This music moves, and it is also moving. Though the individual parts by themselves seem disconnected and foolish, when connected together with the other pieces, they create a masterpiece. Each stanza of the song propels the song toward one moment of glorious conclusion. In this way, "tonal music exhibits not the temporality of a single straight line but that of a multi-leveled matrix of waves of tension and resolution, in which the temporal modes interweave within an overall directionality." [241] The idea that music is transient and is best embraced as a journey, a story, and a painting of audio colors is also expressed in the ethic of God's story. In Ephesians 1:5, we see it expressed that God's song clearly has a beginning point:

> Blessed be the God and Father of our Lord Jesus Christ, who has blessed us in Christ with every spiritual blessing in the heavenly places, even as he chose us in him before the foundation of the world, that we should be holy and blameless before him. In love he predestined us for adoption as sons through Jesus Christ, according to the purpose of his will.

Although our beginning started with God's plan, as devised apart from any part we played in it, God chose to work us into the means. Ephesians 3:9-11 shows that Paul is a songwriter, raised up in the middle of this ongoing song in order

> ... to bring to light for everyone what is the plan of the

mystery hidden for ages in God who created all things, so that through the church the manifold wisdom of God might now be made known to the rulers and authorities in the heavenly places. This was according to the eternal purpose that he has realized in Christ Jesus our Lord.

God's introduction clearly keeps hidden certain aspects and intentions. His main transpositions and soft movements were concealed until their appropriate times. He knew we would Fall, He knew we would need the law, He knew Jesus would come, and He knew that He would redeem humanity. All this He knew so that, through the church, He might make known these secrets to the whole of creation. All this was a plan to unfold His wisdom, His glory, His un-searchability, and His Majesty. All this was to provide the journey with an element of mystery and surprise. This journey goes and changes keys, but all the endings lead to one ending—the glorious return of Christ:

Revelation 19:11-16: Then I saw heaven opened, and behold, a white horse! The one sitting on it is called Faithful and True, and in righteousness he judges and makes war. His eyes are like a flame of fire, and on his head are many diadems, and he has a name written that no one knows but himself. He is clothed in a robe dipped in blood, and the name by which he is called is The Word of God. And the armies of heaven, arrayed in fine linen, white and pure, were following him on white horses. From his mouth comes a sharp sword with which to strike down the nations, and he will rule them with a rod of iron. He will tread the winepress of the fury of the wrath of God the Almighty. On his robe and on his thigh he has a name written, King of kings and Lord of lords.

All of this is a culmination of history's rising and falling. Like each note sounds, music is always dying and giving way. Music emerges from transience, from the coming into being and dying of tones. It's the only way that dynamic qualities can be sensed. Journeys like this are defined by different segments of time that are played out in different ways and different lengths in order to bring the glorious order to completion.

. . .

Movement

When we are born, long before we can place our eye to the lens of a microscope or complete an equation, we learn how this movement works. "Movement is our first language. We move in the womb, and experience the movements and heartbeats of our mothers. Rhythm, well-being, joy, anxiety, distress are all communicated through these early movement experiences." [242]

I can remember my son before he was born, kicking, moving, and almost jumping through my wife's abdomen. You could almost tell what he was going to be like before he even emerged into the world. Once he was born, he moved. This child still begins to move and gyrate whenever he hears music. No one had to tell him to and no one could keep him from doing it. It's just in him. It is part of the worship and imaging of the Creator God. This natural movement in how people process God can be seen to be fully understood even back into Scripture and into ancient sources like the Talmud. All of these sources together give sample demonstrations that sacred dance was a normal part of everyday Jewish life, not as an attempt to manipulate natural life-forces, but as worship of Yahweh. [243] Dance was understood as natural reflection not only of response, but of the nature of childlike faith.

Sadly, children who once moved grow up to become adults who, all too often, become still. They embrace the pattern of the world that life is not a vibrant movement played unto God, but a scientific exercise that is best measured in a tube, a beaker, or by a formula. Western Christianity, especially, has inadvertently screened out whole swaths of human reality and offered us a preferred flavor of being a Christian: cerebral, disembodied, male, emotionally controlled, hierarchically ordered. Very often, we have portrayed Jesus in similar terms and at the same time attenuate our capacity to relate to him: typically, we know him only with our minds and allow him to know *only* our minds. [244]

The mind is not enough. As we have presented, it is important, but it's not complete. There are limits to what we can understand. There are limits to what a child can understand, limits to what a teenager can understand, limits to what a middle-aged person can understand, and limits even to what a dying man on his deathbed can understand. This means that learning and faith cannot thrive in isolated periods of time, but that they have to move dynamically in order to be shaped. It's like a moving car! If you try to steer that car when it's stopped, it's nearly impossible to move the steering wheel. If you put the car in motion, the steering wheel kicks into gear and can freely direct the car.

This is precisely why God inspired the Bible in the manner He did—through progressive revelation. Slowly, as humanity grew and spread, God unveiled more of His plan. This is a how a parent raises their children. The parent doesn't expose the child to everything all at once, but rather exposes pieces of information along the way as the child is ready to understand and deal with their processed response. If the journey were to be unveiled too quickly and using concepts and ideas that make no sense to the child, the learning attempt proves useless. It is important that movement be considered in learning. Though maturity changes over time, simple truths from previous stages are not to be altogether forgotten.

Hebrews 5:12-14 teaches the importance of moving but not losing lessons along the way. The writer says, "For though by this time you ought to be teachers, you need someone to teach you again the basic principles of the oracles of God. You need milk, not solid food, for everyone who lives on milk is unskilled in the word of righteousness, since he is a child. But solid food is for the mature, for those who have their powers of discernment trained by constant practice to distinguish good from evil." The truths were not the problem, it was the people's lack of use of them in practice. The audience here was predominantly unconverted Jews who held all the truths of the Old Testament in their hands. However, though progressive revelation had revealed these truths in infant ways to them as Jews, the people had never moved from crawling in immaturity to walking in maturity. The truths themselves remained steady, but the people did not embrace how the truths interacted with the journey, and therefore their maturity did not grow. Thus, their beliefs became a set of cerebral precepts but were in no way a dynamic dance.

EMOTIONS

Movement doesn't just reflect the shaping of the mind, but it also allows time to account for a person's emotions as well. Emotions are extremely transient, and they change pitch very easily as the journey produces different experiences. We've discussed previously in the chapter on pitch, how life rises up out of notes and chords that may contain various groups of notes; the notes may sound pretty or they may sound dissonant. Though we've discussed that life is more than a series of peaks and valleys and railroad tracks, but rather one continuous song, we must look at the musical expression of how our emotions play into this journey.

A quote by Jeremy Begbie states that, "some would argue that there is a resemblance between musical patterns and emotional patterns in the mind. Essentially, emotions are states of mind which music in some way resembles: to say that music expresses an emotion is simply to draw attention to the resemblance." [245] What Begbie is stating here is that music portrays externally what the mind is doing internally. Music, in a sense, is a "creation of forms symbolic of human feeling." [246] Music then helps us to understand the cognition of feelings rather than the feelings themselves. [247]

A person may be experiencing excitement, fulfillment, release, tension, sudden change, and even different speeds of tempo (stress, anxiety, depression), but until they are divulged, they may or may not be visible. As a person experiences these things, their mind packages them into a meaning, and the mind determines how to show its results. For emotions to be sparked, they have to originate in a stimulus, they have to be formed and embraced in us by a motive, and then come out of us in an action. Emotions always have to have a cause. A scary moment causes us to fear, a heated moment causes us to panic, and a tragic moment causes us to weep. Emotions become barometers for what is going on in our soul. These emotions are not only vital to our well-being but are essential to helping us gaze a little bit into what is going on within us. What results is that a journey can take a person in various directions resulting in different types of reacted responses.

When the emotions come out, they become an outwardly recognizable and visible display of a person's true desires, beliefs, or actions. Though this is not always a perfect science, it is very telling and helpful. A Biblical case of this can be found in the list of the fruit of the spirit. God says that the Spirit's fruit, if He resides in us, should show forth in some manner of love, joy, peace, patience, kindness, goodness, faithfulness, gentleness, and self-control. In other words, as the Spirit works inwardly, the fruit of the Spirit shows outwardly. It is interesting to note how much of the Spirit's fruit is emotional. In the exact opposite case, if the Spirit is not dwelling in someone's heart, out will come fleshly and worldly fruit: hate, depression, stress, anxiety, bitterness, indifference, selfishness, disloyalty, harshness, and indulgence. Life's moments and responsive interactions are similar to the moments in music. Music creates stimuli that impact the emotions and invoke a response—whether it be weeping, cheering, raising our hands, or leaving to get a refund at the box office.

Life and Death in Musical Notes and in Life's Song

Remember how I said that musical notes are forever dying and giving way? This is what promotes the movement and the expression. Life is then a series of these deaths and births. Life is very experiential and very emotional. Psychologists will even address this from a scientific point of view. They will talk about moments of grief (dying away), and they will express how a person goes through a process of denial and isolation after a tragic death. This might be the death of a loved one, the death of a vision, the death of a belief, or the death of an expectation. This death causes a person to enter into a time of anger, when they lash out to try to regain what they've lost. Then and only then do they realize the reality that this lost thing is never coming back. The anger then subsides, and a person will begin to bargain. They'll begin to say, "If only I'd done this, if only I'd done that," and then the regrets will pour in. Their soul will be overwhelmed with depression until they reach a point of acceptance that the thing that has died is never coming back.

This is called the grieving process, and I call it the freeing process. I call it the freeing process because, most times, the things we consider to be losses are things we need to do without anyway. God frees us in taking them away. To understand this, let's take, for example, the history of Israel in the Book of Numbers once again. They had just been freed from slavery by an Almighty and All-Loving God, and as soon as they got out into the desert, they started complaining about the weather, the laws, the leadership, and their food. Almost immediately they wanted to go back to the bondage they had just left. Why? They were grieving. They'd been in hell, but they'd gotten used to hell. They had gotten used to its false protection, its false promises, and its false hopes. They had eaten its fruits and digested its foods, and now when God offered them something different, they first needed to accept that something in the past had died.

So the travels of Israel continued, and so do ours. Our journeys are filled with moments of the freeing process. God sends us out into the world and very emotionally deals with us. He unearths deep patterns of rebellion in us. He awakens deep places of woundedness in us. Sometimes, His energy is like the fast-paced introduction to a classical tune, and sometimes it wears on in a slow melody. Sometimes, He pushes right through patterns of false thinking, and sometimes He repeats the stanza. He might even have a first, second, third, and even fourth ending as He repeats the same discipline, the same lesson, and the same truth in our lives only to drive it deeper and deeper into our meditation. Sometimes, His lessons come in bunches. We have a term in music for this called *polyphony*, which is a texture consisting of two or more simultaneous lines of independent melody. God may, at the same time, have two different types of melody going on in our lives—happy and sad, mad and hopeful, life and death, etc.—in order to grind us, shape us, and remake us.

A Reflection on Discipleship

The reason I mention this drastic approach to life and living is because I am always drastically shocked by how discipleship methods are ill-equipped to deal with this reality of the journey. Hard and static curriculums are developed out there for rehabilitation purposes, and their approach is cerebral, disconnected, and detached. It seems as if, in entering into the real moments of people's lives, that many discipleship tools and methods are theologically inadequate. They go after the mind, which is good, but they ignore the affections. This is not true to real life, and it leaves something to be desired in how we are forming people.

If you'll permit me to vent in an area of particular concern to me, it is in regard to how we disciple in our services and liturgies. I'll be in a service that will push through eight hymns in which we sing every verse (and some of them have eight verses), and though the lyrics are filled with great truths, the time is never given—the fermata and pause—to digest these great truths. As we push through these words as if we're trying to prove how smart we are, I ask myself, "Is this true to real life?" Life doesn't function like this. When God teaches us in monologues (where He speaks), He always stops to let us think, have conversation, and have a dialogue. He'll often let us sit and rest as He plays the lasting note, or He might stop in silence and reflection after the French horns have just sounded a powerful chorus.

Also, in churches like this, everything tends to be more scripted. The prayers are written before-hand. Everything is somber, quiet, and reverent. The calls and responses are planned. The communion is the same every time, and the service offers no real feel of "humanness." I ask myself, "Is this true to real life? How are we forming people?" Yes, it is true that sometimes we follow a script and obey the directions. Yes, it is true that we are to have a place for reverence and awe before the Lord. Yes, it is true we need familiarity, ritual, and planning. With all of this I agree, but is this the whole story of the human journey? NO!

What about on the flip-side in the services where we sing six praise songs loudly and happily, have a short off-the cuff prayer, then go to the altar to receive prayer for the umpteenth time in two weeks, and, lo and behold, there's never communion. Is this theologically correct? Is this true to real life and the reality of God? No! Yes, life is spontaneous, loud, and happy at times, and yes, we need prayer and counseling that focuses on our needs. Yes, we need times of informality and casual expression. But is this all there is? No! If this is the only diet a person gets, I ask myself, then what are they going to do with grief? Where are the lament and the training for how to deal with anger? That's real! Where are these services addressing when a person is too desperate to pray off-the-cuff prayers, so they simply resort to form: "Our Father, who art in heaven, Holy be Your name … deliver me from evil."

Music has the capacity for breaking open the gospel in a way spoken words cannot: by giving a broader scope and context. [248] It has a way of embracing, mimicking, and also challenging the dynamics of real life. This is how disciples should be formed. It is broader, it's all-encompassing, it's complete!

The Tempo of Discipleship

So what does this mean for us?

Theology: This means that theology has to be true. What do I mean? True means that it's true in every time and space. For example, the health, wealth, and prosperity gospel cannot be true. Why? The reason is because not every culture can achieve it or relate to it. Therefore, it's not

The Tempo of Discipleship

true. To put it another way, if we have a theology that even Jesus can't fit into, we have a problem. Jesus was poor, without a place to lay His head, lacking any material wealth, sick to the point of bleeding tears. His friends didn't understand Him, Judas betrayed Him, and the Pharisees angled to kill Him! This is real life and real experience in a fallen world.

Theology has to form itself in real life. Yes, we interpret life with the Scriptures, and not the other way around. The Scripture is our absolute truth, and we believe what it says over what the world says, but we cannot use this as an excuse to disconnect real truths from real cultures and real people. If theology doesn't address praise and suffering, plenty and want, love and hate, life and death, joy and sadness, loud and quiet, beginnings and ends, then our theology is no good. The Bible embraces the whole scope, and so should we.

BIOGRAPHY: THIS MEANS THAT DISCIPLESHIP'S CONTEXT IS A JOURNEY. OUR lives are going to travel like a song. Sometimes, the pieces won't make sense, but it all progresses forward to one momentous end. This may mean that God keeps us moving while the rest of the song and world are at rest. This may mean that God keeps us at rest while everyone seems to be moving on in the song ahead of us. It might mean that God repeats lessons over and over in our lives, and it may mean that God has to transpose keys for a while into something that doesn't make sense to us, only to allow our lives to serve the purpose of the whole song. It also may mean that God has to *fermata* our lives and hold a section out in order to let it resound and have its full effect.

In the life of Israel, I'm sure the manna and the quail didn't make sense. I'm sure the forty years in the desert seemed like a repeating and revolving detour. I'm sure that Moses and Aaron, their leaders, dying right before they stepped into the Promised Land must have seemed confusing, but it was all part of God's plan of education. God designed the education of His people, and it involved times of plenty and want, and it involved detour and disaster. At the time, the Israelites may not have understood tragedies, such as the deaths of Moses and Aaron, in the broad scope of history, but we now know why things went down as they did: "And all these, though commended through their faith, did not receive what was promised, since God had provided something better for us, that apart from us they should not be made perfect." [249]

. . .

Doxology: What this means for our lives and praise is two-fold. Firstly, our gathered worship and formation needs to be overhauled. We need to be deeply conscious about how we are formed and how we are forming disciples. As presented before, we need to fully embrace life in our liturgies as we plan regulatively and normatively. We need to have one eye on the Bible and one eye on the culture. This means that understanding what Scripture says is as important as understanding what the people are truly going through. Emotions should flare and be considered. Times of life and death should be savored in the life of the local church. All these moments have something to teach us. The next time we breeze through that line of a hymn all strung together without a pause or we neglect a reflection, a prayer, a time of ministry, a bow, or a tear, let's ask ourselves if we are forming people for real life. Next time we amp up the volume in praise, encouragement, speed, and excitement, all the while skipping over tradition, formed responses, and times provided for heart care and compassion, we need to just think twice.

Our scattered worship needs a face-lift in like fashion. As we go out to *be* the church to people, we need to ensure that, as people are around us, they feel that we understand their journey. They should not feel attacked with a line of truths or judgments that sentence them to hell, nor should they feel we validate everything they're doing by never speaking God's mind. There needs to be a balance. God's rhythm holds within this journey of all human life. There are times when the journey requires a pronouncement and a call to repentance, but it may be that the moment requires the touch of God's compassion and listening ear. Jesus demonstrated this in dealing with the two Marys at Lazarus' tomb. Lazarus' death caused them both to grieve over their friend's loss of life, and as they ran to Jesus for consolation and explanation, Jesus' response is telling. He rebuked one Mary for her lack of faith in His ability to heal Lazarus. On the other hand, as the other Mary approached Him with similar sorrow and objection, it says that, with her, "Jesus wept." Two responses to the same situation, but were driven by an understanding of what was needed in each person's journey in order to "bring them along."

12

Sustain and Resolve

We have been discussing the very real dynamics of God sending us out into the world. We have come face to face with the reality of how rhythms form us and how life's rhythms come in form and complexity within the timeline of a real journey. Now we turn our attention more towards the overarching theme of life as being sent by God. We consider how music can help us cope with these various elements of this reality.

To begin a discussion that will carry us through the next section, I'm going to discuss in brief detail what is known as a musical cadence. Cadences are when a group of notes that create sustaining tension are held in dissonance only to then be resolved. Music creates moments that stress the listener's ear only to finish off by providing the listener with relief. These cadences, though easy to understand in concept, are difficult to explain to the untrained musician (or even the trained musician, for that matter). Cadences are more easily heard than explained. For this reason, allow me to indulge you in this next section as I explain in brief how these cadences work. As I communicate in regard to these cadences, please grab onto the big idea through it all. I'm going to stress the importance of music's ability to create moments of sustaining tension and then to bring tensions to wonderful resolve.

. . .

Musical Cadences

In the following section, I'm going to list the most common types of musical cadences, and provide a brief description of how they function in music. Here's there first one,

Authentic Cadence (V-I | IV V I)

The Authentic Cadence is the one that is most natural to the human ear. It can be explained in brief by showing the major scale once again:

e.g. G A B C D E F# G

The strongest note in this scale (G in this case) is known as the *tonic* pitch. Because it is the most dominant sound, all the other notes either pull our ear up to that note, or down to that note. This is authentic. The authentic cadence uses the most pronounced "pulling" notes to let the listener know that we're going back to the tonic. In this case, A pulls hard down toward G, and F# is the neighbor that pulls up hard toward G. The authentic cadence tells the ear that we are about to go strongly back to the tonic in some way, shape, or form.

Perfect Authentic Cadence (V-I | V-i in minor keys)

The perfect authentic cadence holds the same idea, but when switching from chord to chord, it makes sure that the root pitch of each chord is in the top and bottom. For example, if I were to play a D chord, the notes would be D F# A. The root is the note that we call that chord. In this case, it's a D chord. If I were to put another D on top—D F# A D—this would set up nicely for a perfect cadence moving to G. "This strong cadence achieves complete harmonic and melodic closure." [250]

Imperfect Authentic Cadence

The imperfect authentic cadence implies, in the simplest form, that it is exactly like the perfect, but it does not have the tonic in the top and bottom notes. You can take chords in this cadence and do what is called *inverting*. This is when you take a chord like D F# A D and you put the F# on bottom—F# A D. This would be a first inversion chord because it's the first time I changed it. Now, for you musicians who understand all this mumbo jumbo, you can also replace the vii° and still end on I. Regardless, closure is created.

Half Cadence (Preceded by V, but ends ii, IV, I)

The half cadence is basically a cadence that sounds strong but ends weak. Because it sounds incomplete or suspended, the half cadence is considered a weak cadence that calls for continuation. [251] If a person hears this cadence, they may feel a sense of hanging, like a movie that ends on the words "to be continued." It is many times a beautiful end, but the listener feels a bit open-ended and unsatisfied.

Plagal Cadence (IV – I)

This is what's known as the "Amen" cadence. It's the one that ends many hymns that finish the song with a resounding Amen. The IV chord does not contain the tugging notes that pull to the tonic, but it completes nonetheless.

Interrupted (Deceptive) Cadence (V to any chord but I)

This cadence tricks you in that you think it is bringing the song back home to the tonic, and you feel the resolve coming, and then it takes you another direction altogether. This gives the feel that the song still has something to say. The deceptive cadence most likely holds in a section of a song only to ultimately conclude later as the song goes on, but it may throw a bit of confusion into where the song will actually end up.

Jazz (Turnaround)

In jazz, we have a unique style that can take numerous turns, and is highly improvisational. Though jazz moves unresolved around various chord changes, it eventually begins its descent like an airplane on a landing strip that brings you back to the tonic or back to the original idea. It's called a turnaround.

THESE CADENCES PROVIDE US WITH A GOOD CASE STUDY IN HOW ANALYZING music can have a lot to teach us about the nature and tempo of discipleship. The primary function of cadences in music is to bring places of tension to moments of completion and resolve. The authentic and perfect cadences do this more fully and naturally, whereas jazz turnarounds and deceptive cadences might throw a few surprises in the mix before finally ending. The end game is always the same— the cadence's function is to bring the song to a place of decision.

Life, very similarly, brings with it these tensions. There are moments that seem to flare up, yet they are quickly resolved in perfect and strong "tugging" ways. There are also moments that seem to carry on for a while. Though many of life's struggles do resolve, they sometimes seem to be like a half cadence in that they never feel like they fully reach a place of full closure. Further, there are moments in our journey that seem to be deceptive, or even long in their duration, like the jazz cadence. These areas of stress in our lives seem to hold in apprehension for long periods of time and seem to divert to other issues and fuel other major problems. They carry on for what seems like forever, and maybe if we're lucky, they might finally turn around and squirrel their way back down the tree to finally come back under control.

TENSION THAT SUSTAINS

Our experience within the world provides us with many similarities to that of the cadences of music. The world presents various patterns of tensions and closures, sufferings and resolves, and characters of antagonism and decree. These hardships and pressures often present themselves in various ways. One stress may be more severe than another. One relational conflict might seem to hit us really hard but may be as complicated as Jazz with ever-changing turnarounds. One pain may not be as intense, but it may linger on for a long time. Some worry is answered quickly, and some can carry on, spinning and swerving in different directions, almost never seeming to reach a point of finality.

The fact is, music was created to teach us about how suffering works in tandem with resolve. One author, in analyzing music's lessons in this regard, even was so bold to say that "musical experience can be described as enjoying the tension." [252] The point of the statement seems to imply

The Tempo of Discipleship

that within music, the tensions and "sufferings" of the notes, as they linger without closure, almost seems to keep the listener engaged. The tensions create music that is vibrant and engaging and almost make music that much sweeter when the victories finally reach their cadence.

This perspective is somehow unsettling if we are to blow it up into a real life analogy in dealing with real world pain and suffering. Much of the suffering within the world can be described as anything but "enjoying the tension," but I believe what music teaches us is far deeper than enjoying the tensions themselves, but seeing through to where the tensions lead. For example, Jesus never said he enjoyed the cross, but in Hebrews 12:2 it states that "for the joy" set before Him, He "endured the cross." The exclamation mark in Jesus' suffering was not the endurance itself, but it was the joy of having His family back together again that caused Him to revel in what He was suffering. His suffering was opening a doorway to a whole world's healing. The suffering He experienced was working a greater good.

This is what music, in some form, teaches us. Many times, when I speak to people who are disgruntled with the fact that there is so much suffering in the world, I discern that they possess misunderstandings of the nature of suffering itself. They will use these misunderstandings as a platform from which to launch into their hatred and rejection of a very real, good, and loving God. People simply cannot connect and reconcile the possibility of having a loving God all the while living in a world that contains so much suffering. It just doesn't seem to compute.

When people come to these kinds of conclusions, I use it as an opportunity to explain how the Bible outlines two broad categories of suffering—rewarded and unrewarded suffering. In a very general way, I'll begin to explain these concepts to the person in tension by asking, "Do all people suffer?" Their reply is an emphatic "YES!" Then I proceed to ask them, "Well if all people suffer, would you rather receive a promised reward for that pain, or suffer and receive nothing for it?" The answer to this question is always, "Well I'd rather suffer for a purpose or to receive something as a result." My conclusion to this is that the God of the Bible promises a reward to all suffering, but the little wannabe "god" of this world (Satan) promises nothing—just suffering. My reasoning brings me to conclude that I'd much rather spend time trying to unweave this problem of suffering alongside a God who promises me a reward in my search rather than learning suffering at the hands of a task master demon who will only beat me, leave me, and do it all without completing me. This God of the Bible, the Trinity, clings to the promises underlying suffering so much so that He'd send His own Son, Jesus, to help us see the joy through it. Because of His promises, I can at least give Him my attention.

Just as there are many kinds of tension provided in music, there are also many kinds of suffering found within the world. It is not helpful to simply dumb down all types of suffering into one category—"just suffering." All suffering is not the same, just like all cadences are not the same, nor should we treat, reason, or deal with all suffering the same. It will help our discussion if we take some time to make some distinctions. Mark Driscoll, in a post from the Mars Hill Church blog, notes 15 different kinds of suffering in the Bible: [253]

Adamic Suffering

Driscoll states that "because Adam is our first father, representative, and head, when he sinned all of us were implicated; we inherited a sin nature (Rom. 5:12-21) and were born into a fallen world (Rom. 8:18-23)." This fallen nature did not make us wiser in regards to good and evil and therefore make us into highly evolved, naturally selected "good" people. This event caused the human race to fall into bondage and brokenness. Because of this, humans, though we may "evolve" in our technological advancement, will forever use our advancements to create betters ways to kill, steal, and destroy.

Punishment Suffering

This is the kind of suffering that was brought upon Israel by God's hand when He exiled them into slavery under the hands of nations like Egypt, Assyria, Babylon, Persia, and even Rome. God's people, deserving death for their Adamic sin, deserved death, but God granted them life. Therefore, punishment was itself a grace. God decided, in His mercy, not to obliterate His people but to punish them for a specific time and in a specific way in order that they may turn from their wicked ways and follow Him.

Consequential Suffering

The Bible teaches us a principle that we reap what we sow. If we sow in laziness, we will reap broken-down houses and fields. If we sow selfishness, we will find ourselves left without friends. If we amass debt, we will forever be enslaved to that debt until it is paid off in full. Sometimes suffering arises in our lives due to the very real consequences of our very real sin. These consequences are to serve as teachers and warnings that instruct us not to travel down the crooked path again.

Demonic Suffering

This suffering includes torment (Acts 5:1), injury (Acts 8:4-8), false miracles (2 Thess. 2:9-10), accusation (Rev. 12:10), and death (John 8:44). Satan carries the intention to harm all those within this world. Even when he tempted Jesus in the Garden, he tried to convince Jesus that he (Satan) was lord over Jesus. Jesus responded, "I am the Lord YOUR God." Satan's pride over time has puffed him up to the point that he is ruthless in trying to convince us that he is in control. This is an illusion and a magic trick. Believing his accusations, his false miracles, and his fake light only ends up landing us in torment, injury, and sometimes death.

When I speak of such things, a personal encounter comes to my mind of a lady who came to our church severely demonically possessed. She had been used as a blood and sexual sacrifice in the Satanic church since she was two years old, and her oppression and abuse had led her to live in such darkness, that she literally could no longer see colors or smell scents. After thirteen hours of intense counseling with this individual, and leading her through confessing her sin in the "Name of Jesus," she was delivered of her strongholds. She fell on her face crying, and the first thing she said was "I can see color." This is a dramatic testimony to Satan's influential power, but more so that his power is not ultimately lasting and real. When its exposed for the nothingness it really is in light of Jesus' name, we see that Jesus holds the true power.

Victim Suffering

I've been in ministry for over 15 years, I've served all around the world, and it is still staggering to me the number of people I meet everywhere who have been abused spiritually, emotionally, verbally, socially, or physically. I remember a girl who gave up her Muslim faith to follow Jesus, and her father came after her to kill her in what they call a "drowning ceremony." She had left the faith and become a traitor, and therefore she deserved death. I've met kids whose parents refer to them as a "little *%*$," and I've met countless women and men who have been sexually assaulted, raped, or molested. I remember a teenager coming to my youth group and confessing that he was gay. His only memory of his mother was her strangling him without her shirt on, as her breasts hung in his face. This is victim suffering.

Collective suffering

This happens by virtue of being born into a people who are suffering. Those born into Rwandan genocide, or females born into the Chinese cultures that uphold destruction of women, are given over to suffering just by nature of the culture they're in.

Apocalyptic Suffering

This is increased suffering that signals the end of this age. Examples include the prophecies of the Old Testament (e.g., Isaiah 24–27; Jeremiah 30–33; Ezekiel 33–48; Daniel 2–12; Zechariah 12–14) and Jesus (Matthew 24–25; Mark 13). Jesus was very clear that we cannot predict the end of the age, but He is very clear that suffering will happen as a judgment from His hand upon the world that turns against Him.

Disciplinary Suffering

God chastens believers in order to mature them. Examples can be found in such places as Proverbs (3:11; 13:24; 15:5), the prophets (Zeph. 3:7), and the New Testament (Heb. 12:7). This type of "suffering has a way of causing believers to remember what really matters. As painful as suffering is, trials are treasures because they separate triviality from reality." [254] God's intention in discipline is to train our hearts to do righteously. I'll use an example in how I discipline my children to explain.

When my children do something wrong, I do two things. In the wake of an extreme disobedience, I'll first sit them on my knee and spank them. I tell them that their heart is like a cookie jar. At the bottom of that cookie jar is a cookie we can't reach, so to get it out, we have to turn it upside down and bang on the end. In the human heart, that cookie is sin, and to dislodge folly in a child's heart, it needs to be removed—that's why God commands us to spank. [255] The next thing I do is embrace them, pray with them, and lead them to repent before God and before the person(s) they failed to love. With love, I tell them that I'm trying to train them that sin always hurts, and sin always complicates things. I explain to them that I would rather teach them that sin is always followed by pain by swatting them with a lovingly controlled spank. I'd rather this than they ignore sin's consequences and touch a hot burner, run out in front of a car, or grow up to go to a party where they are date-raped. In this manner, God disciplines us to teach us that sin is followed with pain. He trains our hearts to enjoy playing within His safe boundaries.

Vicarious Suffering

Servants of God suffer because the ungodly oppose them. This is brought on by persecution and false slander, like in the case of Nehemiah when he was provoked by Sanballat and Tobiah while he was trying to obey God in rebuilding the wall around Jerusalem.

Empathetic Suffering

This is best shown in the incarnation. When God considered our lost state, He had compassion for us and entered into our suffering to save us, taking on human form. When brought to the cross to be crucified for our sins, the Bible tells us that he provided us an example to follow in in our suffering, as well. 1 Peter 3:21-23 says, "For to this you have been called, because Christ also suffered for you, leaving you an example, so that you might follow in his steps. He committed no sin, neither was deceit found in his mouth. When he was reviled, he did not revile in return; when he suffered, he did not threaten, but continued entrusting himself to him who judges justly." This verse clearly shows how Jesus suffered, but later in the next chapter, Peter writes that husbands are to consider their wives in the same way Christ considered us. The consideration of Christ spoken of here is when he looked upon us and consider what we needed for our betterment even while we were crucifying Him. This empathy caused suffering in Him in places that could have easily and normally been avoided or suppressed, but God's mercy causes us to willingly embrace pain in order to better love and serve His world.

Testimonial Suffering

This is suffering that tests and proves a believer's faith, thereby confirming to them they are true believers, strengthening fellow Christians, and serving as an evangelistic testimony to unbelievers. Like us, the apostle Paul begged for his suffering to be taken from him, but he learned that God's grace is enough in the midst of them. He learned that, when we are weak, God makes us strong in Him (2 Cor. 12:10). Paul taught that part of the maturing process includes suffering just as Christ suffered (Phil. 3:10) and that suffering is actually promised to the believer (Phil. 1:29). [256]

Revelation Suffering

One example of this type of suffering is Hosea's marriage to Gomer. Hosea's allegiance to Gomer, a prostitute, is to model and provide us with a live drama in order that we might understand the depths to which He loves us His people. Hosea committed to her, even while she reveled in her filth and folly in order to reveal to humanity the covenant love that God has toward us.

Doxological Suffering

This suffering is not because of sin, but rather to teach us a lesson about God so that worship of Him can increase. Examples include Joseph's imprisonment in Egypt and the man born blind in John 9:1-3. Jesus clearly stated that these moments were planned by the hand of God in order that people might see His glory revealed in a profound way.

Preventative Suffering

God gives us nerves for a reason. They are to tell us when things are hot and cold, and alert us to when things are sharp and soft. This kind of pain prevents us from doing things that are harmful to us physically.

Mysterious and Providential Suffering

Job's life provides maybe the strongest example of this. Though we do not fully know why God chose to point Job out to Satan, He did it for a reason. I'm sure Job, after being up in heaven for a while, has asked God a few times, "Why did you point me out; Satan wouldn't have seen me otherwise?" However, God's intention, though we can see His plan to use Job's life to teach us about true faith and true suffering, is not fully known to us.

I feel Driscoll's list above is very sound and complete in many ways. If I could, I would add a couple types of suffering that I believe can be considered. First, I'll mention what I call Prosperity and Disparity Suffering. In James 1, we are taught about how various kinds of trials are going to come our way, and when they do, we are to seek God's wisdom in how we respond. In verse 9, James says this; "Let the lowly brother boast in his exaltation, and the rich in his humiliation." This implies that, at whatever state we are in, we are going to be tested; if we're poor and in despair, we're going to suffer and find it difficult to praise God. God uses poverty to test our hearts of worship toward Him. On the other hand when we are rich and prosperous, we're going to struggle also to praise God. God also uses riches to test our trust in Him to see whether or not we will acknowledge Him in all seasons as our truest satisfaction. What this means is that we are to count ourselves blessed and loved in Christ through highs and lows, but I also think this implies that times of Prosperity and Disparity produce times of suffering in us—a crisis of worship. Proverbs tells us that not only is a man tested by despair, but also by the praise he receives. Sometimes God causes us to suffer by keeping us from getting what we want, and sometimes He exposes our hearts by giving us what we want. We feel both of these as suffering, discomfort, stress, and pressure, but the Lord intends them all the same to unravel our unsavory pride.

The final type of suffering is one that most certainly deserves its own category, and that's Sacrificial Suffering. Galatians 1:4 tells us that Jesus "gave himself for our sins to deliver us from the present evil age." Jesus, in laying down his life, paid once for all the sins of the world. To describe this flavor of suffering that Christ endured on behalf of my sin and yours, a new word had to be added to our language—*excruciating*. Christ excruciatingly paid a debt that was not His to pay and incurred the suffering from it. This was a wild act of love!

Resolve

It would seem there are different kinds of cadences in the suffering of humanity. With these tensions come different resolves. Like the authentic and perfect cadence, some suffering comes to a dramatic and perfect end. Jesus' suffering was tense, but it resulted in a final decision, resurrection, and ascension into heaven. This perfect resolve is never to be questioned because it perfectly "tugs" toward the tonic of creation's song. In the same way, though on a much smaller level, we can experience this in circumstances in our lives. Buying a home or a car can produce real suffering and can resolve perfectly in a purchase. Consequences can come as quick as a teenager hitting a lamp post and getting grounded for a week. These sufferings are short, but their tensions resolve profoundly and sweetly with release.

We might also go through our little half-cadence sufferings. It may often seem like things continue toward resolve, but never do. We all are currently in one of these at this very moment. Adam's sin brought death, sickness, disease, tears, and decay into creation. Though Jesus died to save us, we still await the kingdom where one day we will feel no pain, and every eye will be a dry eye. There's a sense in our soul that the kingdom is now and not yet, all at the same time. We may also encounter a deceptive cadence. This suffering is tainted with ploys from the enemy that are thrust into our sphere of existence for the purpose of leading us astray. It's the ploy of the enemy to tempt us to move outside of the safety of God and to steal, kill, and destroy. However, like the deceptive cadence, though it continues to give the impression that it will never return to the home and tonic note, it undoubtedly does at some point. We see in faith that every ploy of Satan is completely overseen by God—the composer—and allowed by God within His song. Though Satan tries to distract us with suffering, God always directs the enemy's deception back to a resounding tonic pitch—He makes sure everything in all of creation always glorifies Christ.

There are also cultural and long-lasting sufferings that seem like a Jazz turnaround. These sufferings feel as if they linger on forever in our story, but though they turn around and redeem themselves slowly, they turn around all the same. Two case studies present themselves of this type of suffering in the lives of Esther and Joseph in the Bible.

Joseph was born a dreamer. His brothers hated his dreaming and pride, and so they ditched him in a hole, only to turn around and sell him as a slave in Egypt on the black market. Joseph was then introduced to the wife of his new master, Potiphar. She quickly thought Joseph was pretty cute and tried to seduce him, and when he fled, this woman falsely accused Joseph of coming on to her; this landed him in prison. During his time in prison, he spent time working and meeting people who had once worked alongside the Pharaoh and had since done something to tick him off. Lo and behold, one day the Pharaoh released one of these men to come back into his courts. When the Pharaoh had a dream one night, which frightened and puzzled him as to its meaning, the ex-prison mate of Joseph brought Joseph to Pharaoh to interpret his dream. Joseph, who began as a wise-guy-dreamer, interpreted Pharaoh's dream, which led to the ultimate provision and prosperity for all of Egypt.

Esther, on the other hand, was born a mere disgruntled and faithless Jew who lived in the land where an evil King named Xerxes lived. Xerxes threw wild parties where he would parade ladies, including his wife, naked before his armies. One day, his wife said no more to his perversion, and Xerxes ousted her and held a talent competition in his castle that would enable him to find a new wife. He picked Esther, the faint-hearted, duplicitous, and most likely low-lying Jew—nonetheless a follower of Yahweh. Esther won the show, became Xerxes' wife, and went on living in the castle clearly having no problem with Xerxes' escapades, until one day a man named Haman got in an argument with Esther's relative, Mordecai. Haman was so mad at Mordecai that he tricked the King into sending out a decree into all the land that ordered the annihilation of Mordecai and all his people—the Jews. Esther was one of these Jews! For the first time, Esther stood up in courage by throwing a dinner party in order to discuss and expose this matter to the King and to fight for her faith and for her family. At this dinner party, she informed the King of the plans in place that would lead to the death of her and her people, and the King connected the dots and realized that Haman was the man who orchestrated this little deception. Haman, the Satanic figure of the story (trying to kill God's people), was symbolically hung on a cross in a story of a huge reversal of redemption—a turnaround. Though God appeared absent in the story, His cadence resolved all the same. The Israelites were saved, and they threw a huge feast called Purim that concluded their long-standing tension with a glorious resolve.

Sovereignty

Though there are many types of suffering presenting themselves at various times, places, and for different durations, there are a few factors that remain constant even amidst the seeming flux of the music. One manner in which the nature of music will help us to theologize regarding the nature of suffering is to think upon the relationship that the composer has with a piece of music. We must ponder the idea of God's Sovereignty through and over all human suffering, and music provides us the best vehicle to think through this issue.

The song writer, artist, or composer involves themselves only in part when they partner with their work to maneuver the tones to create a beautiful piece of music that brings with it great emotion and intensity. Though the piece itself involves a journey with notes and musical variations that are constantly changing, the composers themselves do not change. In this way, the composer is outside of the time signature and the timeline of the song and is truly more existent than the song itself. Though the song itself is merely a creation of the artist's mind, the composer is a true being—of the truest reality. The song has no bearing on the creation of the composer. The song also cannot define the composer; it can only allude to him. The composer, the only true being, is more genuinely existing than temporal beings (songs), for they (the artist) are more genuinely present and untainted with past or future. [257] In this relationship between creation and creator, we see genuine insights emerge for how we are to think about God's handiwork surrounding suffering within our own lives and songs.

God is the composer and though He writes time and can freely move within it, He can also exist completely and freely outside of it. When He writes the score to humanity's masterpiece, He's able to craft the notes of each individual moment in a way that contributes to the song's beginning and end. He's inside of this framework of creation only so much as He allows Himself to experience the symphony itself. The song does not change Him, nor does it contain Him, but in bringing the score to life with the sounding of various instruments as they erupt in a live performance, we feel God erupt into the story as He too hears it and experiences it. As the composer becomes the conductor, He moves the notes along to move the song along in such a manner that it moves the audience toward the affections that He deposited into His writing. However, the composer's free movements are always contained within the parameters that He Himself places on the notes. The limits of the song's shape and how He responds limits how He acts, but He Himself is the very one who imposed these restrictions. Because of this, the opus of God's symphony plays one resounding note: it sings His sovereignty.

Like a composer or artist, God maintains strict control over His piece. The piece never masters Him, the piece never changes Him (unlike what Process Theology might suggest), nor does the piece ever envelope Him or turn Him into the piece itself (the view of Pantheism). Rather, He is at every moment crafting, shaping, tugging, pulling, and resolving each beautiful note to tell the story that He designed it to tell (He's involved in time, unlike the view of Deism). This ensures that God's perspective over the timeline of His opus is much broader than that of the individual instrumentalists. Whereas a flute player is self-contained to their part and the percussionists highlight their part, God Himself has designed all the parts to work toward a greater goal, which He alone sees.

The Tempo of Discipleship

In Figure 11.1, there is a diagram displaying how God views this timeline of humanity from a Sovereignty perspective. We, as His players, only see the moments we are in. We cannot perceive the end from the beginning. God, however, can push Himself up and out of time into a proverbial helicopter view of life and reality. He can then see from the horizon of the beginning to the horizon of the end, all at the same time. This affords Him the opportunity, in stories like Joseph and Esther, to take the "long view" on things like suffering. He sees the deceptions. He crafts them and allows them to be written by His composer's pen. He sees the half-resolves, and He sustains them until their appropriate climax. Like a song writer, God is not shocked when the chorus of a song plays again or the bridge takes a while to reach a turnaround in order to explain the situation, for He Himself has designed it this way. This shape that He puts to music resembles how His Sovereignty works.

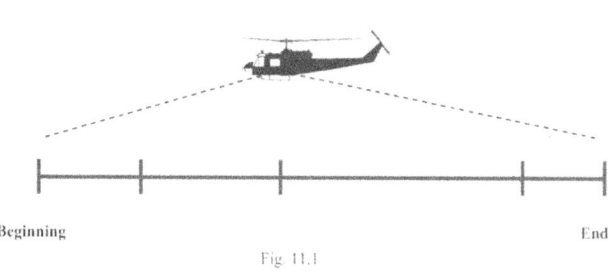

Beginning End

Fig. 11.1

IT IS BENEFICIAL TO THEOLOGIZE IN RELATIONSHIP TO THE COMPOSER AND the composition itself; doing so in order to better understand how God works in and through our suffering, and to help us to ponder one other aspect of the song. We will find it particularly enlightening if we turn our attention to also consider the key within which the composer sets the notes. As we've discussed previously, a key is a grouping of eight notes that tell the songwriter what to play and what not to play. For example, the key of G contains the notes G A B C D E F# G. Any of those notes are in the key. Any notes outside of this framework, like an A# (sharp) or Db (flat), for example, is foreign to this key. In music, if these foreign notes appear, we call them *accidentals* and sometimes passing tones. These accidentals provide moments of tension but always emerge in relation to the key in which they're set. They can only move so far and accomplish so much unless the songwriter decides to switch keys, and again this is the decision only of the composer. The passing tones often are just that, passing. These are tones introduced only for the purpose of moving to greater notes that are within the key. They are not lingered upon for long, but they provide the song with interesting shift and movement.

The truth is that amongst all this movement, "there is a background against which tones 'move'…our sense of melody depends on the place of the pitches within the key." [258] The composer sets this key when he/she begins writing, and this is analogous of how God wrote the cosmos. As a songwriter sets a key, as an athletic coach marks the boundary lines, or the construction engineer erects the walls of a home, God puts structure to His creation's boundaries. He writes the container so that the contents themselves can move.

The key in music allows for the instrumentalists to sound rightly as they play. The boundary lines in an athletic event enable the players to improvise with freedom and within safe limits. The walls of a home provide shelter and protection as the family lives life openly and independently within its shade. Only in remaining inside of these keys does true reality makes sense. This is what the Bible calls the Kingdom of God. Anything outside the kingdom's parameters produces confusion, complication, and out-of-bounds play.

The Tempo of Discipleship

This brief glimpse into music's philosophical look regarding the Sovereignty of God and the suffering of man should be basic to a disciple's understanding. Unfortunately, all too often, a view of God's overarching plan, as it couples with human willing, is not presented and understood in depth by God's sons and daughters, and it produces an anemic chorus. There are three "hands" in how we can treat this matter. In one hand we can treat this matter in a way that leads us to *hate suffering*; growing embittered, disillusioned, and confused at God and at His allowance for these events. This can only lead toward disbelief and rejection of an all-loving and good God. The second hand is to misunderstand the various flavors of suffering and sovereignty, thereby paralyzing ourselves in dealing with it. This can cause us to move toward assuming all suffering is from the Devil, all suffering is from God, or all suffering is from sin, when the truth is that all these colors exist in God's rainbow plan for redemptive suffering. Theology, as true to the Bible, must make room for all these possibilities. Lastly, in the third hand we must see sovereignty and suffering within the symphony of God. This view allows us to embrace tensions and hope for resolve. It allows for confidence to form in how God composes the various parts to collide, intertwine, and make peace with one another. In this construct, we can understand His goodness and song-writing skills and seek Him as the answer for why each note was written into His work.

THEOLOGY: THIS IS WHY DISCIPLESHIP SHOULD SHAPE THEOLOGY IN USING art forms as well as academic forms, not only music but also things such as "poetry, which often do a better job than prose at communicating the paradoxical theologies of scripture in a way that both maintains the tensions of scripture and leads us to devotion of praise." [259] All too often, sheer artful understanding only embraces the grey (leaving everything in question), whereas sheer academia tries to resolve everything into black and white (leaving nothing to faith). When poetry of a theologizing kind embraces and combines both realms of creativity and form, then a world of color emerges.

What this aids in when dealing with topics that are as volatile as the nature of God's Sovereignty or the nature of human suffering, is the allowance for holistic thinking. This means that hard lines are not drawn, nor are the lines altogether ignored, but rather a world of wonder and love is created in dealing with these subjects. We can marvel at how the fabrics intertwine, and we can love appropriately in the little moments of tension that God allows for us to experience.

Further, what this also implies is that discipleship is really a rhythm of tension and resolve. Discipleship should not ignore these tensions, minimize these tensions, gloss over these tensions, or take them lightly. God may compose a time in our story that lingers deeply with darkness and minor harmony. He might trip us up with quick accidentals that go outside our box and key. Rather than rejecting these moments of dissonance as altogether useless, we can submit our thinking to their purpose and begin to unlock some of the deeper motifs that are written within our song. These strains on our lives and experiences lose their weight of despair and produce in us hope for their purpose and their ultimate resolution as we see the reason for our suffering.

BIOGRAPHY: IT IS OUR JOB TO EMBRACE EACH ENCOUNTER AND UNDERSTAND it for what it is. Sometimes, it's an attack that needs to be rebuked. Sometimes, it's a discipline that needs to be deeply received. When push comes to shove, life is not just a clean cookie-cutter existence, and I think it's helpful that God and music embrace this fact. God enables us to sing the song of suffering and to taste its bitter stress only so we can awaken to it fully when it resounds its anthem decision.

The only question in the wake of this fact remains, "Will our suffering be rewarded or reward-less?" Reality tells us that everyone will taste suffering, but some will do so with a disdain for the hand that dealt it. Some will so reject suffering that they'll never taste its sweet fruit as it grinds us down to our most real shape. At the end of the rebel's journey will only come eternal punishment, where they will forever suffer and gnash their teeth over the fact that they missed the point. They missed the point that their suffering was trying to prove! The point to suffering is hidden in the reward, not the suffering itself. Those who seek to find and receive the lessons and deep truths of God's sovereignty within the opus of suffering will find for themselves a pot of gold and enjoyment beneath its seemingly destructive façade. In wading through the complex issues that suffering dredges up, the greatest reward is produced when we find ourselves crippled to answer the questions with satisfaction. In reaching a point of surrender and abandon, we are forced to lean upon a greater mind, a greater hand, a greater satisfaction, and a great faith! Our reward is then found in what the suffering drives us to—a dependence more upon the Supremacy, the Glory, and the Majesty of Christ!

DOXOLOGY: THOUGH AN ULTIMATE STRAIN WAS INTRODUCED INTO OUR world through the disobedience, tyranny, anarchy, and sin of Adam, God reminds us that Jesus has entered into the verse of our agony and provided a profound chorus and resolve. In Hebrews 12, the Bible instructs us about Jesus' suffering and teaches us the implications it has upon our response: "Therefore, since we are surrounded by so great a cloud of witnesses, let us also lay aside every weight, and sin which clings so closely, and let us run with endurance the race that is set before us, looking to Jesus, the founder and perfecter of our faith, who for the joy that was set before him endured the cross, despising the shame, and is seated at the right hand of the throne of God. Consider him who endured from sinners such hostility against himself, so that you may not grow weary or fainthearted." This verse does not cloud the nature of human suffering, but rather explains its true end. Though the suffering itself seems unbearable for a moment, it works to strip us of our world of sin, evil, and death and enter us into a conclusion of joy and rest.

Take a look and notice that Christ's joy came *through the cross* not *around* it. This is important, but it also indicates what we are now to do in our own suffering. It tells us to consider His suffering so that we may not grow weary and fainthearted in our same fight. This verse implies that there is a rest in contemplating the excruciating death of Jesus. Where most people try to find rest by vegging in front of a TV or getting away and hypothetically "turning their mind off," Jesus says to activate our minds to find rest in deeply pondering one thing—His suffering. I believe the reasoning here is because, in this one moment in human history, suffering and sovereignty collide. God not only related to our own human experience by suffering agony and death, but He planned His own. Written into God's very true song is the moment of Jesus. We are not to cut this moment out and despise it, nor are we to remain indifferent to it and fail to unwind its meaning, but we are rather exhorted to leave it in the song and link all human pain and suffering to it. All relational betrayal, assault, abuse, stress, anxiety, worry, doubt, pain, striving, pride, despair, shame, guilt, etc., is to be reckoned with at the cross of Christ. We find, in one moment, not a moment when our pain was denied or simply dismissed, but a moment in time when it all is dealt with and resolved.

13

Sound and Silence

A squealing peal of rapidly accelerating tires through a bustling metro city produces uniquely distinctive sound. Bright lights and billboard signs squawk for attention, commuters blare their horns in the midst of traffic contention, and adrenaline becomes the drug of habit. Amidst such a scene, our attention is drawn to one crossing sign after the next, to one vendor shouting over another vendor, and to a million messages assaulting our conscience and appetite all at once. This is noise. This is loud, this is intoxicating. But it cannot all function like this. The soft country road still holds its allure. Even the most highly decorated and most prestigious CEO of a Fortune 500 company needs a day off once in a while. The yearning in the human soul to meander and rest is always present. When the high-octane leader slips away from the bustle and grind, they inevitably find a secluded beach, a quiet meandering river through a mountain scape, or a field covered with cattails only to be accompanied by a picnic blanket, on which lays all the items to make for a bonafide romantic country meal. The serene scenery is medicating and quiet. It is just what a weary soul desires to return to normal.

Sound and silence. Work and rest. God, in sending His people out by His hand to be a reflection of His image, expects this real dynamic of going and waiting to be part of the flow of His Kingdom. God drives a kingdom Cadillac with both a gas pedal and a brake, and both are essential to us arriving safely at His destination. The right amount of work with all diligence brings profit [260] and provisions, [261] health for every situation, [262] great reward and pleasure, [263] respect from others, [264] and can be an outlet for our love for God, [265] a saving grace and hope to those who don't believe, [266] and a major way for us to act like our Father in heaven. [267] Similarly, moments of loudness magnify the Lord's holiness and bring about reverence and trembling, [268] and can portray victory and joy in the truest sense. [269] Loud exclamation can biblically resound God's worship [270] and can herald and proclaim God's truth in a transforming and dynamic way. [271] Hidden within this dynamic of the busy, the loud, the noise, and the *doing* is God's glory.

The cruel dichotomy is that work and sound, when used haphazardly without brakes, can become like a poison and a pollution to the soul. Overwork can rob us of a quiet and simple life. [272] Overwork leaves us empty when we place in it all our trust; [273] it can expose disorder in us, [274] it causes us to gratify ungodly passions, [275] it shows forth our discontent, [276] and it can even distract us from Jesus. [277] Sound and busyness can also be used to sound bitter cries; [278] they can outlet a stubborn hardheartedness, [279] they can outlet much sin, [280] they can attract undue attention and become a curse, [281] they can be the voice of the demonic, [282] and they can even be heard out of the crucified Messiah's lips, as all the weight of humanity's sin bore down on him: "Jesus cried with a loud voice, saying, *Eloi, Eloi, lama sabachthani?* which is, being interpreted, My God, my God, why have you forsaken me?" (Mt. 27:46) The weight of the Messiah's words express the true depth of sin's destruction as the weight of the world fell upon Him.

On the same token, within rest and silence is the same double-edged sword. The right amount of rest is a grace from God [283] and shows forth an attitude of trust in our Savior that He can deliver us from every fear. [284] Rest cultivates an attitude of contentment in simple provisions, [285] a right perspective on work, [286] an awareness of the body's limitations, [287] a conscious awareness of God's work in spite of our weakness, [288] and a belief that utter safety and completion is found in God and God alone. [289] Restful waiting and silence before the Lord causes us to stop folly before it starts and it gives way to thoughtful cultivated wisdom. [290] Silence accepts God's defense of us on our behalf, [291] can aright our heart to receive instruction [292] and to hear God speak, [293] and can even be a humble way of admitting that we are wrong. [294] Too much rest, however, and a person becomes lazy and a sluggard; [295] too much silence shows a lack of courage and justice [296] and can even enable demons to run rampant to the most evil degree. [297]

It appears that the most important issue in this discussion is not on whether work and rest are important, but in what way we can balance them so we can reap their truest fruits and avoid their most detrimental evils.

Music and this Dichotomy

Music has a lot to teach us about how this rhythm works itself out in the life of a human being. Each tone in music as it sounds, does so in a distinct way. When a note sounds, it often sounds very loudly and in a pronounced fashion. Behind the sound of a trumpet is the work of the trumpeter's breath. Behind the weight of the heavy bass drum is the work of the drummer's powerful swing. In the very DNA of music, there is encompassed within its structure an interaction between the artist and the sound itself. Sound is produced by work and effort, and the weight of the effort determines the volume of the sound.

Without the sound, there would be no notes, but greater still, without the source of breath in the performer, there would be no sound at all. The audio is made available only by the work of the player. Depending on breath speed, velocity, vibration, and the size of the instrument, the notes sound forth with intensity. The instrument can sound across a whole measure, across a half measure, across a quarter measure, etc., depending on what the music calls for and what the player can provide.

Combined with these sounds are also periods of silence, rest, and decay. For one pitch to sound, another has to die away. The music may call for the pitches to die away for a split second (1/32) or they may call for the pitch to die away for two counts, four counts, or even a cluster of measures. The fact is, the written music tells and prescribes for the instrumentalist times of work and sound, and times of rest and silence. This is where the great dynamic of music comes forth. If everyone were always playing the music loudly, it would be forceful, but at the same time incoherent and horrible. People would vacate concerts, worship services, and venues in hopes just to escape the noise. If everything were silent, then the club would be shut up, closed down, having bars across the windows. There'd be no excitement.

Rest has to remain in balance with work. When certain instruments bellow on or tweet sweetly, other players lie dormant. This rest amplifies the work of the others, and the other's work exalts the rest of their counterparts. It's a rhythm. It's a conversation. It's an interaction. Without rest, one cannot understand work. Without work, there's nothing from which to rest. These concepts in music and in life have to hold hands and walk in tandem.

WORK AND SOUND

The first combination of work and rest entered Creation when God spoke and there was light. When the sound came out of the ordered, revelatory, and wise mouth of God, it shouted out in a loud "Bang!" The array of God's light hit the disarray of the dark and formless earth like a wrecking ball. As a cue ball crashes into pool balls and sends them parading toward their pockets, this collision sent Creation into a scattering sprint. God broke the darkness, the void, and the quiet with a sound. His voice produced the work of Creation. For six days God spoke and Creation worked in response. The lights took their place, the fish swam around, and the land pole-vaulted into the sky to create the mountain's timberline. Mount Everest exploded, Canis Majoris ignited, and the Great White Shark whisked around playfully in his new home. When the seventh day arrived it wasn't God who was tuckered out and tired, but the creation itself. It had been hog-tied, stripped, ordered, re-shaped, and changed in dramatic fashion. The Bible does not purport a God who, on the seventh day, needed sleep as if He was tired from the work, [298] but it would seem fitting that He knew that a rhythm of work and rest must fill all of creation for the betterment of its own maintenance. After God poked and prodded and unleashed His power on an un-expectant world, God gave it rest.

Before we get to that rest in detail, let's take time to mention one thing. On the sixth day, God created man. When he fashioned Adam out of dust and breathed into him the Triune image and life, Adam's first experience on earth as a living being was to hear God speak. God sounded His voice into Adam's restful and waiting ears, and God filled Adam with the same ethic for work. In Genesis 1, He tells Adam to have dominion over the animals, to be fruitful and multiply, to fill and subdue the earth, and to cultivate for provision and life.

Before Adam even kicked back a yawn and ate his cream of wheat, God woke him with his alarm clock voice. Adam had been officially placed in Creation as a gatekeeper. Theologians call Adam here the Federal Head. He is the source from which all other humans would come. The mission and work given to him would also be the work of his children. This Adam, this man, was to take the provisions of God and provide for the animals. This man, who had been given a safe haven of protection, was called to subdue the uninhabitable, unprotected wilderness around him and make it rich like the Garden—a haven of safety.

Adam was the priest, and he was filled with the power and presence of God. Before Adam even reached the moment when he would give this safe haven up for a measly prohibited apple, God had called him to responsibility and work. This ethic was present in the Garden. Work was not a result of the Fall. God had sounded this call. Work was not a curse, it was a blessing.

As the sixth day passed, and Adam's commissioning was over, he awoke on the seventh day to start his new job. What we must observe is that Adam awoke on the seventh day when God rested. God's last day of creating was Adam's first day of serving. God had been creating for six days and took a day of rest on the seventh day. When man came along, rest began humanities' work. Man did not have to work *for* anything, but rather worked *from* everything. Man had been given everything, and this rest was a symbol to Adam. It was a symbol to Adam. It shaped his attitude in how he would do everything. There was no striving in the Garden, no competition, no vain conceit or passion. Adam and his wife, Eve, had everything, and the mentality of working "for the weekend" evaded him. He was working from the week beginning.

Then it happened … tragedy hit the Garden. Work and rest were interrupted by a new sound, the voice of a serpent. His voice took up home in Adam's and Eve's ears and caused them to put their hands to work in a different fashion. Rather than enjoying God's freedom, they placed their hands on the words of Satan and were forever bound to be enslaved by the land, enslaved to each other, and alienated from the life of God. The Garden's rest was forever filled with a curse. God looked upon the serpent and humanity as cancers that had disrupted His perfect safety and all that He pronounced good (by good, He meant perfect). As a result, God proclaimed that the ground was cursed, the womb was cursed, and the marriage was cursed, and would seemingly never regain what it had lost.

Work was forever dismayed. Work took up home in the man's heart not as a blessing but as a weight. It now defined his identity, and he forever felt compelled to use work to work *for* his worth, dignity, and value, not *from* it. From that day on, all of humanity now works to prove something. They work to prove how rich, how smart, how popular, how significant, how hip, how cool, or how desirable they are.

WORK AND SOUND RESOUNDED

Genesis tells us that God provides a solution to this problem. Though humanity is forever in conflict with the world and the Devil, God produced a Deliverer in the form of His own Son, Jesus. When Jesus showed up on the scene, and in Luke 4 entered the desert before He began His ministry, what transpired was more than a temptation by the Devil in a dry, dusty place. The Devil came to Christ just like he did Adam. He tempted Christ with the provision of bread. Christ denied it. He tempted Christ with the false power of imaginary kingdoms, and Christ denounced it. He tempted Christ by offering Him false protection, and again Jesus declined. Jesus, in denying Satan's false claims, emerged sinless and perfect. He adequately oversaw his temple-garden as a priestly man. He took up the chair of protector, provider, and the owner of dominion upon the earth. He turned humanity's ear back to the voice of the Father. The sound was heard anew, and it resounded back into Creation in the perfect life, death, and resurrection of Christ, and because of this, all of humanity can now return to work *from* God instead of *for* "god" or *as* God.

This reality is what causes Jesus to challenge the Jewish idea of rest. Up until Jesus' arrival on planet earth as a man, the Jews had attempted to follow suit with God's teaching in Genesis that the seventh day, the Sabbath day, was their rest. They believed God Himself had been at rest since the seventh day of Creation. So, when Jesus showed up, as John records, claiming that His "Father is still working," [299] all the while claiming that He Himself is God's rest and the personification of the seventh day, the day of rest, one can understand why the Jews wanted to crucify Him. In Matthew 11:28-30, he proclaims, "Come to me, all who labor and are heavy laden, and I will give you rest. Take my yoke upon you, and learn from me, for I am gentle and lowly in heart, and you will find rest for your souls. For my yoke is easy, and my burden is light." Jesus entered into a tired, stressful, anxious, worried, and enemy-infiltrated humanity and claimed to be the absolute sleep aid and depression medication. He re-awakening humanity to the fact that their identity in God had been lost, and that God Himself now produced in human flesh the work they had failed to do in Adam. Jesus was their good. Jesus was being perfect for them. Jesus put an end to every high-flying jock who earns popularity through rims and sports cars. Jesus stamped an "A" on every high-strung student proving their worth by a grade. Jesus put an end to every high-octane leader stamping worth on life by defining it as money and power. Jesus ended competition between His family members, and Jesus put an end to the story of human strife.

Now the Dichotomy

We see a bit of where the dichotomy of work/loud and rest/silence comes from. The Bible clearly states that if we work for our glory and attempt to self-prove our worth, we will be loud, obnoxious, evil, distracting, full of sin, embarrassing, disgracing, and have a mouth that just has one giant foot in it all the time. This is where lies come from, this is where murderous intent comes from, this is where coveting and competing comes from; it is based in the work of the Fall, not the work of Christ. In like manner, rest and silence plays its role in the Fall's work. Not only was true rest hidden from humanity, but it was perverted. Satan got humanity thinking that vegging in front of the TV is rest; spending millions of dollars is rest; the life of movie stars is rest! This is false advertising.

The pure, unadulterated work and rest tandem comes gloriously colliding together in and through believing in Christ. The work, done in Christ, has now put us back in the Garden with the same ethic and place as Adam. We have God's provisions, His power, His protection, His presence, and we are His priests. Because of this returned and redeemed glory that was and is bestowed afresh on any human who believes and follows Christ, the Bible says that the work and rest we now perform is altogether different because of Christ's work. The Bible says that the work of the Christian is now to be a witness to this story of Christ. This was the intended work of Adam from the beginning in that, being fruitful and multiplying, he would expand the Kingdom of God upon the earth and would make God's name known. This paradise lost is the restored value and ethic under Christ. All of Creation is to once again hear about the Garden culture. The world needs to know about what life in God is like. This is what the Bible calls a sweet and fragrant message. The fragrance can't be spread unless it's allowed to waft freely. God in the New Testament calls our work a fragrant offering, because our fragrance flows when we share this good news of God's work with others' [300]; when we scatter His good news with finances and giving, [301]; and when we glorify His fame, His Honor, and His greatness in worship as we move along. [302]

What this implies is that all work is God's work if done with witnessing in mind. What this also implies is that all work not done with witnessing in mind is not work at all, but fraud. The motive is what makes all the difference. It is true that for the gospel to spread, there needs to be designated preachers, evangelists, and teachers to teach the good news, but, for the Gospel to be financed and fueled, there are to be equally faithful people in the high rises of economic society pulling in the big bucks and modeling Christ-like integrity in ways that bring new Christians out of the world and into the church; supplying them with the provisions of God to be gathered, taught, responded, and sent all over again. This is what led Charles Spurgeon to say, "Every Christian is a either a missionary or an imposter." [303] The fact remains that true work is foundationally missions. Work is defined as something that is establishing God's grace-filled message and witness in areas of business, government, media, arts, entertainment, education, the family, or in faith.

The Trinity's Rest

Now that we have a proper definition of work and a framework for it, we must realize that this impacts our rest and silence. Not only does this change the nature of how we perceive and do work, but it changes how we perceive and do rest. To understand this rest, we must first go back to the source of rest; it's found in the Trinity. The Father, Son, and Spirit create a relationship culture that is owed our respect and serious contemplation. Hypothetically, if one were to sit down to dinner with the Trinity and participate in the culture that is between them, one would find very dominant colors to the mood of their domain.

The Trinity's table most assuredly gives off the sense of lovely perfection. Because perfection is around their table, this determines how they relate to and experience each other. This means they can trust each other, enjoy each other, and speak with one another freely. Though they are all knowing, all present, all powerful, and all One together, there remains no hidden thing amongst them. There are no shadows to their community, and there is no divide to be found anywhere within them. They are not worried about any identity wars, competition, or social norms that confuse things and create atmospheres of intimidation, jealousy, greed, and the like. There is the most profound intimacy between them. Their perfection breathes only love and rest.

Out of this untainted union, God created humanity, called them good, and pronounced His blessing of rest over all creation. God's rest should not be interpreted as a nap, but His rest is summed up in the idea of perfection. His rest is encapsulated with unadulterated and sheer intimate community. Nothing is hidden in darkness between them, and everything is freely exposed and out in the light. Sucked up into this vortex of love and light were Adam and Eve. They were profoundly caught up around God's table and were placed within the intimate community of the Trinity. They dined with God in His Garden, they communed and walked with Him, and they were seamlessly a part of God's family.

This colored everything Adam and Eve did. Though they worked the Garden and expanded its borders with hard work and labor, the flavor of their attitude in their work reflected the Trinity's image. Their attitude was predominantly one of enjoyment. Their hands were hard at work in serving God, but all the while they had one hand to the ground, they were seamlessly feeling, sensing, embracing, resting in, and feasting upon the pleasure that God had in them. There was no strife or worry, only pure worship.

The problems arose when Adam and Eve decided to invite anarchy into this perfect utopia. They made the decision to usurp God's rule and reign and to reign for themselves. When they did this, they were reduced into finite beings of limited knowledge, limited love, and limited capacity and power. Humanity lost its sharpness, its edge, and its perfection. All rest was lost. In thinking about God's presence and what it feels like in complete disclosure and intimacy, Adam and Eve now seemed only to want to withdraw and hide. The reason they hid is because they knew that if a person, like our sinful selves, was to again walk into a Trinitarian community after breaking the first rule, the law of love, and come carrying shame, guilt, secrecy, insecurity, and doubts with them before God, they would enter such a union of Oneness as the Trinity and immediately feel out of place.

The perfection would burn and pierce through us like a flaming stone. Insecurities can not handle being exposed and penetrated in such a manner.

Marked in history, this is the first day that humanity no longer found rest in God of their own accord, but would forever search to fill that now gaping hole with various modes of false promises. Right out of the Garden, humanity's stain began to multiply in the bitter jealousy of Cain, who murdered Abel, and the flood of evil which then resulted in the great flood. Abraham lied to conceal his secrets; Jacob played family favorites; Judah had sex with his daughter-in-law; nation slaughtered nation, kings enslaved people, and all in all the world turned not into a place of rest, but into a place of strife.

Sabbath

Into this forgetfulness and absolute revulsion toward God and His ways of rest, God introduced a people. He did not give up on humanity, but He created a people who would be examples to the world. They were to not only be put on display to model humanity's frailty, but also to show forth God's continual commitment to His people. God chose Israel. He chose them not because of their ability but because He had to start somewhere. He gathered them around, gave them laws, and formed their community.

One of these laws that He instituted into their dynamic was that the idea of Sabbath. Up until Exodus 16, there was no record of anyone keeping the Sabbath, nor of any decree, but the first mention appears in Exodus 20:8-11, where God calls the people to remember His ways by observing this "memorial rest from creative activity." [305]

God's intention was to institute a rhythm into a very frail world. This rhythm would serve to remind us of paradise lost. The Sabbath was never to be an end in itself; it was to remind Israel of a Trinitarian culture they had lost, and it was to encourage them that a day was coming when this culture would be restored. On the Sabbath Day, the people were to cease from their work, rest in God's work, embrace enjoyment, and feast in celebration. This was God's grace given to His people to cause them to experience what life had been like in the Garden.

Unfortunately, human sinfulness snuck in once again as the people of Israel turned the Sabbath into a law of command rather than a gift of grace. The deception became so dogmatic, forced, and legalistic that by the time Jesus came on the scene in Mk. 2:27, He had to remind the people that "the Sabbath was made for man, not man for the Sabbath." The Jews turned a gracious day into a day of works. They inserted their strife back into it all over again and enforced rules and regulations upon the Sabbath that went beyond its intent. Their goal was not to observe the Trinitarian ethos, as was intended in the Sabbath, but they went so far as to prohibit people from lifting a finger to do anything on the Sabbath, even so far as to prohibit acts of love, service, sacrifice, and the like.

Jesus very quickly dealt with this shift with the intensity of a lion and the gentleness of a lamb. He quickly dispelled the myths surrounding the Sabbath and proclaimed that the Sabbath, all along, was about His Lordship. [306] This Sabbath, in Jesus' mind, is a shadow that was given in the Old Covenant [307] and was held as a reminder of Garden times—only for a time—until the Garden would once again visit humanity in Jesus. Ephesians 3 clearly states that Jesus abolished this law and its ritual enforcement in ceremonial law when He came to the earth. Hebrews 8:13 states the nature of Jesus' new Covenant in rest in this: "When He said 'a new covenant,' He has made the first obsolete. But whatever is becoming obsolete and growing old is ready to disappear."

Jesus regained the Sabbath that Adam lost. He completed the redemptive work [308] by restoring rest to the Garden (all of creation). The work of Christ [309] satisfied the Father's perfection in the resurrection and ascension, [310] leading again to divine rest. [311] Jesus was and is the Sabbath rest. [312] The Apostle Paul said, "Therefore no one is to act as your judge in regard to food or drink, or in respect to a festival or a new moon or a Sabbath day—things which are a mere shadow of what is to come; but the substance belongs to Christ." [313] Jesus is the Yeshua (Joshua) that leads God's children to the Promised Land. [314] He is the Jubilee [315] that cancels debts, [316] and in Him alone we find our rest. This is why Paul rebuked the Galatians for attempting to add the observance of the days to Christ's sufficient work. [317] He realized that a legalist enforcement of such laws was a violation of the new ethic in Christ. Sabbath observance was now a shadow in the wake of Christ. To continue its observance would be demeaning of Christ's work. This is why the church changed to Sunday observances: in light of the day that Christ rose. [318]

. . .

Sabbath Heart

In the New Testament a shift in emphasis takes place regarding the Sabbath. The stress is not placed on a festival or a weekly location and time, but to a heart location. God had penetrated the anarchic heart of Adam's and Eve's humanity. The sin of our first parents, which caused them to approach the table of the Trinity with fear, shame, guilt, and strife, now is a table restored in Christ. Christ came and bore the weight of our wrath incurred. He took the anger due us and the judgment we deserve. Though we deserve condemnation, He refused to allow us to wallow in worry, anxiety, and regret. Hebrews 4:1-16 tells us that He removed all of it! He now beckons us to enter his rest, and at the head of His feasting table is Jesus Himself. Ultimately, this all will culminate in one glorious, unveiled Garden Feast in Revelation 14:13, where God's creation will be restored, [319] and the curse will never again be felt. [320]

In placing the context of the Sabbath within the human heart, we are heightening its significance, not lowering it. The work is for more complete and far greater in its penetrating depth. However, it still remains to be asked, are we to observe a literal Sabbath Day as Christian disciples?

I think there is indication that it's still a beneficial rhythm, [321] and I also think it was a rhythm put into God's designed schedule even before the Fall of humanity in Genesis. The *principle* of observing a Sabbath is still helpful. The framework however with which we approach it is crucial. It is not merely a day to take a nap, entertain ourselves, and avoid work, but rather to be intentional about enjoying our work, taking joy in creativity, feasting with and serving in and amongst God's family, and embracing all of life's little subtleties. It says on the seventh day of Creation that God ceased His work in creating. The idea of ceasing a task is in order that all the emphasis must be placed on the relationship. God spent the day of Sabbath around the Triune family. Sabbath heightens our commitment to the relationships in our lives that are most important.

The Sabbath should be a welcomed weekly rhythm, but it should also be a daily carried reality. The day itself really should remind us of a mentality that is carried into all of life. All of life has been put to rest in Jesus. The heart's position before God, people, and culture is really what's at stake here. We are encouraged to have a Sabbath heart. Just as breathing in and breathing out, our day is to be filled with moments of exerting our energy and saving our energy. We are to develop rhythms in our day of working hard and resting hard, laboring for Jesus and remembering Jesus in our labor.

I really believe that God crafts in us this heart of Sabbath through three specific avenues:

Waiting: God instills in our lives seasons of waiting and seasons of seeing, seasons of planting and seasons of harvest. He may use an illness, a crisis, an abnormality, a stress or worry, an unresolved issue, or even a suffering to linger in tension while He teaches us to rest and be at peace with Him. In waiting on Him, He reminds us to return to the ethic of the Garden. The ethos of the Garden is enjoyment. Waiting is God's way of saying, "Enjoy me!" God causes us to wait for things that our heart believes will satisfy us in order to give our heart truly what it needs—God Himself.

Silence: God teaches us to make a place for him in silence. In speaking to Elijah in 1 Kings 19:11-13, God's work came not in fire and an earthquake, but only after the noise subsided does the text tell us that God's voice spoke in a whisper. I think this is revealing as to how God uses the tension of loud and soft in our lives. He allows us to deafen our ears with noise, busyness, and stress in order to reawaken our Garden craving for peace. In the distress, our heart cries out and yearns only for silence. When the silence comes, we are so prepared for it and ready to embrace it that we are more humble and open to listen. Elijah realized this. After the devastation of a fire and an earthquake, the land was barren and looking for relief. In that moment, God can meet the broken and ready heart.

Rest: The Bible tells us that God gives rest to those He loves. I believe this is far deeper than a nap or a good eight-hour sleep (although this is included [322]). Rest is an all-encompassing Deliverance. Deliverance happens when relational conflict is reconciled, when the unemployed receive work, when the woman in labor gives birth, when the man trusts God to provide, and when the child submits and obeys their parents. It is when things make their way back to how they were intended in the Garden. These are all examples of rest. It is when we fall in line with the perfect ethic of the Trinitarian kingdom of God. When we begin to accept

His culture, His language, His mission, His family dynamic, and His method for doing things, we find that our waging war returns to peace in our surrender.

The Tempo of Discipleship

This is the profound truth that music teaches us about the very real rhythms of life. We cannot have work without rest and vice versa. We must learn the nature of what it is to sound good notes that contribute to the song in beneficial work, and also how rest is beneficial to the song we are playing. Too much flux either way could be disastrous, and it is important that a follower of Christ recognize this. Too little work and the disciple will fall prey to idle hands; too much work and the disciple will fall into idolatry. On the other hand, too much rest and the disciple will fall into lazy incoherency, and too little rest will weary the soul.

Theology: In observing how the theology of work and rest can be taken to the extremes, we must first observe that all beliefs can be taken far beyond the limits that God provides. This tendency was seen in the Jews' tendency to "over-ruleify" the Sabbath, and it is seen in all of human tendency in how we can over-law the things we do. We tend to take good things and turn them into objects that we worship and serve. We must realize that God places real parameters on His Garden work, but only to enable the freedoms of His people within the borders of its rest. The borders are there to protect perfection, not restrict our enjoyment. In our fallen state, we tend to restrict with our beliefs on issues because we're trying to recreate the Garden habitat just like Adam and Eve did. We must choose to accept that God's limits are, at times, wider than ours or narrower than ours. This is about observing His Garden culture, not ours.

Biography: There need to be moments for work. Work is a Godly thing, not a God thing. We are not to worship work, but our work is to fill everything we do with the fragrant witness, giving, and expression of the story of Christ. Whether we are working to plant a church or we are flippin' burgers down at the local McDonald's, the purpose of work remains the same: people need Jesus! Everywhere, people need Jesus. Our work should not just be to get a paycheck, but it should be a place where we *image* and portray the Trinitarian culture of enjoyment, community, and rest to a broken world.

This means that our witness and hard work need to be followed by times of rest. As in music, rest comes after work and actually ensures that the notes played do not overwhelm the ear. I would contend that silence and rest in music is, indeed, an intrinsic element of music, not only because without it the sounds in a musical piece cannot be appreciated, but also because it is an intrinsic element of rhythm. [323] All rhythm is essentially is the combination of *sound* and *silence*. The rhythm that space creates between sounding notes is similar to the space we need between our sounding schedules. We need to leave room between meetings, room between decisions, and room between events to simply enjoy waiting, being silent, and resting. Only in this rhythm will we truly enjoy life. "The essential temporality of everyday life means that humans experience not only the passing of time, but also the necessity to wait until one temporal process has run its course in order for another to begin." [324] Life and music have rhythm; you can speed it up, but it becomes incoherent. My hope is that we would embrace a Sabbath heart that does not long for speed, but rather ceases, rests, feasts, and embraces everything God has to give. The observance of a carefully planned day off or a carefully scheduled vacation is fantastic. A one-day rest however will never replace a heart that walks and works in this peace—peace with the Creator.

DOXOLOGY: THE VISION OF MUSIC AND WHAT IT TEACHES US ABOUT THE totality of life is that all of work is filled with purpose and meaning. All we do has Garden-like potential. "Music is taking the raw material of sound and rearranging it to give us sounds that are meaningful, that lift us, change us, and help us. An architect takes the raw material of the earth and creates a bridge or a building or a street, and these are things that human beings need if we are going to live in community or if we are going to survive the winter. Writers and actors act out stories. They take the raw material of human experience and create stories that teach us or help us or give us meaning. A venture capitalist is someone who takes the raw material of an idea (or a talent) and resources and puts them together, and you have new enterprises, new products that add value to life, and new jobs. All work is rearranging some kind of raw material to give people what human beings need." [325] The end game to us producing what humans need is not the creative object in and of itself. What this forming and fashioning does is retool our hearts to understand the labor and love by which we were formed and fashioned. The hard materials remind us of our hard hearts, which God continues to shape in great love and patience. The hope is that, in the raw material, there is a hope for creating a work of sense, and so also is there a hope for redemption in God making sense of us.

14

Encore

As we now arrive at the grand finale of this short contribution to the discussion of music, theology, and discipleship, I think it would be beneficial to complete such a work with a short recap of its contents. The goal in summarizing this book's aims and contributions is not to merely solidify its presentation in our minds as a finale to its song. Rather, this book should expose us to a new discipleship tool and way of thinking that leaves us at a place of *encore*.

In a musical setting, the encore comes when the crowd is so awestruck by the performance of the band in concert that they clap, cheer, and beg the band to come back on stage for one last song once their show has seemingly ended. I'm not supposing that this book will have that effect on you, but what I mean is that our encore will drive us to keep theologizing through music in ways that lead to better methods of crafting and creating disciples. The encore is that we take the information we learn in this book and we play it in one last song. We bring it into real life, to a real awaiting crowd, and to souls hungry for true formation and transformation. What music teaches us about discipleship is not just dried-up theories and pragmatic application, but it teaches us a whole thought process, timing, and approach to discipleship that is both thoughtful and expressive.

It has been proposed in this book that we need a new *Tempo for Discipleship*. This book in no way attacks other discipleship models, nor even assumes to propose one, but rather seeks to uphold discipleship efforts by equipping those within their constructs with the right approach and expectations in the endeavor.

Gathering in Melody and Participation

Those making disciples and those who are themselves following Jesus and learning from Him need to understand that He is gathering us. He gathers us around one melody, one song, and one image. That image is the very image of the Trinity. Not only does He gather us around His nature, but He invites us to participate, to sing along. What this implies is that we are to consider all the ways the culture of the Trinity interact. We are to ponder their community, their reasoning, their organization, their scriptural language, and their mission together. This is holistic and total. The Trinity demands every part of us.

Only in getting caught up in thinking through the make-up of the Trinity can we begin to know what it's like to live the Kingdom of God. The Kingdom of God, made up of sons and daughters of the King, takes place in very real environments. God Himself has a culture around the dinner table (community); He holds a real philosophy system and value structure for how His home runs (reasoning); He has a very real way in which His home, His government, His workplace, and His people are to be deployed and managed; and He has a very real curriculum of education that we are to learn in order to develop a kingdom IQ. When we begin to wrap our imaginations around this melody of complete in-sync audio, resounding from the bosom of the Trinity, only then can we truly build His Kingdom on earth *as it is in heaven.*

The Word in Rudiment, Pitch, and Song

When God gathers us, He begins to teach us through His Word about His ethics. He begins to transmit what is in His mind and heart into real words and creative movements that put on display for us what is really important to Him. It's important that we pick up and learn these fundamental rudiments of His nature. Learning them is important in understanding the mind of Christ. These vibrations of learning do not come to us in dry and still black-and-whites, but they resound with audio pitch and song that are vibrantly distinct and unique. Discipleship, therefore, is not formed alone in simple dogmatic routine and doctrinal correctness (although this is also stressed in importance), but it has to be played out and informed by the real flux of life. Pitch teaches us everything about how a disciple is formed. It's not a static experience, but a dramatic one, lived out and acted out on a living stage.

Faith, in this way, does not only take place in one environment, but the truths of God reach into every expanse of human history. They define the old as they establish the familiar and even on into how they create and recreate the new. This is how God's words come to us. They come to us in framework and an old song of tradition, but they transpire in us along the roads of a journey, which births out of us new songs of deliverance and exuberant thanksgiving.

The reason that the emphasis upon the Word is included within the framework of this book in the manner in which it is, has not been to judge or demerit discipleship methods from around the globe. Raw materials are needed only so much as they are combined with methods of learning that are oral and transmittable. This work serves to merely imply character and context to how discipleship is carried out. Discipleship has a very real character, and it is not flat line. Discipleship has a very real context, and it is not the classroom. Discipleship principles need to form a tempo that flows as life does, with pitch, form, and with ancient future.

Responding, Remembering, and Transposing

When God gathers, He speaks, and when He speaks, He causes us to think through all that He implies—that it might bring about in us some sort of upheaval of change and repentance. This is how God collides with His world. When this reality in fact happens, we tend to position ourselves in one of two ways. The only choice we have is simply to respond, but this leaves open to us two options: to reject or to receive. In God creating a dialogue with us with musical intensity, we are given the opportunity reject His song or receive it. If we reject it, we forget it. If we receive it, then we respond in the second fashion, to remember it.

The gospel depth enters into our very stomachs like a nutritional meal to be digested down to the last enzyme. Our stomach ruminates upon, breaks down, transports, and embraces all the nutritional quality that God's truth proposes and outsources it to the rest of the body. As this nutrition fires out from the center of our bodies, it enables the body to function, to run and amass energy. This energy then finds its outlet through activity and transposition. This energy lays its senses upon things. It lays its touch upon kinesthetic learning, its taste upon pleasures, its sight upon right indulgences, its ears upon opuses, and its smell upon fragrances.

All of the nutrition that comes from God's word races through us and affects everything we do and comes out into everything we do. If we receive God's truth, we will remember God's truth, and then we will position ourselves in a fashion that enables us to outlet His energy and nutrition into the veins of society; causing His truth to flow into the bloodstream of commerce and flow throughout culture in a way that they too can be energized by it.

SENT INTO A JOURNEY

As blood courses through the veins, a disciple equipped with real nutritional content surges into a real bloodstream—life! Life is motivated by pulses and real cardiological rhythms. The pulse of the heart pushes the truths ever deeper and broader throughout the body and understanding of a follower of Christ. A disciple is pushed into daily beats and habits in life that allow the truths of God to permeate their being and their culture.

We must remember this context of the disciple's journey. This *sending* is the real classroom. This journey is the real book. This *going* provides the very real operating room in which the hearts of disciples are operated upon. Discipleship must remember this. Staying conscious of this is easy in theory, for you're reading a book, but in reality, this carries with it real animated flesh and bone, and it's hard to maintain the patience and diligence to hang with real people. It's oftentimes hard to be patient and hang with ourselves. But the fact that remains is that, ever so slowly, in work and rest, in suffering and resolve, in transience and stillness, God slowly grinds His image against our frail frames. We buckle, we erupt, we cripple, and we buck, but at the end of the day, God's glory shines through in the limps and in the healing.

MY HOPE

The Tempo of Discipleship

My hope in writing this work is that discipleship will undergo some real tempo shifts on behalf of all of us. My prayer is that we, as followers of Christ who are shaping other followers of Christ, would place our expectations rightly and have the long view in mind when fashioning God's people. I'm praying for an outlook change.

My prayer is also that we would resonate with the fact that everything is deeply and profoundly forming. Everything! If music teaches us anything, it's that we are to be inclusive rather than exclusive in our limits as to what we believe crafts us. From the gimmicks that we embrace in media advertising to the clothes we wear, and into the very shape of our worship services on Sunday morning, these reflect our hearts and they are profound enough to be considered. Music provides us with a healthy way to analyze in this regard. It embraces a construct that teaches us how to form our beliefs about God. Music teaches us that the loud moments and the soft, the reverent and the celebratory, the empty and the full, the wordy and the quiet, the work and the rest, the call and the response, the gathering and the sending, the tension and the finale, the lament and the joy, the acceptance and the rejection, the form and the improvisation, the trust and the risk, the certainty and uncertainty, the melody and the harmony, and the new and the old are all vitally important! These dynamic ranges should help us to shape our worship, shape our homes, shape our churches, shape our world, and ultimately shape ourselves.

So I leave you to your tempo. How are you moving? What's forming you? Consider your life as you step out on stage before a watching world. Give the world a life worth watching; a life that causes the world to erupt in a resounding cry unto Christ as you grow as a member of His family. This is the greatest encore of all!

15

Endnotes

Introduction

1. Rom. 3:11 *(All Scripture references are from the ESV version unless otherwise noted)*

2. Gal. 2:20

3. 2 Tim. 2:4-6

4. Ibid.

5. 1 Sam. 18:7

6. 2 Sam. 11

7. 2 Sam. 6:12-23

8. 1 Cor. 3:10

9. 1 Cor. 3:10-15

10. 1 Cor. 9:26-27

11. 1 Th. 1

12. 1 Pt. 1:3-6

13. 1 Cor. 3:8

14. 2 Tim. 2:4-6

15. Eph. 4:12

16. Mt. 16:18

17. Jn. 10:27

18. Jn. 15:1

19. Rev. 19:16

20. Rev. 19:6-9

21. Zeph. 3:17

22. Bryan Chapell, *Christ-Centered Worship* (Grand Rapids: Baker Academic, 2009), 21.

23. Jeremy S. Begbie, *Theology, Music & Time* (Cambridge University Press, 2000).

24. Ibid., p. 4.

25. Calvin R. Stapert, *A New Song for an Old World: Musical Thought in the Early Church* (Grand Rapids: Eeerdmans, 2007), Kindle Location 1371.

26. Donald J. Grout, Peter Burkholder, and Claude V. Palisca, *A History of Western Music* (New York: Norton and Company, 1973), 8.

Chapter 1:

27. Duet. 6:4-15

28. Victor Zuckerkandl, *Sound and Symbol: Music and the External World* (London: Routledge and Kegan Paul, 1956), 297-99.

29. J. R. Middleton, *The Liberating Image: The Imago Dei in Genesis 1* (Grand Rapids: Brazos, 2005), 27.

30. James K.A. Smith, *Desiring the Kingdom: Worship, Worldview and Cultural Formation* (Grand Rapids: Baker Academic, 2009), 163.

31. Jn. 6:38

32. Mt. 28:18; Eph. 1:21-22

33. John 1:29

34. Gen. 12:1

35. Gen. 9:15

36. Gen. 15:9-11, 17-21

37. Victor P. Hamilton, *The Book of Genesis* (Grand Rapids: Eerdmans, 1995), 430.

38. Ex. 24

39. 2 Sam. 7:12-13

40. Mt. 1:1

41. Acts 2:22-26

42. Gal. 3:24-25

43. Eph. 3:11

44. Jn. 1:1

45. Constance Cherry, *The Worship Architect* (Grand Rapids: Baker Academic, 2010), 2.

46. Mike Cosper, *Rhythms of Grace* (Wheaton: Crossway, 2013), 30.

47. *Encyclopedia Brittanica*, "Harmony," (accessed October 8, 2013), http://escola.britannica.com.br/article/110125/harmony

48. Elizabeth Elliott, "The Essence of Femininity: A Personal Perspective," in *Recovering Biblical Manhood and Womenhood: A Response to Evangelical Feminism*, John Piper and Wayne Grudem, eds. (Wheaton: Crossway, 1991), 395.

49. Darrow L. Miller, *Nurturing the Nations*, (Colorado Springs: Paternoster, 2007), 120.

50. Stephen D. Kovach, "Egalitarians Revamp Doctrine of the Trinity," *CBMW News*, vol. 2, no. 1 (Dec. 1996): 4.

51. Harold Best, *Unceasing Worship* (San Francisco: Harper SanFrancisco, 1993), 21.

52. Cosper, 184.

53. Stapert, Kindle Location 1371.

54. John Tavener, *The Sacred in Art*, an unpublished lecture, provided by Chester Music, source unknown, no date.

55. Chalmers, "The Expulsive Power of a New Affection."

56. Cosper, 186.

57. Joseph H. *When the Church Was a Family: Recapturing Jesus' Vision for Authentic Christian Community* (Grand Rapids: B&H Publishing, 2009), 141.

58. Ibid., 170.

59. D. A. Carson, *Showing the Spirit: A Theological Exposition of 1 Corinthians, 12-14* (Grand Rapids: Baker Book Group, 1996), KL 270-281.

60. Kenneth Berding, *What Are Spiritual Gifts?: Rethinking the Conventional View* (Grand Rapids: Kregal Publications, 2006), Kindle Locations 181-182.

61. Ibid., 182.

62. Ibid., 131.

Chapter 2:

63. Louise Maeve Heaney, *Music as Theology: What Music Says about the Word* (Princeton Theological Monograph Series: Pickwick Publications, 2012), 81.

64. Dorothy Retallack, *The Sound of Music and Plants* (Camerillo: Devorss & Co, 1973).

65. Zeph. 3:17

66. L. Wilson, J. Moore, *Digital Storytellers: The Art of Communicating the Gospel in Worship* (Nashville: Abingdon Publishers, 2009), 38.

67. ESV Translation, *emphasis mine*.

68. David Rhoads, "Performance Criticism: An Emerging Methodology in

Second Testamental Studies—Part 1 & 2," *Biblical Theology Bulletin*, 36 (2006), 164-84.

69. Botha Pieter, "Cognition, Orality-Literacy, and Approaches to First-Century Writings," *Society of Biblical Literature*, (2004): 37-63.

70. A. K., Bowman & G. Woolf, *Literacy and Power in the Ancient World* (Cambridge: Cambridge University Press, 1994).

71. C.M. Bechtel, *The Old Testament for Christian Worship* (Grand Rapids: Eerdmans, 2008), KL 610-613.

72. Ibid., 164-84.

73. Richard Ward, "Pauline Voice and Presence as Strategic Communicator," *Semeia*, vol.65, sec. 54, (1995).

74. J.A. Loubser, "Orality and Literacy in the Pauline Corpus: Some New Hermeneutical Implications," *Neotestamentica*, 29/1 (1995): 61–74.

75. R. N. Longenecker, *New Dimensions in New Testament Study* (Grand Rapids: Zondervan, 1974), 281–97.

76. Martin MacGuire, "Pauline Voices and Presence As Strategic Communication," *Reformed Liturgy and Music* 30:2, (1996): 185.

77. Jana Childers & Clayton J. Schmit, *Performance in Preaching: Bringing the Sermon to Life* (Grand Rapids: Baker Academic, 2008).

78. Alla Bozarth Campbell. *Word's Body: An Incarnational Aesthetic of Interpretationn* (Alabama: Alabama University Press, 1979).

79. Jana Childers & Clayton J. Schmit, *Performance in Preaching* (Grand Rapids: Baker Academic, 2008).

80. R. Prior, "Orality: The Not-so-Silent Issue in Mission Theology," *International Bulletin of Missionary Research*, 35, no. 3 (July 2011): 143-147.

81. John D. Arcy May, ed., *Living Theology in Melanesia: A Reader* (Goroka, PNG: Melanesian Institute, 1985), ix, x-xi.

82. Mohenoa Puloka, "An Attempt at Contextualizing Theology for the Tongan Church," in *South Pacific Theology: Papers from the Consultation of Pacific Theology, Papua New Guinea* (Oxford: Regnum Books, 1987), 84-85.

83. Kambati Uriam, "Theology and Practice in the Islands: Christianity

and Island Communities in the New Pacific, 1947-1997" (Doctoral Thes., Australian National Univ., 1999), 133-34.

84. Simon Chan, *Liturgical Theology: The Church as Worshiping Community* (Downers Grove: InterVarsity Press, 2006), KL 297-299.

85. Michael A. Rynkiewich, "Mission, Hermeneutics, and the Local Church," *Journal of Theological Interpretation* 1, no. 1 (2007): 50.

86. Carol M. Bechel, *Touching the Altar: The Old Testament for Christian Worship* (Grand Rapids: William B. Eerdmans, 2008). KL 1218.

87. Smith, 2009, 27.

88. Ibid., 39.

89. Heb. 9:21

90. Robert Webber, "Is Our Worship Adequately Triune," *Reformation and Revival Journal* 9/3, (2000) 121-29.

91. Chapell, 35.

92. F. Russell Mitman, *Worship in the Shape of Scripture* (Cleveland: Pilgrim Press, 2001).

93. Robert E. Webber, *Ancient-Future Worship: Proclaiming and Enacting God's Narrative* (Grand Rapids: Baker Books, 2008), 110.

94. Cosper, 94.

95. Cosper, 79.

96. Heaney, 285.

97. Cosper, 90.

98. Cosper, 71.

99. D.A. Carson, *Worship by the Book* (Grand Rapids: Zondervan, 2002).

100. A.J. Torrance, *The Self-Communication of God: Where and How does God Speak*, an unpublished paper delivered at the Annual Conference of The Society for the Study of Theology.

101. Chapell, 144.

102. Chapell, 99.

103. Edmund Clowney, "The Singing Savior," *Moody Monthly*, July-August (1979), 42.

104. Smith, 2009.

Chapter 3:

105. Robert Louis Wilken, *The Spirit of Early Christian Thought: Seeking the Face of God* (New Haven: Yale University Press, 2003), xiv-xv.

106. Gal. 4:3

107. Gal. 4:9

108. Col. 2:28

109. Heb. 5:12

110. Col. 2:20

111. 2 Pt. 3:10-12

112. Mt. 7:8

113. Jaroslav Pelikan, *Quote*.

114. Peter Ditzel, *Are You Following the Weak and Beggerly Elements, Rudiments, and Principles of the World?* (accessed Oct. 1, 2013) http://www.wordofhisgrace.org/elements.htm

115. Rom. 7:12

116. J.B. Lightfoot, *The Teaching of the Apostles* (accessed October 2, 2013) https://www.christianhistoryinstitute.org/study/module/didache/

117. C.H. Dodd, *Gospel and Law* (Cambridge: Cambridge University Press, 1951).

118. Kevin Perotta, "A Distinctive Way of Life" in *Leading Christians to Maturity*, ed. John C. Blattner (Lake Mary: Creation House, 1987), 94-98.

Chapter 4:

119. Example provided in "Changing Meaning through Word Stress 2," (accessed October 15, 2013), http://tx.english-ch.com/teacher/christin/level-a/changing-meaning-through-word-stress-2/

120. H. E. Dana and Julius R. Mantey. *A Manual Grammar of the Greek New Testament* (New York: The Macmillan Company, 1927), 176.

121. Stephen W. Paine. *Beginning Greek: A Functional Approach* (New York: Oxford UP, 1961), 41.

122. Paul Achtemeier, "Omni Verbum Sonat: The New Testament and the Environment of Late Western Antiquity," *Journal of Biblical Literature*, 109 (1990): 3–27.

123. Albert Mehrabian, *Silent Messages: Implicit Communication of Emotions and Attitudes*, 2nd ed. (Belmont, CA: Wadsworth, 1981).

124. David Rhoads, *Reading Mark, Engaging the Gospel* (Minneapolis: Fortress Press, 2004), 176-201.

125. David Rhoads "Biblical Performance Criticism: Performance as Research," *Oral Tradition*, 25/1 (2010): 157-198.

126. Shimon Levy, *The Bible as Theatre* (Porland: Sussex Academic Press, 2002), 15.

127. Ibid., 41.

128. **Community:** Psalm 12, 44, 58, 60, 74, 79, 80, 83, 85, 89, 90, 94, 123, 126, 129

INDIVIDUAL: PSALM 3, 4, 5, 7, 9-10, 13, 14, 17, 22, 25, 26, 27, 28, 31, 36, 39, 40:12-17, 41, 42-43, 52, 53, 54, 55, 56, 57, 59, 61, 64, 70, 71, 77, 86, 89, 120, 139, 141, 142

129. Psalm 6, 32, 38, 51, 102, 130, 143

130. Psalm 35, 69, 83, 88, 109, 137, 140

131. **Community:** Psalm 65, 67, 75, 107, 124, 136

Individual: Psalm 18, 21, 30, 32, 34, 40:1-11, 66:13-20, 92, 108, 116, 118, 138

132. Psalm 8, 105-106, 135, 136

133. Psalm 11, 16, 23, 27, 62, 63, 91, 121, 125, 131

134. Psalm 8, 19:1-6, 33, 66:1-12, 67, 95, 100, 103, 104, 111, 113, 114, 117, 145, 146, 147, 148, 149, 150

135. Psalm 50, 78, 81, 89, 132

136. Psalm 2, 18, 20, 21, 29, 45, 47, 72, 93, 95, 96, 97, 98, 99, 101, 110, 144

137. Psalm 46, 48, 76, 84, 87, 122

138. Psalm 15, 24, 68, 82, 95, 115, 134

139. Psalm 1, 36, 37, 49, 73, 112, 127, 128, 133

140. Psalm 1, 19:7-14, 119

Chapter 5

141. Paul Ricoeur, "Naming God" (Ph.D. diss., Catholic University of America, 1998).

142. R.P. Martin, *Worship in the Early Church* (Grand Rapids: Eeerdmans, 1964), 43.

143. Emily R. Blink & Bert Polman, eds., *The Psalter Hymnal Handbook* (Grand Rapids: CRC, 1998),

144. J.A. Smith, "The Ancient Synagogue, the Early Church and Singing," *Music & Letters*, 65/1 (1984), pp. 1–16.

145. Stapert, Kindle Locations 1317-1319.

146. Eph. 3:10-11

147. Gen. 8:20

148. Gen. 12:8

149. Gen. 26:24

150. Gen. 31:13-Gen. 32:22-32

151. Ex. 17:14

152. 1 Kngs. 18:30-31

153. Exo. 20:24

154. Barry Liesch, *The New Worship: Straight Talk on Music and the Church* (Grand Rapids: Baker Books, 2001), 40.

155. Stapert, KL 2579

156. Eph. 4:14

Chapter 6:

157. Bata Drumming, (accessed October 2, 2013) http://batadrumming.com/drums

158. J. Gleick, *The Information: A History, a Theory, a Flood*, London, (Fourth Estate, 2001), p15.

159. Cherry, 54.

160. Mark H. Lane, *Bible Numbers for Life*, (accessed October 16, 2013), http://biblenumbersforlife.com/

161. Amos 5:8; Job 38:31, 9:9; Ps. 29:6

162. Heaney, 161.

163. J. Begbie, *Beholding The Glory*, (Grand Rapids: Baker Academic, 2001), 60.

164. Jhn. 10:27-28

165. Ibid., 167.

166. 1 Cor. 2:16

Chapter 7:

167. Marcel Kinsbourne, "Hemisphere Specialization and the Growth of Human Understanding," *American Psychologist*, April 1982, pp. 411-420.

168. Ibid., 410.

169. *Center for Advanced Study Newsletter*, April 2004.

170. No Author Listed, *Article*, (accessed October 15, 2013), http://musicandmemory.org/

171. Sally P. Springer and Georg Deutsch, *Left Brain, Right Brain* (W. H. Freeman, 1981).

172. AryahKaplan, *Jewish Meditation: A Practical Guide* (New York: Schocken, 1985), pp. 165.

173. Cosper, 32.

174. See also how the Israelites observed important Feasts and Celebrations, and how they reflected the coming of Christ: In the Spring was Passover (Pesach) Lev. 23:5, in which the Unleavened Bread *(Chang Ha Motzi)* was prepared the morning after (Lev. 23:6). Look at the matzah (unleavened bread) and see that it is striped—"By His stripes we are healed"—and pierced—"They shall look upon me whom they've pierced,"—and pure, without any leaven, as His body was without any sin. The Passover custom of burying, hiding and then resurrecting the second of three pieces of matzot (the middle piece), presents the Gospel *(Afikomen)*. There was then the Feast of the First Fruits *(Reshit Katzir)* in Lev. 23:11—representing the fertility of the land—Christ's resurrection—Easter. The Feast of Pentecost *(Shavu'ot)* in Lev. 23:16—marked summer harvest—bread baked with leaven—church comprised of both Jew and Gentile. The Fall Feasts like the Feast of Trumpets *(Yom Teru'ah)*—blowing trumpets—sign of victory. There was Atonement *(Yom Kippur)* in Lev. 23:27 where the blood was poured on the mercy seat—Jesus is our mercy seat (Rom. 3:25—propitiation). And the Feast of Tabernacles (Sukkot) in Lev. 23:34—Where God's shelter and protection of Israel in the Desert was remembered.

175. Luke 4

176. Jhn. 6:35

177. Acts 2:42

178. Maeve Louise Heaney, *Music as Theology: What Music Says about the Word* (Princeton Theological Monograph Series: Pickwick Publications, 2012), 81.

179. Tim Chester, *A Meal with Jesus: Discovering Grace, Community, and Mission around the Table* (Wheaton: Crossway, 2011), KL 1351.

180. Begbie, 167.

Chapter 8:

181. Jhn. 4:24

182. C.S. Lewis, *The Weight of Glory* (San Francisco: Harper, 1980), 109-11.

183. Andy Stanley, *Communicating for a Change* (Grand Rapids: Multnommah, 2006).

184. Vern S. Poythress, *Symphonic Theology* (Phillipsburg: P&R Publishing, 2001).

185. Richard Pratt, *What is Biblical Theology*, (accessed Oct. 17, 2013), http://theresurgence.com/2011/03/22/what-is-biblical-theology

186. Duvall and Hays, *Grasping God's Word*, (Grand Rapids: Zondervan, 2012), 24.

187. Bryan Chappell, *Christ Centered Preaching* (Ada, MI: Baker Academic, 2005).

188. Duvall and Hays, 2012.

189. Cosper, 38.

190. Smith, 27.

191. Matt Boswell, *Doxology & Theology* (Nashville: B&H Publishing, 2013), 142.

192. Heaney, 191.

193. Acrostic taken from *Dare2Share* ministries.

Chapter 9:

194. C.S. Lewis, *The Screwtape Letters* (Harper Collins, 1996), 139.

195. David P. Goldman, "Sacred Music, Sacred Time," *First Things*, no 197N (2009), 31-36.

196. "Clave Rhythm," *Wikipedia*, (accessed October 3, 2013), http://en.wikipedia.org/wiki/Clave_%28rhythm%29

197. David Peñalosa, *The Clave Matrix; Afro-Cuban Rhythm: Its Principles and African Origins* (Redway, CA: Bembe Inc., 2009), 81.

198. Godfried Toussaint, *The Geometry of Musical Rhythm: What Makes a "Good" Rhythm Good?* (Boca Raton, FL: CRC Press, 2013), 17.

199. 2 Pt. 3:8

200. Psa. 31:15

201. Isa. 57:15

202. Rev. 22:13

203. Heaney, 205.

204. Nicholas P. Wolterstorff, "Thinking About Church Music," in *Music in Christian Worship: at the Service of the Liturgy,* ed. Charlotte Kroeker (Collegeville: Liturgical Press, 2005), 3-16.

205. Cherry, 207.

206. Cherry, 208.

207. Ps. 5:3

208. Lam. 3:22-23

209. 1 Cor. 6:19-20

210. Cherry, 244.

211. Oliver Davies, *Theology of Transformation: Faith, Freedom, and Christian Act* (Oxford, 2014), 3.

212. Smith, 2009.

213. Ibid., 68.

214. Ibid., 47.

215. Ibid., 42.

216. Ibid., 57.

217. Heaney, 281.

218. Israel C. Stein, "Sacred Space and Holy Time," *Jewish Bible Quaterly,* 34 no 4 O-D (2006), 244-246.

219. Smith, 26.

220. Mt. 11:28

Chapter 10:

221. S.W. Carruthers, *The Westminster Confession of Faith* (Manchester R. Aikman and Son n.d.).

222. 2 Cor. 11:14

223. Jhn. 8:44

224. Eph. 2:1-3

225. 1 Cor. 14:33

226. Rev. 12:9-11

227. 2 Tim. 4:2

228. 1 Cor. 11

229. 1 Tim. 2:1

230. 2 Cor. 8-9

231. Col. 3:16-17

232. Matthew M. Boulton, *God Against Religion: Rethinking Christian Theology through Worship* (Grand Rapids: Eerdmans, 2008).

233. Mark Driscoll, *Religion Saves; Regulative Principle,* (accessed Sept. 31, 2010), http://marshill.com/media/religionsaves/regulative-principle.

234. Heaney, 93.

235. John, Webster, *Barth's Ethics of Reconciliation* (Cambridge: Cambridge University Press, 1995), 71.

236. D. Bailey, *Improvisation: Its Nature and Practice in Music* (London, British Library).

237. Mt. 27:51

238. See John Sailhamer's *Genesis Unbound*. In this book, John Sailhamer discusses the Hebrew word *reshit* in Genesis 1 where God says, "in the beginning he created the heavens and the earth." The word *reshit* refers to an undetermined period of time that took place in God creating, which

could be long or short in duration. This preparation in Genesis 1:1 is separate from God's literal 24 hour, 7 day preparation of the specific land of the Garden. Therefore, the book of Genesis leaves room for the earth to be old, but the actual creation account to also allow for a literal 24 day creation.

To understand this, the following analogy is helpful. If I were to assemble a fish tank, I would go and buy various elements to do it correctly. I'd have the tank itself, the pump, the fish, the plants, the rocks, and other various items. The items themselves come from all different places and are various ages. The tank could be from a yard sale down the street where a grandmother was getting rid of some old possessions; the plants and coral could be many years old, having been harvested out of the sea; and the fish themselves could be babies, teenagers, or old in their age. However, when the aquarium pieces are separate, they are not "habitable" for life. To "prepare" them, it may take a literal hour to assemble all of these items of various ages and backgrounds together in order that the environment is right for the fish—habitable for life. In this way, the tank is old and new at the same time. This is the idea of Genesis 1:1 in that God implies that His creation of the pieces of creation could have taken place over an undetermined length of time, but when He actually prepared the Garden for life, He assembled it in a literal 7 day period.

239. See Peter J. Gentry and Stephen J. Wellum's *Kingdom through Covenant*. In brief, the authors discuss God's covenant in dealing with Israel, but they also look at how God dealt with those outside of Israel in different ways at different times (implying dispensation). Though God's covenant love has always remained the same to His people, the Israelites were led to respond differently to the outside world at different moments in history, per God's command. Sometimes, their relationship to the Gentile world was through withdrawal and spiritual priesthood, and other times it was through monarchy and the advancement of war. Now, in the New Covenant—though it continues the covenant thread of love in Jesus—it also commands an ethic for how we are to relate to the unbelieving world. God now stores up His wrath and uses His church to express His love and proclaim His good news through the gospel. Ultimately, again this dispensation for unbelievers will change in Revelation, when God will remain faithful to His believing family as He saves them to glory, but His dealings in this dispensation will change when His withheld wrath will flow unrestrained once again to end the plight of false religion and rebellion. In this

sense, the thread of covenant and dispensation can run through Scripture in unity.

240. See Romans 9-11

Chapter 11:

241. Begbie, 2001, 92.

242. Jeremy Begbie, *Beholding the Glory* (Grand Rapids: Baker Academic, 2001).

243. Begbie, 2001, 67.

244. Ibid., 72.

245. Begbie, 16.

246. Susanne Langer, *Cognitive Poetics: Goals, Gains and Gaps* (Berlin: Walter de Gruyter GmbH & Co., 2009).

247. Simon Frith, *Performing Rights; On the Value of Popular Music* (Cambridge University Press, 1988), *238*.

248. Paul Westermeyer, *The Heart of the Matter* (Chicago: GIA Publications, INC., 2001), 35.

249. Heb. 11:39-40

Chapter 12:

250. William E. Caplin, *Classical Form: A Theory of Formal Functions for the Instrumental Music of Haydn, Mozart, and Beethoven*, (Oxford University Press:; 2000), 51.

251. Jonas Oswald, *Introduction to the Theory of Heinrich Schenker*, (1934), 24.

252. Kathleen M. Higgins, *The Music of Our Lives*, (Philadelphia: Temple University Press, 1991), 164ff.

253. The following 15 categories for suffering, unless otherwise marked, are taken from Mark Driscoll's post entitled *15 Kinds of Suffering*, (accessed October 21, 2013), http://marshill.com/2009/02/01/15-kinds-of-suffering. Most of the commentary under each heading is original content, but it borrows phrases and wording from Driscoll's post.

254. Kelley, Michael, Eric Geiger, & Philip Eric Nation, *Transformational Discipleship: How People Really Grow* (Grand Rapids: B&H Publishing Group, 2012), KL 2034-2036.

255. Prv. 13:24

256. Kelley, 2012

257. See Leftow, *Time and Eternity* (1991), 84.

258. Begbie, 2001, 49.

259. Lester Ruth, "Observations on the New Hymns Movement Part 2" (accessed October 1, 2013) www.cardiphonia.org/2012/01/19/observations-on-the-new-hymns-movement-part-2

Chapter 13:

260. Prv. 14:23

261. Prv. 12:11

262. Prv. 12:24

263. Prv. 12:14

264. Prv. 22:29, 31:31

265. Col. 3:23

266. 1 Tim. 4:10

267. Jhn. 5:17

268. Ex. 19:16

269. Ez. 3:13

270. Ps. 150:5

271. Rev. 5:2, 6:10

272. 1 Thess. 4:11

273. Jhn. 6:27

274. 1 Cor. 14:40

275. James 4:3

276. Heb. 13:5

277. Luke 10:40

278. Est. 4:1

279. Pro. 7:11

280. Ps. 10:19

281. Pro. 27:14

282. Mk. 5:7

283. Ps. 127:1-3

284. Prv. 3:24

285. Prv. 17:1

286. Ps. 127:2

287. Mk. 6:31

288. Ex. 20:8-11

289. Ps. 23:2

290. Pro. 17:28

291. Ex. 14:14; Mt. 26:63

292. Job 6:24

293. Job 33:33

294. Mk. 9:34

295. Pr. 13:4

296. Hab. 1:13; Isa. 65:6

297. Lk. 4:35

298. Isa. 40:28

299. Jhn. 5:17-18

300. Eph. 5:2

301. Ph. 4:18

302. Num. 4:16

303. Charles Spurgeon, "A Sermon and a Reminiscence." A short sermon from the "Sword and Trowel" (March, 1873).

304. Robert E. Webber, *The Biblical Foundations of Christian Worship*, Vol. 1 (Nashville: Star Song Publishing, 1993), 186.

305. These subcategories were taken from Marva Dawn's work, *Keeping the Sabbath Wholly* (Grand Rapids: Eeerdmans Publishing Company, 1989). In the book Marva discusses various elements of how humanity is to keep the Sabbath. Her discussion eludes to the glorious union of how the Trinity communes with Himself.

306. Lk. 6:5

307. Ex. 31:16-17; Neh. 9:14; Eze. 20:12

308. Jn. 4:34; 5:36

309. Jn. 17:4; 19:30

310. Rom. 1:3-4; Gen. 1:4

311. Heb. 10:11-12

312. Mt. 11:28-30

313. Col. 2:16-17

314. Mt. 1:21

315. Lev. 25:8-10

316. Lk. 4:18-19

317. Gal. 4:9-11

318. Ac 20:7; 1 Cor. 16:2; Jn. 20:1, 19

319. Rev. 21:4; 22:10-12

320. Rev. 22:3

321. Num. 28-29

322. Lk. 8:23

323. Heaney, 104-105.

324. Weigert, 1981, 227.

325. Tim Keller, "Hope For Your Work" (Sermon transcript, 25 October 2009), (accessed October 1, 2013),. http://redeemercitytocity.com/content/com.redeemer.digitalContentArchive.LibraryItem/503/Hope_for_Your_Work.pdf)

www.ingramcontent.com/pod-product-compliance
Lightning Source LLC
Chambersburg PA
CBHW022100090426
42743CB00008B/664